Before Albany

J.W.Bradley

This was the first
book sold.
JB

Before Albany

An Archaeology of Native-Dutch Relations in the Capital Region 1600–1664

by JAMES W. BRADLEY

New York State Museum Bulletin 509

2007

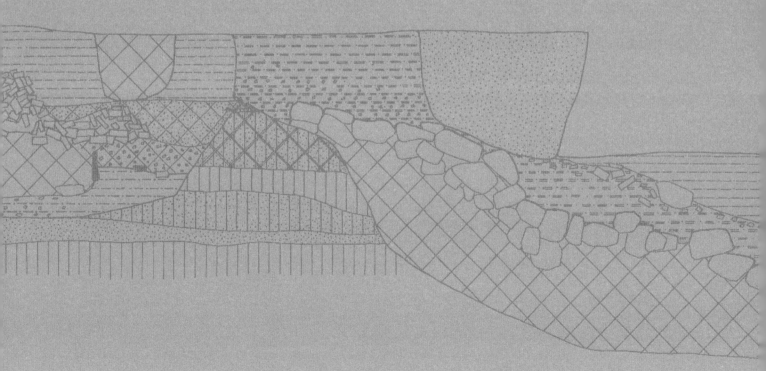

The University of the State of New York   The State Education Department

This publication has been made possible
in part through generous support of:

The Bender Family Foundation
Furthermore: a program of the J.M. Kaplan Fund
The Goldberg Charitable Trust
The Hogarty Family Foundation
McCarthy Charities
The Netherland-America Foundation

Additional support has been provided by: Matthew Bender IV,
Wesley and Barbara Bradley, William and Gail Bradley, Jeff and Mark Bryant,
Charles and Charlotte Buchanan, Jane T. Friehofer, Karen Hartgen,
Assembly Member John J. McEneny, William and Stephanie Swire
and Janet Walker.

This book is printed on Fox River paper (Starwhite Tiara Smooth 80lb. Text)
made by the Fox Valley Corporation of Appleton, Wisconsin and generously
donated to the Before Albany project.

Copies may be ordered from:

Publication Sales
Room 3140 CEC
New York State Museum
Albany, New York 12230
518.402.5344
518.474.2033 (Fax)
www.nysm.nysed.gov/publications.html

Printed in the United States of America

Library of Congress Catalog Number: 2006935436.

ISSN: 0278-3355

ISBN:155557-238-3

TABLE OF CONTENTS

continued next page

LIST OF FIGURES

LIST OF TABLES

This book is dedicated to

PAUL HUEY

whose work on Fort Orange
set the standard, and

KAREN HARTGEN

who has proved that good archaeology
is good business.

ACKNOWLEDGEMENTS

Good scholarship is always a collaborative effort and this book owes its existence to the generosity and support of many people. While it has been my privilege to put the story together, a broad community of friends, colleagues and supporters has made this possible. The initial idea grew out of a series of lunch discussion in the spring of 2002 with Paul Huey (Senior Scientist, Archeology, New York State Office of Parks, Recreation and Historic Preservation) and Karen Hartgen. (President, Hartgen Archeological Associates, Inc.). The subject was the need for a popular book on the archaeology in the Capital Region. Three more people soon joined us as project partners: John Hart (Director of Research and Collections, New York State Museum), Charles Gehring (Director, New Netherland Institute), and Michele Vennard (Executive Director of the Albany County Convention and Visitors Bureau). This is the group that brought the project to life. Two other individuals have also played key roles. Len Tantillo used his exceptional talents to help us visualize what several of these sites might have looked like when people lived there. He also has been wonderfully generous, permitting me to use several of his paintings and drawings in this book *pro bono*. Matt Bender has been another extraordinary friend, not only in building a financial base for the project, but in sharing his passionate commitment to the Albany area with me. Without the support and guidance of these people, this book would have remained just one more good idea.

A book is created in several stages. First is assembling the information from which the story will be written. It is the generosity of many friends and colleagues that made this possible. In addition to Paul Huey, Lois Feister and Joe McEvoy at OPRHP were invaluable. Several individuals at Hartgen Archeological Associates, Inc. shared their thoughts with me, especially Kevin Moody and Adam Luscier. In addition to Charly Gerhing, Janny Venema of the New Netherland Project was a great help. Nearly everyone in the Anthropology and Ethnology Divisions of the New York State Museum provided assistance. Particular thanks go to George Hamell as well as to Andrea Lain and her excellent Collections staff who were always patient with my endless requests. Thanks also go to Stefan Bielinski and Craig Williams of the History Division, and Fred Bassett of the New York State Library, Manuscripts and Special Collections, for their help. Many other people offered information, made critical comments and pointed out errors. These include: Lisa Anderson, Monte Bennett, Gary Bernhardt, Marge Bruchac, Robert 'Bobby' Brustle, Elizabeth Chilton, Steve Comer, Joe Diamond, Shirley Dunn, the late Chuck Fisher, William Fitzgerald, Tammis Groft, Jerome Hall, Robert Kuhn, Lucianne Lavin, Henry Miller, the late Jim Petersen, Marie Lorraine Pipes, Greg Sohrweide, Fred Stevens, Bly Straub, Jim Walsh and Tom Weinman. Special thanks go to Wayne Lenig for sharing his vast knowledge of Mohawk sites and collections as well as the collected wisdom of the Van Epps – Hartley Chapter, NYSAA.

Many friends and colleagues in the Netherlands also provided generous assistance and support. These include: Jerzy Gawronski, Wiard Krook and Michael Hulst (Amsterdam Bureau of Monuments and Archeology), Margriet de Roever

(Amsterdam Municipal Archives), Don
Duco (Pijpenkabinet Museum, Amsterdam),
Maarten Poldermans (Haarlem Bureau of
Archeology), Tosca van der Walle-Van der
Woude (Hoorne Bureau of Archeology) and
Alexandra Gaba-van Dongen, curator of
applied arts at the Museum Boymans Van
Beuningen, Rotterdam. Particular thanks
go to my friend and colleague Jan Baart.
I am very grateful to all these individuals.

Once the manuscript is written, the
processing of making it into a book begins.
Here again, I have been fortunate to have
great support and assistance. Several individuals read the draft manuscript and made
substantial comments. My thanks go to
Matt Bender, Penny Drooker, Charly Gehring,
Paul Huey and Wayne Lenig for their patience
and perspective. Joanne Moryl provided
excellent editing and Martha D. Shattuck
compiled the index. A manuscript does
not become a book all by itself. It has been
my good fortune to have Booth Simpson
(Booth Simpson Designers) provide the
graphic design and layout. Artwork was
provided by Ellen Chase, Gordon DeAngelo
and Gene MacKay. Many of the photographs
were provided by Joe McEvoy (OPRHP),
Ted Beblowski (NYSM) and Wiard Krook
(AHM/BMA). My thanks go to these gentlemen as well as to all the other individuals
and institutions that allowed me to reproduce
images from their collections. Finally, it
has been my privilege to work with John B.
Skiba, Manager of the Office of Cartography
and Publications at the New York State
Museum, whose guidance turned the
manuscript into a published volume.

All this takes money, and many organ-
izations and individuals contributed the
funds and materials that made publication
possible. These include The Bender Family
Foundation, Furthermore: a program of the
J.M. Kaplan Fund, The Goldberg Charitable
Trust, The Hogarty Family Foundation,
McCarthy Charities and The Netherland-
America Foundation. Individual contributors
include Matthew Bender IV, Wesley and
Barbara Bradley, William and Gail Bradley,
Jeff and Mark Bryant, Charles and Charlotte
Buchanan, Jane Friehofer, Karen Hartgen,
William and Stephanie Swire and Janet Walker.
Assembly member John J. McEneny provided
additional support through 2003 Legislative
Grant. Finally, this book is printed on Fox
River paper (Starwhite Tiara Smooth 80lb. Text)
that was generously donated by the Fox
Valley Corporation of Appleton, Wisconsin.

To all those who contributed, I offer my
profound thanks. I hope you enjoy the story
you have helped to bring to life.

INTRODUCTION: When Worlds Collide

There are times in history when events simply outpace our ability to understand them, when technological innovation, political instability or natural disasters change our world in ways we cannot foresee. While we may live in such times now, this was certainly the case during the first half of the 17th-century.

In the fall of 1609, when Henry Hudson anchored far up the river that now bears his name, two very different worlds collided. One was the world of Native American people whose ancestors had lived along the river for thousands of years. The other was the world of the Dutch Republic, a new nation born out of bitter religious conflict and shifting economic realities. These two worlds could hardly have been more different in terms of their technology, conception of religion and views on everything from personal morals to governmental authority.

What happens when two radically different cultures meet? Usually the results are catastrophic. The technologically superior culture dominates and distrust, exploitation, even annihilation of the other culture are the result. But something different happened in the upper Hudson Valley when Dutch entrepreneurs came first to trade and then to settle. Although conflicts certainly occurred, these very different people learned to live together during the first half of the 17th-century. And they did so in a manner unlike that of the other Native–European interactions in New England, Virginia or elsewhere in the Americas. This different relationship was based on a sense of mutual opportunity, of seeing more advantage in cooperation than in conflict.

As contacts grew, this tendency to work together was enhanced by a gradual increase in understanding, and occasionally even respect, in spite of the profound cultural differences. This collaborative quality produced important results. One was a viable fur trade, successful because it was a joint economic venture. Each side had a measure of control, and each side got what it wanted. More cordial relations with Native

people also made possible the establishment of stable Dutch communities such as Beverwijck, the predecessor of present-day Albany. A measure of Beverijck's unique success is that it was one of the few European settlements never attacked by Native people in spite of its remote frontier location.

At its simplest, this is a story with two strands, one Native American and one European. But since all Native people were not the same, any more than were the Europeans, these two strands quickly became four. On the Native side were two distinct peoples–the Mahicans, the Algonquian-speaking people who lived along the Hudson River Valley, and the Mohawks, their Iroquoian neighbors who dwelt farther west. On the Dutch side, two strands were also evident, especially after 1629. One was the West India Company, the entrepreneurs who built Fort Orange and saw the wealth of New Netherland primarily as an asset in their war against Spain. The second was Rensselaerswijck, a vast private colony established by Kiliaen van Rensselaer and envisioned as a source of agricultural products for feeding the new colonies of America. During the first six decades of the 17th century, an ever-shifting set of alliances, rivalries and hostilities characterized the relationships among these four groups. There were also plenty of internal feuds and factions within each group. However, by 1660 an overall pattern had emerged, one in which Mahican people chose one way to deal with the Dutch, while the Mohawks chose another. The Dutch in turn had resolved some of their internal disputes and settled into a pattern that lasted long after the English conquest in 1664. Taken together, these choices formed the basis for many aspects of what we call our "colonial" American history – the fur trade, the Covenant Chain and other treaties with the Five Nations, and the building of successful communities, such as Albany, deep in the interior of the continent.

How did this happen? How did the Native people of the upper Hudson Valley respond to Europeans, their exotic appearance, materials and ideas? How did the Dutch react to this new land and its Native inhabitants? How were these interactions reflected in the changing nature of the fur trade? In short, what was it that made the relationship between Native people and the Dutch on the upper Hudson successful? One objective of this book is to examine answers to these questions.

A second objective is to explore this story from an archaeological point of view. Archaeology is the science of understanding human behavior by looking at its material remains. These can range from objects – artifacts such as tools fragments, pieces of pottery and beads – to trash pits, building foundations and even the landscape itself. Wherever human hands have left their mark, archaeology seeks to understand the motivations behind the actions.

Archaeological inquiry is often divided into two different methods, both of which are used in this book. The first focuses on past cultures where people did not keep written records. This approach is used to study human evolution and the emergence of cultures around the world. This is also the approach used to understand most Native American sites. With the exception of descriptions made by early Europeans, and any oral traditions that were recorded, we have no documentary sources to help us

interpret what we see in the ground. As a result, while the patterns of archaeological evidence can tell us a great deal about Native people, how they lived and responded to the changes occurring around them, we still see them abstractly, as a general group. Rarely can we identify them as individuals.

By contrast, historical archaeology focuses on sites for which some kind of written record is present. Here the excavated evidence can be compared with documentary records. Often the families and even the individuals who lived or worked on a particular site can be identified. This, in turn, allows the archaeological evidence to be examined more precisely. Because the Dutch were meticulous record keepers, we know a great deal about the early settlers. While the archaeological evidence from these sites is modest, it has been possible to identify several sites that can be linked to specific individuals. We will follow the story of several people, but one man in particular, Arent van Curler, provides a particularly good example of how the documentary and archaeological evidence can fit together.

We will use two kinds of archaeological evidence as we explore this story – sites and artifacts. Sites are the physical locations where past people lived or worked. Archaeologists also use this term to describe where a particular excavation takes place. The decision on where to live tells us a great deal about past people and what they considered important. The degree to which site locations change over time, or remain the same, can also reveal much about the decisions they made. This story involves many kinds of sites, Native and Dutch, and we will examine several of these in some detail.

Artifacts are the archaeologist's other primary source of information. These are material objects that past people left behind, intentionally or otherwise. Often referred to as "material culture," this physical evidence can range from the smallest seeds and animal bones to large-scale landscape features. We will look at artifacts in three ways. One is to understand the material culture of the region's Native peoples. A second is to reconstruct what kind of material goods Europeans brought with them to trade for fur. Finally, we will also look at the wide range of objects Europeans brought for their own use when they came to settle.

Like the people who used them, the story of these three different groups of artifacts, or assemblages, is one that blends and braids together. How did the material culture of the region's Native people change as result of contact of Europeans and their things? Conversely, how did the material culture of Dutch traders and settlers change as they learned to live in a new and very different environment? Of particular interest is the issue of "trade goods" – what they were and where they came from. We will examine this by looking at several specific classes of objects – shell and glass beads, tobacco smoking pipes, firearms – and how the combination of Native demand and increasingly specialized European production converged to reshape the world's economic system.

Understanding what artifacts mean is perhaps the greatest challenge in archaeology. We are complex creatures and nowhere is this more evident than when we try to define "meaning." This is especially the case in a cross-cultural setting. What did a copper kettle or string of glass beads mean to a Dutchman in 1609? Certainly not the same thing they meant to a Native person. Nor

would either have viewed these objects in the same way fifty years later. This is a story in which meaning changes not only across cultural boundaries, but over time as well.

Archaeologists commonly use a set of conceptual tools when they look for patterns in the information they have collected. We will use them as well. Think of these as rules of grammar as we learn the language of archaeology. There are four:

Visibility – How much of the evidence do we really see?

Context – How reliable is a piece of information? How reliable is its source?

Sample – Do we have enough information to answer our question?

Scale – Are we asking the question at an appropriate level? Is the information too specific or too general?

With these questions in mind, we can examine how the archaeological evidence helps us understand the complex changes that are the heart of this story.

One final comment on archaeology and history: Both are powerful ways to understand the past. However, since Europeans made all the written records, they are strongly skewed towards that side of the story. Archaeology is less partisan. Everybody leaves trash behind and, if we can decipher that evidence, we have the potential to see the story of Native-Dutch relations from both points of view.

This story is told in five chapters. Chapter One focuses on the Native people of the upper Hudson. We will look more closely at both Mahican and Mohawk people, their origins, sites and material culture. Based on this, we will examine the similarities and differences in how both Algonquian and Iroquoian people lived from pre-Contact times to Hudson's visit. We will also explore their relationship before Europeans showed up, how they responded to this unexpected occurrence and how it began to change their traditional ways of living.

Chapter Two shifts to the other side of the Atlantic and the Dutch Republic. Born of changing times, this new nation and its largest city, Amsterdam, quickly became engines of change themselves. Their influence was felt around the globe. This was especially true in terms of international trade, and we will look at the independent traders and early trading companies who were quick to follow up on Hudson's accidental discovery. We will also look at how Mahican and Mohawk people responded to the more regular presence of Dutch traders between 1609 and the establishment of Fort Orange in 1624 when the traders also became settlers. Finally we will look at the changes that resulted from these increased contacts, not only in terms of Mahican and Mohawk sites and material culture, but their relationships with one another.

Chapter Three looks at the period 1624 through 1640 as the Dutch struggled to create permanent settlements, establish good relations with their Native neighbors and build a viable economy. In part, this is the story of how an organized fur trade began to develop out of the free-for-all activities that preceded it. This is also the beginning of the Rensselaerswijck story, Kiliaen van Rensselaer's private colony and its sparring relationship with the West India Company, its inept and distracted parent. Permanent European settlement, no matter how tenuous, gave Native people a vastly greater exposure to European culture. From different objects and technologies to alien concepts of property ownership and deadly new diseases,

the impact of Dutch culture is increasingly clear on the sites, the material culture and the politics of the region's Native people.

Chapter Four focuses on the period 1640 to 1652. This was a period of intense rivalry between Rensselaerswijck and the West India Company, resulting in the establishment of Beverwijck in 1652. It was also the period when Dutch newcomers settled in and learned how to live more comfortably in a new and challenging land. Building long-term relationships with both Mahican and Mohawk people was essential, and this part of the story is examined through the experiences of Arent van Curler, Kiliaen van Rensselaer's grandnephew and business agent for the growing colony. As a farmer and successful businessman in the fur trade, Van Curler exemplifies how traditional Dutch culture and values began, not only to take root in a new place, but also to evolve into something new.

Chapter Five traces the growth of Dutch communities from the establishment of Beverwijck through the English take over in 1664. Although the focus is on Beverwijck and its distinctly Dutch character, this is also the story of how the Dutch began to branch out and establish a second generation of communities. This chapter also looks again at the Native people of the region and how more than a century of European contact, and fifty years of intense trade, had re-shaped their lives.

A final epilogue looks at the pattern of Dutch settlement and Native response that was firmly in place by the time the English took control in 1664. That pattern would define many of the political and cultural conflicts that dominated the next one hundred years, issues not resolved until the American Revolution.

I am often asked why I care about all this old stuff. It is a fair question and deserves a thoughtful answer, or perhaps two. The first is that this story, although far removed in time, is still very much connected to us. The complex relationship between the Dutch and Native peoples, and how it resolved, is not just their story. It is the beginning of ours, of who we are as Americans.

The second reason is a little more abstract. When the worlds of Native people and Europeans collided early in a new century, no one knew what would happen. It is only now, with the comforting knowledge of how things turned out, that the results seem so predictable, so straightforward. At the time, however, things were every bit as confusing, disorienting and stressful as our world is today. Although the technical details of our times are different, human behavior and the problems we face are remarkably the same. Environmental change, global economic shifts, political instability and factionalism all continue to cloud our vision and challenge our ability to find solutions. Looking back may not provide the answers we need, but it is comforting to know that, in similar or even worse circumstances, good solutions to intractable problems are possible.

CHAPTER ONE: An Old World, Native People of the Upper Hudson Valley

When Henry Hudson left the Dutch Republic in March of 1609, his official destination was the East Indies. Hudson was convinced that the quickest way east was to sail west, around the globe. Ignoring his orders to find a Northeast passage to the Spice Islands, Hudson set out across the Atlantic. What he found was not a New World – by this time America's existence was well known – but a country of people more ancient and diverse than he or his contemporaries could have imagined.

This was an Old World. Native people had lived along the great North river and its tributaries since the end of the last Ice Age, for at least 13,000 years. This made them longer-term residents of their lands than some Northern Europeans since portions of that continent were not de-glaciated until much later. As in Europe, the indigenous cultures of northeastern North America had changed over the millennia – the result of environmental fluctuations, new technologies and the movement of people.[1] By the time of Hudson's arrival, two distinct groups lived along the river and its tributaries.

The Mahicans – People of the River

As Hudson sailed upriver, he began to meet a "friendly and polite" people, a distinct change from the more hostile reception he had received downriver. Indeed, these were a "very loving people" who offered the Dutch maize, pumpkins and venison as well as tobacco, furs and great strings of beads.[2] These early descriptions, though few, provide a glimpse of Mahican people and how they lived when the first Europeans arrived early in the 17th-century.

One of the ways scholars differentiate the region's Native people is by language. The Mahicans were part of the broad linguistic family of Algonquian speakers that stretched from the mid-Atlantic coast to the Canadian Maritimes. The Mahican language itself was probably most similar to the Munsee spoken along the southern portion of the Hudson River and adjacent Delaware drainage, but was also related to the Algonquian dialects of northern New England. According to their own traditions, the Mahicans believed their ancestors had migrated into the region from the west.[3]

Archaeological evidence provides us with a more detailed view of how the Mahicans lived during the Protohistoric period – the time between 1525 and 1609 when European materials had begun to reach Native people but before Europeans themselves came this far inland. We will look at this evidence by first focusing on sites and patterns of settlement, that is, where did Mahican people live and what did these sites look like? Then we will look at the evidence for subsistence and territory. How did Mahican people get the food, shelter and other fundamental resources they needed and where did they find them? Finally, what kinds of pottery, tools and other artifacts have been found on Mahican sites and what do these tell us about how people lived?

Sites and Settlement. At present, more than thirty Protohistoric Mahican sites are known.[4] These sites occur primarily along the Hudson River and extend from Fish Creek in Saratoga County, up the Mohawk River past Schenectady and south through Columbia and Greene counties. In general these are small sites spread across the landscape, places where an extended family group lived during certain times of the year. Not surprisingly, favored locations were used year after year, probably over many generations.

The great majority of these sites are located on the rich soils of the river's flood plain. A smaller number are on higher ground, often near where tributary creeks join the river. A few are located in the uplands away from the river. Virtually all these sites are less than one-half an acre and appear to be informal in their layout. Most contained only a few dwellings – probably a combination of small domed structures known as a *wetu*, or wigwam, and somewhat larger, rectangular longhouses. The former had a frame of bent and lashed poles covered with mats of cattail and bull rush while the latter were covered with bark. These small camps or hamlets also contained a wide range of cooking hearths, storage pits and racks, and areas for processing the plants and animals that provided the basics for everyday living. No large village sites dating from this period are known, nor is there any evidence that these sites were enclosed within a palisade.

In general, little archaeology has occurred on these Mahican sites. Given their location along the river, many have been destroyed by erosion or the growth of later communities such as Albany, Troy, Athens and Hudson. Their small size also makes them easy to miss, even when they have survived. In fact, the only Mahican site of this period that has been systematically excavated is the Goldkrest site located in East Greenbush.[5]

Subsistence and Territory. Mahican people were primarily foragers and fishermen, people who lived by an ecological sense of time. Their sites reflect a keen awareness of when and where essential resources were available. This pattern of seasonal movement had evolved over hundreds, even thousands of years. By the early 17th-century, this way

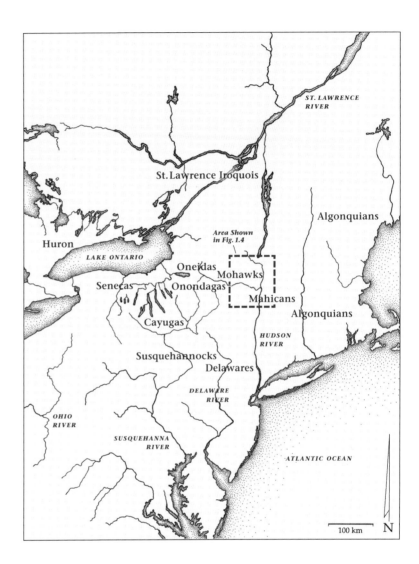

of life followed a well-established pattern of seasonal movement.

In the spring, as soon as the ice was gone and the first floods had subsided, Mahican people moved back to sites along the river or its major tributaries for the spring fish runs. Alewives, shad and especially sturgeon were caught with nets, spears and weirs. Spring was also the time to gather a wide range of wild plants and to plant crops such as maize, beans, squash and tobacco in the flood-replenished soil.

FIGURE 1.1
Map of the Northeast during the Protohistoric period.
Map by Ellen Chase and Booth Simpson.

SITE PROFILE 1

The Goldkrest site

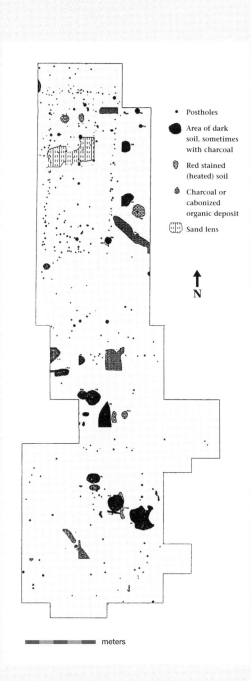

- • Postholes
- ● Area of dark soil, sometimes with charcoal
- ⬭ Red stained (heated) soil
- ◗ Charcoal or cabonized organic deposit
- ⊞ Sand lens

↑
N

FIGURE 1.2
Excavation plan of Locus 1, the Goldkrest site
After Lavin et al 1996:126, figure 11

meters

The Goldkrest site was discovered in 1993 during an archaeological survey for a new gas pipeline. Located along the east bank of the Hudson River near Papscanee Island, the site was deeply buried beneath several levels of alluvium, or flood-deposited soil. Subsequent excavation indicated a complex series of occupations dating from the time of European contact back at least 1,600 years.

Since excavations were limited to the right-of-way, the actual extent of the site is not known. Still, three loci, or areas of concentrated activity, were found within an area less than an acre in extent. The outline of two structures, as traced by postmolds, was uncovered in one of these areas, Locus 1. The first structure was oval in shape with dimensions of eight by eleven meters. This shape and size are consistent with the style of *wetu* or wigwam traditionally used by Algonquian people. The second structure was rectangular, four meters wide and eleven meters long. With a series of large centerposts, this structure was surprisingly similar to the long-houses traditionally used by Iroquoian people. Fragmentary outlines of other structures were discovered in Locus 3. These dwellings are important not only because they indicate two different styles of buildings were used, but because they are the first Mahican dwellings to be documented archaeologically. In addition to these houses, the Goldkrest site also contained several hearths and other kinds of features.

A small but significant assemblage of artifacts was also found at Goldkrest. These included fragments of several Garoga horizon pots found in the late pre-Contact or Proto-historic period levels. These vessels have a

10

well-formed collar with a deeply notched base and are decorated with incised motifs. Only a small number of stone tools were recovered, primarily triangular points of local Hudson Valley chert. Two small pieces of sheet brass were also found in association with a hearth (Feature 59). Large quantities of floral and faunal remains were retrieved from this hearth and other features on the site. Plants included charred hulls from butternut and hickory, several kinds of seeds including raspberry and elderberry, maize kernels and cob fragments. Animal remains included sturgeon and other fish, freshwater mussels and white-tailed deer.

In addition to the brass, another unusual aspect of Feature 59 suggests the presence of Europeans. The most frequently occurring seeds from this hearth were from the common Buttercup (*Ranunculus* sp.). These seeds are not

edible but were valued by Native people as a medicine and protection against witchcraft. One traditional use for Buttercup was as an anti-venereal.

The Goldkrest site typifies the kind of a small riverside camp that Mahican people, and their ancestors, used seasonally for fishing, farming and foraging. With its small bark houses and abundance of food resources, it also provides the best archaeological evidence we have for reconstructing the Mahican settlements described by Hudson and his crew.

FIGURE 1.3
Fall in Mahican country. "The Goldkrest site"
Courtesy of L. F. Tantillo.

During the summer, most activity remained focused around the river. Fishing remained a major pursuit along with the tending of crops. Nesting birds and fresh-water mussels were important food resources, as were strawberries and a host of other wild plants. Plants were also used for medicines and building materials.

By fall, the focus of activity shifted to harvesting both planted and wild crops, and preparing them for winter storage. Nuts, a valuable source of oil, were particularly important. Fall fishing added to the growing larder of supplies for the winter, as did the hunting of summer-fattened game.

By early winter the sites along the river were abandoned in favor of winter camps. These were usually located in more protected, interior settings, often near a pond or marsh. Here, ice fishing and upland hunting for deer, bear and smaller animals such as beaver, otters and turtles provided additional food until spring when the cycle started anew.

Native people and Europeans had a different relationship to the land on which they lived. For Native people, there was no formal sense of ownership. People belonged to the land rather than land to people. Native people saw the land and its resources as commonly held. Territory was defined primarily by what resources the group needed and where those could be obtained. As a result, territorial boundaries tended to be fuzzy rather than sharp. In addition, some resources, such as a particular fish run or quarry site for chert (a flint-like stone from which tools were made), may have been important to several Native groups. In this case, these groups might agree to share usage.

For all these reasons, it is impossible to know with certainty what the boundaries of Mahican territory were before Hudson's arrival. Traditional boundaries have been reconstructed based on historical documents,[6]

but it is unclear whether these reflect the situation during the 16th century. A different approach is to map the distribution of archaeological sites that date from the late pre-Contact and Protohistoric periods.

These sites fall into three geographic clusters. The first extends from Fish Creek in Saratoga County south to Waterford. It also encompasses the lower Mohawk Valley east of Schenectady and includes Ballston and Round Lakes. The second cluster includes both sides of the upper Hudson, from Waterford to the Vlomankill on the west, and from Lansingburg to Schodack Island on the east. Essentially this is the area encompassed by present-day Albany and Rensselaer counties. The third cluster extends along both sides of the mid-Hudson, from Four Mile Point to Inbocht Bay on the west, and from Little Nutten Hook to the Roeliff Jansen Kill on the east, basically Greene and Columbia counties.

It is no coincidence that these site clusters are located around the prime fishing areas and on the best agricultural land. From these areas of concentrated settlement, Mahican hunting territory probably extended eastward into the Taconics, possibly as far as the Housatonic. On the west side, Mahican hunting territory may have included the northern Catskills and reached as far inland as the Schoharie Valley.

In sum, the Mahican pattern was one of foragers and fishermen. Although they also grew maize and other crops, their culture emphasized mobility and flexibility. They seem to have preferred small, dispersed settlements rather than large, consolidated villages. It is difficult to know how large the Mahican population was, but an estimate in the range of 2,000 to 3,000 seems right. Although bound by kin and clan responsibilities, Mahican people were more loosely organized than their Iroquois neighbors, with individual groups quite capable of independent action.

The Mohawks – People of the Flint

The Mohawks were the second group of Native people who would play a pivotal role in shaping the Capital region during the 17th-century. Their homeland lay less than thirty miles (48 km) west of the confluence of the Mohawk and Hudson rivers. The Mohawks were the eastern-most tribe of the Five Nations Iroquois or *Houdenosaunee* (People of the Longhouse). In their own language, the Mohawks referred to themselves as *Kanyu?keha:ka* (People of the Flint).[7]

Although it is unclear whether any Mohawks met Hudson in 1609, they certainly encountered another European. Earlier that same year, Samuel de Champlain and his northern Algonquian allies traveled south along the Richelieu River to explore the lake we know by his name. Along the way, they ran into a large Mohawk war party headed for the St. Lawrence River. The resulting hostilities drew the French into an emerging web of intertribal conflict and helped to establish the Mohawks' reputation as fierce and war-like.

Like the Mahicans, the Mohawks had their own traditional creation stories. According to some of these, Mohawk people had always lived in the same place since they "came out of the earth." Other stories told of living elsewhere and moving into the region from farther west. Archaeological evidence provides support for both points of view. Native people had certainly lived in the Mohawk Valley for a very long time. However, around one thousand years ago, a new group of people ancestral to the Mohawks moved into the region from the south. What is not known is when the Native people living in the Mohawk Valley began to think of themselves as Mohawks.[8]

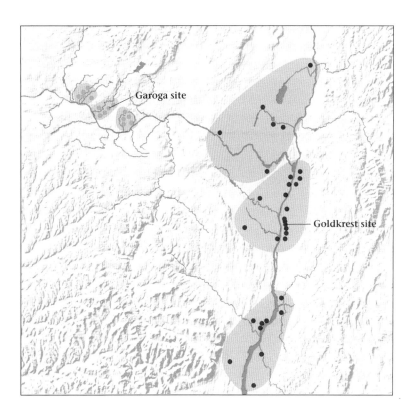

Sites and Settlement. At present more than twenty late pre-Contact and Protohistoric Mohawk sites have been recorded.[9] Nearly all are located north of the Mohawk River between East Canada Creek on the west and Tribes Hill Creek on the east in what is now Montgomery County and the southern edge of Fulton County. In general these are large sites where several hundred people from different clans lived in large communal longhouses.

During the Protohistoric period most Mohawk sites were located in the rugged uplands away from the river, usually on hilltops or high, steep-sided plateaus. These locations appear to have been chosen primarily for reasons of defense. In contrast to the small, dispersed camp sites favored by the Mahicans, Mohawk villages were large, from

FIGURE 1.4

Map of Protohistoric period Mahican and Mohawk sites. Mahican sites and clusters are shown in red. Mohawk sites and clusters in yellow.

For more specific information on these sites, see endnotes 4 and 9.

Map by John Skiba and Booth Simpson

The Garoga Site

The Garoga site is located in the hill country north of the Mohawk River on the upper portion of Caroga Creek. Known to collectors since the 1880s, the site has been extensively excavated. The most recent investigations were conducted by the New York State Museum during the early 1960s.

Garoga is a large site covering two and a half acres. Defense appears to have been a major factor in the site's location. It sits on a high ridge and has steep slopes on three sides. This impression is strengthened by how the settlement was built. A substantial double palisade extended across the narrowest portion of the ridge restricting access to the village. Behind this palisade, more than a dozen longhouses were constructed. The arrangement of houses within the stockade suggests that the village was planned as a unit. Although building lengths vary, several were more than two hundred feet long. Many of these longhouses also reflect expansions or other modification over time. In addition to house structures, more than four hundred other features were excavated. Of these eighty percent were storage pits and the remaining twenty percent were hearths.

Garoga represents a typical large Mohawk village occupied during the time of initial contact with Europeans. Used for perhaps twenty years, it is one of several sites located along Caroga Creek. The large number of houses and extensive refuse left behind indicate a considerable population. Current estimates suggest that between 1,400 and 3,000 people lived at this site. This was a population that relied on hunting and horticulture. Thousands of animal bone fragments attest to the former. Deer is most common, more than seventy-five percent, however, beaver, bear and a wide range of other species are also present. Quantities of plant remains, particularly maize, were also recovered.

A large sample of artifacts has been recovered from this site. These include thousands of pottery sherds representing many hundreds of vessels. The vast majority of these had the deeply notched collar base and opposed triangle motifs typical of Garoga horizon ceramics. A sizable assemblage of ceramic smoking pipes was also recovered. Stone tools are well represented and include triangular arrow points and ovate knives of local Mohawk Valley chert as well as heavier tools for cutting wood and processing plants. Bone and antler were also used to make an extensive array of tools and ornaments. The presence of a few exotic items hints at the changes to come. These include beads and pendants made of marine shell and at least one small fragment of sheet brass or copper, an indication that contact with Europeans had occurred.

Unlike the Goldkrest site, Garoga appears to have been occupied only once. Although efforts to date this site with radiocarbon analysis have been inconclusive, it appears to have been occupied between A.D. 1525 and 1545 based on its relationship with other Mohawk sites.[10]

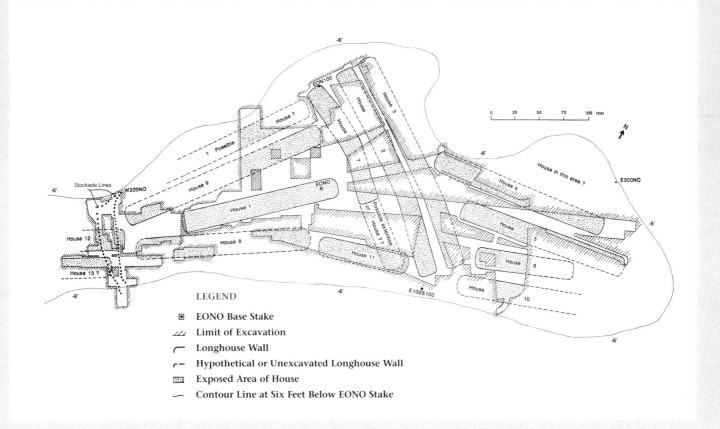

LEGEND

▣ EONO Base Stake

⫽⫽ Limit of Excavation

⌐ Longhouse Wall

⌐‑ Hypothetical or Unexcavated Longhouse Wall

▨ Exposed Area of House

⌒ Contour Line at Six Feet Below EONO Stake

FIGURE 1.5
**Excavation plan
of the Garoga site.**
*After Funk and Kuhn
2003:84, figure 43.*

one to three acres in extent. They were also densely populated and contained as many as a dozen longhouses plus a wide variety of other structures for food processing and storage.

Large villages did not mean that everyone lived there year-round. In the spring and fall, many people went to fishing or hunting camps along the Mohawk River, and probably the Hudson as well. During the late fall

TABLE 1.1: Selected Late pre-Contact and Protohistoric Mohawk Sites

	WESTERN	CENTRAL	EASTERN
Beginning of the Garoga horizon	Otstungo	Swart-Farley #2	Pottery Hill
First evidence of European material	Cairns, Crum Creek Ganada	Garoga,* Smith Pagerie,* Klock*	Caydutta,* Saltsman, Doxstader*
First glass beads (GBP 1 and 2 styles)	Mother Creek* Wormuth*	Englands Woods,* Dewandelaer*	Chapin,* Barker*
	Nelliston*	Schenk #1*	Cromwell*
Polychrome Bead horizon	Wagner's Hollow*	Rice's Woods*	Martin*

* European material recovered

and winter, men hunted well into the Adirondacks. Beyond this, warfare and the opportunity to trade took them even farther afield – north into the St. Lawrence River Valley and south along the Susquehanna River. In all this, the large villages functioned as a base of operations, the center of family, clan and tribal life.

Because of their size, Mohawk sites are much more visible than Mahican sites. They have also survived better since most are located in more remote, rural areas. Much more archaeological work has focused on these sites because of their greater visibility and because they produced large numbers of artifacts. As a result, we know much more about the Mohawks than we do the Mahicans. The Garoga site, located in southern Fulton County, is a good example of an early Protohistoric Mohawk village.

Subsistence and Territory. Like their Mahican neighbors, the Mohawks relied on a wide variety of seasonally available plants and animals. Unlike the Mahicans, this pattern depended more on cultivated crops and upland hunting than on the resources of the rivers.[11] While the Mohawk River contained some fish, the migratory species that made the upper Hudson so rich could not get past the falls at Cohoes. This may have been one of the reasons that Mohawk subsistence was based on farming and upland hunting. In turn, a greater dependence on maize and other crops may have resulted in larger, more sedentary settlements. Fields had to be cleared, planted and tended as well as harvested, all of which required the labor of many people.

However, a larger population also consumed more resources and, not surprisingly, these large Mohawk villages had to move periodically as the soil was depleted and firewood as well as wood for rebuilding were consumed. This pattern of village relocation is very useful for archaeologists since it is allows us to trace Mohawk movement over time.

During the Protohistoric period, Mohawk territory was centered around three distinct and coexisting communities, each of which occupied its own sequence of sites. Each community was located within a different drainage. These included a western community in the East Canada-Crum Creek area, a central community along the upper portion of Caroga Creek and an eastern community in the Cayadutta Creek drainage.

From these three communities, Mohawk hunting territory extended north into the Adirondacks and east toward Lake George. It probably extended south of the Mohawk River into the Schoharie Valley and upper tributaries of the Susquehanna River as well. Although no Mohawk sites have been identified in the Hudson Valley, it is likely that the Mohawks also used its resources, such as the well-known fishing grounds below Cohoes Falls, along with their Mahican neighbors.

In sum, the Mohawk pattern was primarily one of farmers and hunters, rather than foragers and fishermen. They preferred to live in large, more sedentary villages rather than in small, seasonal camps. Estimates of Mohawk population by the end of the period vary widely with some as high as 10,000.[12] A number in the range of 3,000–5,000 seems more reasonable. While the Mohawks probably did outnumber the Mahicans, it is partly their well-defined villages that make them seem so numerous. Mohawk communities were bound together by family and clan ties, and as villages grew larger, it became increasingly important to develop political means to resolve differences and find common solutions to problems.

Friends and Neighbors

Mahican and Mohawk people have often been described as ancient adversaries. Given the differences between the two cultures as well as their ongoing hostilities during the 17th-century, this seems reasonable. However, the two also had much in common and, in all likelihood, were friends and neighbors rather than enemies before the Dutch arrived.[13]

Strong evidence for cordial relations lies in the similarity of the artifacts that were used for everyday life or what archaeologists call their "material cultural" assemblage. Generally archaeologists have assumed that when people speak different languages and live in fundamentally different ways, they also use distinctly different tools. However, as is evident from the Goldkrest and Garoga sites, Mahican and Mohawk artifact assemblages during this time period are very similar. This is especially evident in terms of the pottery each group used. A broader comparison of the assemblages from Protohistoric Mahican and Mohawk sites indicates that this pattern of similarity extends to other classes of artifacts

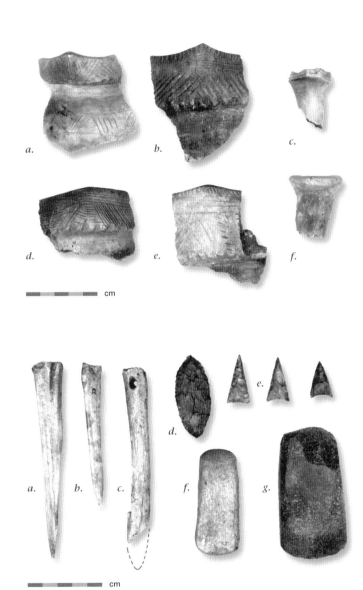

FIGURE 1.6

Top: Ceramic artifacts from the Garoga site.
a., b., d. and e. Four examples of Garoga horizon pottery rims (A-42235.10, A-42236.13, A-42233.18, A-42352.10). c. and f. Two ceramic pipe bowl fragments (A-42363.7, A-42243.9).

Courtesy of the NYSM.
Photo by Ted Beblowski.

FIGURE 1.7

Above: Bone and lithic artifacts from the Garoga site.
a. and b. Two bone awls (A-42349.1, A-42352.5). c. A bone harpoon (tip broken) (A-42357.1). d. A chert knife (A-42243.2). e. Three triangular chert arrow points (A-42887.4, A-42884.1, A-42852.1). f. An antler hammer (A-42369.12). g. A stone celt (A-42541).

Courtesy of the NYSM.
Photo by Ted Beblowski.

FIGURE 1.8

Above: Shell artifact from the Garoga site. A disc bead made from freshwater mussel shell (A-42802-32).

Courtesy of the NYSM. Photo by Ted Beblowski.

cm

FIGURE 1.9

Above right: Garoga-horizon ceramics from the Goldkrest site.

Courtesy of Lucianne Lavin.

as well. These include ceramic smoking pipes, stone tools and a wide range of implements and ornaments made from bone and antler. Where differences do occur, they appear to reflect resource preferences rather than ethnicity. For example, net weights and other fishing equipment are more common on Mahican sites, while chert projectile points occur more frequently on Mohawk sites.[14]

Comparable material cultures support the idea that Mahican–Mohawk relations were friendly prior to the arrival of the Dutch. In fact, there is no evidence of conflict between these groups during this period. Mahican sites were small and unprotected and, while the Mohawks kept their villages strongly fortified, their primary enemies were other northern Iroquoians not the Mahicans.[15] Cordial relations are also indicated by an early 17th-century account in which the Mahicans describe the Mohawks as "their former friends and neighbors."[16]

There were other reasons why Mahicans and Mohawks chose to be on friendly terms. In spite of differences in language and settlement pattern, Mahican and Mohawk people both needed the resources of the Hudson and lower Mohawk rivers. During the Protohistoric period, chert from Hudson Valley quarries occasionally occurs on Mohawk sites as do the remains of fish, such as sturgeon, from the Hudson River.[17] This suggests that the Mahicans and Mohawks were close enough to be friends but different enough not to be competitors.

These cordial relations may also have had deeper roots and may reflect some degree of shared origins. For several hundred years before the arrival of Europeans, Native people ancestral to both Mahicans and Mohawks lived along the Hudson and Mohawk rivers. This earlier culture depended heavily on fish, freshwater mussels and other resources of the river valleys. The cord-impressed pottery that characterizes these sites is widely distributed across upstate New York and New England between A.D. 1000 and 1300. This time period coincides with a climatic interval known as the Medieval Warm Period – an extended period of warm, dry summers and mild winters. About A.D. 1300, this pattern of stable, predictable weather began to shift toward the more variable and extreme conditions often referred to as The Little Ice Age.[18]

Few things influence hunting and gathering cultures more than a change in the environment. A less predictable climate meant that traditional ways of finding food and other essentials had to be re-evaluated, even altered. Faced with such a need, it seems that the ancestors of Mahican and Mohawk people made fundamentally different decisions. Those who became Mahican chose to remain in small, dispersed groups, to live lightly on the land and go wherever the resources were. By contrast, those who became Mohawk chose the opposite – to consolidate

Garoga Horizon Pottery

The similarity between Mahican and Mohawk material culture is especially evident in the pottery each group made and used. Both groups preferred ceramic vessels with globular bodies and a distinctive collar, one with a notched base and finely incised decoration. This style of pottery began to occur early in the 16th-century and is characterized by boldly shaped vessels and precise decorative motifs of horizontal lines and opposed triangles. It continued to predominate on Mohawk and Mahican sites into the first decades of the 17th-century. By then, however, both vessel shape and decoration were more variable and less carefully executed.

The close resemblance of Mahican and Mohawk pottery has been recognized for many years.[19] Recent scholarship has termed these vessels "Garoga-related" and identified them as a time-related style, or ceramic horizon, rather than as a marker of cultural identity.[20]

What does this similarity mean? In both Algonquian and Iroquoian cultures, women were the potters. The strong similarities between Mahican and Mohawk vessels suggest that intermarriage between these groups was common. While further analysis will undoubtedly reveal more variability, these vessels are remarkable for their likeness, not their difference.

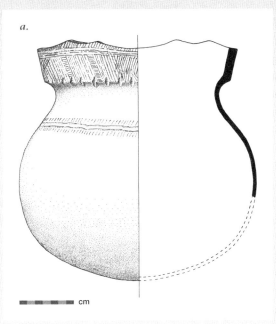

a.

cm

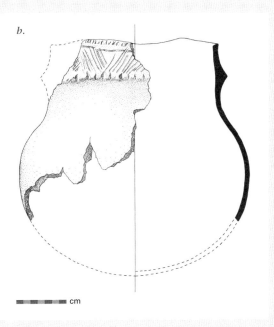

b.

cm

FIGURE 1.10

Two Garoga-horizon pots.

a. An early example with crisp, regular incising on a well defined collar. Also note shoulder decoration.
Swart-Farley #2 (CNJ37/C17-19)

b. A late example with casually done incising on a less well-defined collar.
Swart-Farley #3 (CNJ37/C4)

Courtesy of Wayne Lenig
Drawings by Ellen Chase

FIGURE 1.11
*Brass thunderbird,
Manchester,
New Hampshire.*
After Willoughby
1935:242, figure 130 and
Van Dongen 1995:149.
Drawing by Ellen Chase.

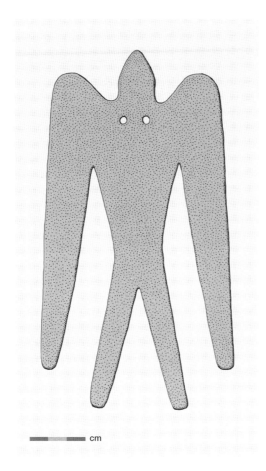

cm

into large, semi-sedentary villages, pooling
their labor and moving only when circumstances required it.

Now, this is certainly simplifying, perhaps
oversimplifying, a complex phenomenon.
But when confronted by difficult choices, even
friends and neighbors can make very different
decisions. These choices reflected a different
set of cultural priorities, and each had its
advantages and disadvantages. Most important, each choice also predisposed how
Mahican and Mohawk people would respond
when confronted by the great challenge of
their time – the arrival of Europeans.

Monsters Thrown Up by the Sea

European contact with Native people was
not one event but a series of encounters over
many years. In northeastern North America,
contact occurred early, within a few decades
of Columbus' voyages. By 1525, Giovanni
da Verrazano had visited the mouth of the
Hudson River. Ten years later, Jacques Cartier
had traveled and traded up the St. Lawrence
as far as present-day Montreal. While
Hudson and his crew may have been the
first Europeans to come so far upriver, the
Native people of the upper Hudson were
already familiar with the existence of these
strange monsters thrown up by the sea.[21]

Like all traditional people, Native Americans
in the Northeast lived at the center of their
own world. They saw themselves as the true
humans, or real man-beings. Their world was
the territory they occupied, one defined by
river basins, mountains and other natural
features. Beyond those boundaries lay increasingly unknown lands inhabited by other kinds
of man-beings, monsters and manitous. While
origin traditions varied, a common belief in
the Northeast was that the world rested on
the back of a giant turtle.

The world which Native people inhabited
was one alive with manitous, spirit-beings of
great power who controlled all aspects of the
natural world. For Native people, the physical
world and the spiritual world were not
separate but fundamentally linked together.
For them the World was an orderly place in
which everything, animate and inanimate,
had spirit and was related to everything else.
As a result, relationships with the spirit world
were of primary importance in preserving
both the natural and social order.

Ritual activities defined how one safely
approached and dealt with strangers –
creatures who might be kin, other man-beings
or even powerful manitous. An exchange
of gifts was one of these rituals and the

substances frequently used – shell, pigments, quartz crystals and native copper – were, themselves, ritually charged. These were the materials of life-enhancing, life-restoring power – the gifts from the manitous.

The Great Manitous. A fundamental aspect of Native cosmology was the division of the World into two parts – the Sky World and the Under(water) World. Each had its own Great Manitou, or Grandfather. These were the most powerful spirit beings. Ancient and implacable adversaries, these two Great Manitous personi-fied the fundamental dualities that structured the Native World.

The Thunderbird ruled the Sky World. Able to transform itself into an eagle or bird man-being, the Thunderbird was the archetypal warrior. Thunder came from the beating of its wings , lightning was the flash of its eyes and storm winds were caused by its flight.

The Under(water) World was the domain of the Great Horned Serpent or Panther. Also able to change its form, the Great Serpent/Panther was usually portrayed as a composite creature with a long body and tail, cat-like features and the antlers (horns) that denoted its chiefly status. As Keeper of the earthly substances of power (shell, crystal and copper), the Great Serpent/Panther was considered the most powerful sorcerer/healer as well as a fierce warrior.

Substances of Power. Humans could obtain both power and protection from these Great Manitous through vision quests, dreams and the exchange of gifts. Such charms, or medicine, assured one of physical, social and spiritual well-being, or in more practical terms, good health and success in courtship, hunting and war. Certain materials were believed to have particularly strong links with the Great Manitous and the power of the spirit world.

The most highly regarded material for ritual purposes was marine shell, especially that of the common whelks (*Busycon* sp.). Valued for its whiteness, shell functioned as the material manifestation of Life and Light. Crystal quartz and mica were also valued for similar reasons. With its bright, shiny surface, pieces of mica (muscovite) were often considered to be scales from the Great Horned Serpent. In several northeastern Native traditions, the Under(water) Panther was believed to have a tail made of copper. The nuggets of native copper found in the Upper Great Lakes and along the Gulf of Maine were thought to be pieces of the Panther's tail. In northeastern North America, the ritual use of shell, quartz, mica and copper and other materials extends back many thousands of years.

When Native people encountered the first Europeans – strange looking, pale man-beings who rose up from beneath the World's rim on floating islands – they tried to make sense

FIGURE 1.12
Mica horned serpent/panther, Brookhaven, Long Island
(NYSM #16079).
Drawing courtesy of Edmund S. Carpenter

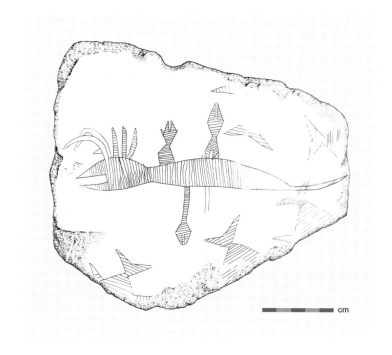

of this unexpected event by reconciling it with what they already believed. To Native observers, the first Europeans looked, and seemed to act, like manitous, traditional beings of power. They appeared to come from the Under(water) World. They could make islands move. They commanded thunder and lightning. Their strange white skin seemed to signify special status, as did the gifts they

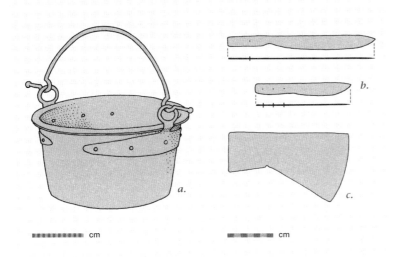

FIGURE 1.13
Basque-related trade assemblage.

a. Large copper kettle banded with iron.

b. Two styles of large, flat-tanged iron knives, side and top views.

c. Large iron axe.

After Fitzgerald 1990:182, figure 29 and Bradley 2005:200, figure 24; 203, figure 26. Drawing by Ellen Chase

offered. While the glass beads, mirrors and copper ornaments may have been "trifles" of little value in European eyes, to Native people these looked like the traditional substances of power – gifts from the manitous.

This first impression changed quickly, especially as interactions between Native people and Europeans became more frequent. It was soon clear that the newcomers were not spirit-beings, but man-beings and not very well mannered ones at that. Early encounters often ended with the Europeans kidnapping Native people and stealing whatever possessions they fancied. As a result Native people soon learned to be more cautious and pragmatic in their dealings with these odd, uncivilized men.

Before Hudson

What were the first European materials, these "gifts from the manitous"? It is difficult to know for sure. Most early encounters were brief. Many were not recorded. Yet even when documents were kept, they often say little. Trade items were usually described as only as "trinkets." Here again archaeology is helpful, especially in documenting the specific kinds of objects used in the early trade.

European traders were a diverse lot and over the course of the 16th century, several different groups were involved. Many of the earliest Europeans to frequent the coast of America were fishermen who sailed from ports across western Europe to catch cod on the Grand Banks. Although fishing was their focus, occasional trading along the Atlantic Coast occurred as well. It was not until the early 1580s that an organized trade for furs began. The initial interest in furs came primarily from French merchants and focused on the St. Lawrence Valley. With a more structured trade came better records and a more clearly defined set of trade goods. Two distinct trade assemblages were particularly important in the decades before Hudson's visit. The first was used by Basque-related traders between 1580 and 1600. Norman traders used a different assemblage beginning about 1600 and continuing into the 1620s.[22]

Basque Traders. Basque interests in the New World initially revolved around fish, but by the 1560s whalers from the Bay of Biscay ports in France and Spain had established numerous onshore whaling stations along the Gulf of St. Lawrence. Here whales were butchered, the oil rendered and packed for shipment back home.[23] After 1580, the demand for furs, especially beaver, grew rapidly and trading became increasingly important.

Archaeologists have defined an assemblage of materials used by Basque traders that combined utilitarian and ornamental objects. Although some may have been adapted from whaling (large flensing knives for example), most seem to have been selected for trading. Specifically, the Basque trade assemblage includes large copper kettles banded with iron. These have a distinctive folded edge and heavy iron fittings.[24] There are also large iron axes, often weighing as much as two kilograms, and long, flat-handled knives. Diagnostic artifacts from the Basque trading assemblage are illustrated in Figure 1.13. Basque traders also used several varieties of glass beads. Based on the work of Canadian archaeologists, these included small round turquoise blue beads (IIa31/40) and larger beads with a ceramic core. We will look at glass beads in more detail in the next chapter and how they, like Garoga-related ceramics, serve as horizon markers. Very few of these early beads have been found on Mohawk or Mahican sites.[25]

Norman Traders. A second group of traders who had a profound influence on the fur trade during the early years of the 17th-century came from northern France. While these traders sailed from ports between Brittany and Flanders, the most important came from Normandy and especially towns along the Seine River. With the ascent of Henri IV to the French throne in 1589, Norman merchants began to receive preferential treatment in terms of the trade. This included a series of monopolies granted to Rouen merchants giving them exclusive control over fur trade along the St. Lawrence River. The most important of these was a ten-year monopoly issued to Pierre du Monts in 1604. During this period, many people including Samuel de Champlain sailed under du Monts' auspices.[26]

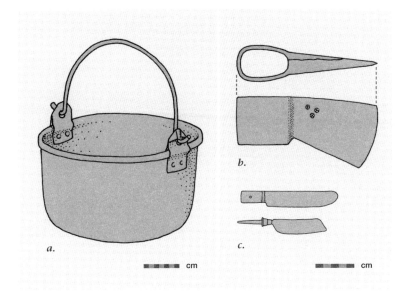

Although Norman merchants used a different set of objects in their trade assemblage, they appear to have paid careful attention to what earlier traders had learned about Native preferences. Most of the items were lighter, more portable versions of those that had been used previously. They include small kettles made of brass, rather than copper, with a rolled lip and sheet brass lugs, smaller iron axes weighing less than one and a half kilograms, and knives with a distinct collar between the tang and blade. A sample of objects from the Norman trade assemblage is illustrated in Figure 1.14. Norman traders also used glass beads as trade goods although, here too, they preferred a different set of colors and styles. Most common are small white and indigo tubular varieties (Ia5, Ia19) and oval beads in the same colors (IIa15, IIa57).[27]

FIGURE 1.14
Norman-related trade assemblage.
a. Brass kettle.
b. Smaller iron axe, top and side views.
c. Two styles of smaller iron knives with raised collars.
After Fitzgerald 1990:182, figure 29 and Bradley 2005:200, figure 24; 203, figure 26. Drawing by Ellen Chase

Recycling a Copper Kettle

To Native people during the Protohistoric period, a copper or brass kettle was an incredible source of wealth, something far too valuable to use for cooking. Besides, Mohawk and Mahican people had plenty of pottery for that purpose. Instead, a copper kettle or even large fragment served as the raw material from which a wide selection of traditional implements and ornaments could be made.

At first glance, this does not seem to be very complicated, however, it is a mistake to underestimate the skill and sophistication of Native metal working. This technology had evolved over several thousand years and displayed a profound knowledge of how copper could be cut and shaped.[28] The first step was to reduce a fragment of kettle to a specific size and shape – not a simple task without shears or an iron knife. One traditional method was to score a deep line on a piece of sheet metal with an antler tine, then abraid away the raised ridge on the opposite side with a piece of sandstone. The result was a clean straight cut.[29] Once cut to size, a piece could be shaped and finished through a variety of techniques. Implicit in this was an understanding that copper became harder and more brittle as it was worked and that it had to be periodically annealed, or softened, by heating before it could be worked further.

These traditional techniques were quickly applied to European copper and brass. As metal became more common during the late 16th and early 17th centuries, the range and complexity of Native-made objects also increased. Figure 1.16 shows some of the more common forms. These included disc-shaped pendants, tubular beads and conical forms that could be used either as ornaments or to line the bowl of a wooden smoking pipe. Implements included triangular arrow points and many varieties of cutting and scrapers tools. Some of these replicated traditional implement forms, others mimicked the shape of European knives. Even the iron bail, or handle, of the kettle was reused. Typically it was straightened, cut into sections and sharpened for use as an awl.

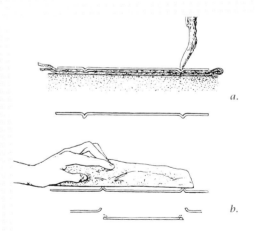

a.

b.

FIGURE 1.15
Cutting copper without an iron knife.
A piece of copper or brass could be "cut" by
(a) scoring it with an antler tine, then
(b) grinding off the resulting ridge. Additional
grinding would produce a clean and precise edge.
After Craddock 1995:102, Figure 3.4.

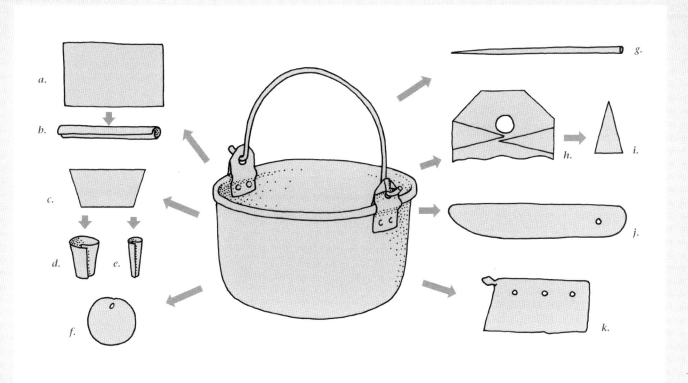

FIGURE 1.16

For Native people, kettles often served as a source of raw material from which other tools and objects could be made. One common practice was to cut a piece of kettle into a rectangular blank (a) that was then rolled into a tubular bead (b). In a similar manner, trapezoidal blanks (c) could be made into conical liners for wooden pipes (d) or bangles. Disc-shaped pendants (f) were produced in this way.

The heavier-gauge metal from the lugs was often used for implements. After being removed from the kettle, the lugs were hammered out flat and scored to be cut into arrow points (h). The finished points (i) could be perforated for easier attachment or not.

Other implements made from kettle pieces included knives that mimicked the shape of European styles (j) or reflected Native taste (k). Even the kettle's iron handle was re-used. After removal, it was hammered out straight and ground down into an awl (g).

Adapted from Bradley 2005:131, Figure 13.

European Material – Native Culture

The European items that reached Mahican and Mohawk people in the decades before Hudson's visit were rare and highly valued objects. Only a few Protohistoric sites produce artifacts of European material and none have

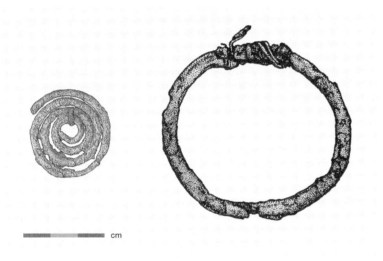

cm

FIGURE 1.17
A brass spiral and hoop.
After Bradley 2005:71, figure 7g, i.

yielded very many. On early Contact sites, such as Garoga, the evidence may be no more than a piece of brass, perhaps reworked into a bead, or fragment of iron. By 1600, more European material is found on the region's Native sites although it is still uncommon. In addition to beads and pendants, these artifacts include knives and other small implements were made from sheet brass and copper. Iron axes and knives occasionally have been found on these sites as well as a few glass beads.[30]

The extent to which these European items were used, and re-used, is one indication of their value. It is unlikely that complete brass or copper kettles reached the upper Hudson during this period. Too valuable to use for cooking, they were cut up and converted into a variety of ornaments and implements. Iron axes and knives appear to have been used until little of the blade was left, although

these too were often recycled quickly. The inclusion of European objects in burials is another indication of how highly valued they were.

Although these small artifacts of copper, brass and iron do not look very impressive, they provide important evidence for how Native people dealt with the changes that occurred after European contact. It has often been assumed that, once Native people had access to metal tools and other European objects, they quickly abandoned their own traditional stone and antler implements in favor of these new, technologically "superior" forms. However the archaeological evidence indicates that something different, and much more interesting, happened.

Two traits characterize how Native people responded to Europeans and their exotic materials. First, they were selective. Perhaps during the earliest encounters, any "gift from the manitous" was welcome but as Native people learned more about these strangers, they became increasingly shrewd about what they wanted. Far from passively accepting whatever was offered, it was Native preference that shaped the trade. It did not take savvy European traders long to figure this out and by 1600, a standard set of trade goods – kettles, axes, knives and glass beads in specific colors – began to emerge.

The second characteristic is that the Native response to European materials was basically conservative. In most cases, European objects were quickly re-processed into traditional forms, both symbolically charged and utilitarian ones. European kettles are a good example. Viewed as a source of valuable raw material, they were systematically cut up and converted into ornaments and implements to meet traditional needs.

While many of these Native-made objects were fairly simple, some show an astonishing degree of complexity. Hoops and spiral-shaped ornaments are examples of this more sophisticated work. These were made from a thin rectangular piece of metal that had been rolled into a long narrow tube, then formed into a hoop or coiled into a loose spiral. These forms are diagnostic of Protohistoric period and examples have been recovered from both Mahican and Mohawk sites. These are complex objects, ones that required great technical skill and control to make. For example, each piece required several anneals, or heat treatments, to convert it from a piece of sheet metal into final form. Because of this sophistication, these artifacts were long thought to be of European origin. However, recent analysis has demonstrated that these objects were made by Native craftsmen from recycled kettle fragments.[31]

What is significant is how little change occurred in the material culture of Mahican and Mohawk people during this period. Traditional skills such as fabricating pottery vessels and making tools from stone, bone and antler all remained strong. Artifacts of European material seem to have supplemented traditional forms, not replaced them.

Summing Up

European contact must have had a huge impact on the world of Native people, especially in the social and political realm. However, most of the evidence we have is archaeological and that limits what we can see. While waves of psychic change may have rolled across the Northeast as a result of contact, the archaeological evidence indicates that the basic patterns of Mahican and Mohawk life – site preference, subsistence strategies and material culture – remained largely unaltered.

For hundreds, probably thousands of years, the upper Hudson River had been a central place whose abundant resources were used and shared by Native people of many cultural traditions. With the arrival of the Dutch and the beginning of direct trade, things changed. What had been a source of mutual interest and cooperation (the river and its resources) became a source of competition and conflict. As they had in the past, Mahican and Mohawk people chose to respond in different, yet traditional, ways.

CHAPTER TWO: A New Country, The Dutch Republic

The Europe of Hudson's day was a very different place from the one we know. It was Europe of the late Renaissance with its church-sanctioned monarchies and empires, its independent cities and principalities. Most of the national borders we take for granted would be established centuries later. It was also a Europe defined primarily by religious differences. The Protestant Reformation and the Catholic Church's response, the Counter-Reformation, had reshaped the political and economic as well as the religious landscape. Religion was the primary criterion for determining friend and foe, business partner or adversary. Business practices were still deeply rooted in the guild system and large-scale production was restricted to a few specialized areas such as Aachen for brass, Cologne for stoneware and Venice for glass. However, if anything characterized this period, it was change, often swift and unexpected.

Two transformations were particularly important. One was the development of modern economic practices. These included the formation of corporations to explore the rapidly expanding world and exploit its resources as well as the financial institutions that made such ventures possible. Second was the emergence of national identities, the tendency to think of oneself as from a country instead of a particular village, town or kingdom.

Nowhere were these changes more evident than in the new Dutch Republic. For much of the 16th century, the Netherlands was part of the Habsburg Empire, ruled first by the Catholic Emperor Charles V (1500–1558), then by his son King Phillip II of Spain. Increasingly unhappy under Spanish rule, the seven largely Protestant Northern Provinces revolted in 1568 and, under the leadership of William

of Orange, united to declare their independence thirteen years later. The war that followed, known as the Eighty Years War, lasted until 1648 when Spain finally recognized the Republic.

While the Dutch fought for independence, they also accomplished another astounding feat. Within fifty years, only a couple of generations, the Republic transformed itself from a small country of traders and farmers into the center of a worldwide empire. Dutch merchants had long dominated the carrying trade in northern Europe, moving cargoes of grain and beer to Scandinavia in their sturdy broad-beamed cogs and returning with lumber, copper and furs. They also brought English wool to the Continent where it was made into cloth. By the end of the 16th century, the Dutch had made significant improvements in their sailing vessels. With larger, deeper draft vessels known as flutes, Dutch merchants expanded their routes into the Mediterranean, taking grain to Italy and bringing back oil, wine and luxury goods such as glassware, ceramics and spices. While the war with Spain put this trade at risk, it also opened up significant new opportunities and encouraged Dutch merchants to undertake ever more ambitious voyages.[1]

The Rise of Amsterdam

Nothing symbolized the spirit of the Republic better than the success of its largest city, Amsterdam. One of several modest Dutch cities until the mid-16th century, the revolt transformed Amsterdam. The precipitating event, known as the "Alteration" of 1578, occurred when the ruling Catholic elite was expelled by Protestants who quickly took control of the city. This was a new generation, one that had grown up with warfare and ready to take risks on new business ventures, not just rely on the established ones. Their opportunity came soon when Phillip's forces captured Antwerp, the international marketplace for the Low Countries, in 1585. With the competition of Antwerp gone, Amsterdam quickly emerged as the Republic's major trading port.[2]

The fall of Antwerp had another profound effect. Tens of thousands of immigrants flocked to Amsterdam. These refugees came from war zones across northern Europe and, along with their families, brought with them professional expertise, craft skills, money and a keen desire to start over. The results were explosive. Amsterdam, which had already doubled in size between 1514 and 1554, doubled again by 1600. This phenomenal growth not only continued but accelerated during the early 17th-century as refugees continued to pour in. Although the city had expanded beyond its walls in the 1580s, building new canals and residential districts, there still was not enough room for the burgeoning population. In 1613 construction of another set of new canals began, employing an army of workers and creating more neighborhoods for start-up businesses and residences. Between 1600 and 1650, Amsterdam nearly tripled in size growing from 65,000 to 170,000 inhabitants. Most were immigrants. These ranged from Portuguese Jews and French Huguenots fleeing persecution to rural farmers and laborers seeking better jobs in this city of outsiders. Whatever their background, one factor united all these new-comers – the desire to improve their lives.[3]

Of all the values that underlay the rise of Amsterdam, this desire for success, for financial gain, was foremost. Money meant many things – the ability to buy property, to start a business, to purchase newly available consumer goods. But primarily it was the means to improve one's life, to move up the social scale and become a respected member of the community. However, it wasn't only

about money. In the emerging culture of the Republic, two other values were equally impor-tant and tempered the quest for wealth. One was tolerance. In a land filled of with refugees,

tolerance was a necessity. This was as much a matter of good business as it was about being a good neighbor. One could not always tell who had the best skills, capital for investment or a good solution to a difficult problem. The other value was a strong sense of community. In a hostile world, whether the threat was from the Spanish or the sea, it was essential to be part of a larger community that could provide assistance and support. These services were provided by local entities such as the church, court and poorhouse. Support of these local institutions was a strong part of the Republic's moral geography.[4] While it was good to make money, one was expected to give some of it back to those organizations that kept the community together.

FIGURE 2.1
Map of the Dutch Republic in the early 17th-century.
After Puype 1985:88, figure 78. Map by Booth Simpson

FIGURE 2.2
A view of Amsterdam in 1611. Print by Claes Jansz Visscher.
Courtesy of the Municipal Archives, Amsterdam

During the first decades of the new century Amsterdam became the hub of a new economic order, one based on international trade and the accumulation of earthly, rather than heavenly, treasure. This entrepreneurial spirit was evident not only in commerce but in all the supporting professions and crafts required for success. By the early 17th-century, Amsterdam was a center for shipbuilding, mapmaking, banking and insurance. It was also the home of a new kind of company, one designed specifically for global trade. Best known was the Dutch East India Company, or VOC, whose primary interest focused on the Spice Islands of the East Indies (now Indonesia). A company like the VOC was a powerful political as well as commercial entity and had the authority to negotiate treaties, recruit soldiers and build forts as well as to trade. With such aggressive potential, the Republic posed a distinct challenge to the

established political and economic powers of the day – Portugal and Spain. In 1494, with the Pope's blessing, Portugal and Spain had divided the newly discovered portions of the world between themselves. Portugal would control the trade with Africa, India, China, the East Indies and Brazil while Spain would rule the rest of the "New" World, especially the vast riches of Mexico and Peru. By the early 17th-century, the Dutch were ready to challenge these claims.

To succeed in this new, rapidly changing world one needed allies, not just enemies. While the Republic certainly made the latter, it also had a small but important friend in England. Both countries were Protestant and, having survived its own internal religious wars during the 16th century, Tudor England strongly supported the Republic in its revolt against Catholic Spain. There were also strong economic ties between the two countries.

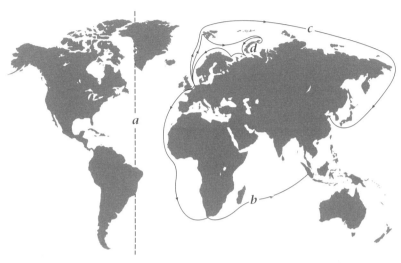

FIGURE 2.3
The 16th-century world.

a. The Demarcation Line, established in 1494, divided the newly discovered lands between Portugal and Spain.

b. The southern route to the East Indies.

c. The proposed northern route to the East Indies.

d. Nova Zembla, 1596.

After Braat et al 1998:11. Map by Booth Simpson

English wool and coal had been essential components of the Dutch economy for hundreds of years. Eventually, economic competition would shatter this cordial relationship but not for several decades.

Independent Traders, 1609–1624

Two important events marked the year 1609 – one great, the other small. The most significant event was a truce in the Republic's long war with Spain. With a break in hostilities, Dutch merchants expanded overseas exploration and commerce at an even more rapid pace. One small part of this effort was Henry Hudson's third attempt to reach the East Indies. The English Muscovy Company had sponsored his first two unsuccessful efforts. When he set sail again in March of 1609, it was under the auspices of the VOC.

Although directed to follow a Northeast route across the Arctic to the Indies, Hudson

quickly reversed his course and set out in pursuit of his real goal – the elusive Northwest passage. By midsummer Hudson and his mixed English and Dutch crew were off the coast of Maine. Here they discovered that Native people were already trading with the French from whom they received knives, hatchets, kettles and beads. However, exploration, not trade, was Hudson's primary interest. Confident of their superior weapons and not trusting the Natives, several of the crew went ashore and, in the candid words of Robert Juet, one of Hudson's officers, "drove the savages from their houses and took spoil of them, as they would have done of us."[5] This was not a good way to make friends.

It was early September when Hudson finally reached the great North River. Here too, suspicion and violence marked *de Halve Maen's* encounters with Native people. It was not until they were far upriver that the situation changed. Having run aground several times, Hudson finally found a good anchorage on September 19th some leagues above the shoals. Here the Dutch were surprised to find the Natives friendly and anxious to trade. Hudson stayed for several days, sending a boat and crew farther upriver to look for a navigable channel farther west.

FIGURE 2.4
De Halve Maen
on the North River,
September 1609
Courtesy of L.F. Tantillo.

In the meantime, there was much socializing on board and ashore as well as a steady exchange of beads, knives, hatchets and other "trifles" for fresh food and furs. Although he found the countryside and its people attractive, Hudson was deeply disappointed when the boat returned on September 22nd to report that the river was "at an end for shipping." The next day he weighed anchor and sailed for home, considering this trip yet another failure.[6]

Hudson's voyage was not the beginning of Dutch commercial interest in North America. The Dutch had been latecomers in discovering the economic potential of Terra Nova and did not frequent the North American coast until the last years of the 16th century. Although initially drawn toward the rich fishing grounds, Dutch interests quickly shifted to

exploring, privateering and trading along the coast of New France. Furs were an especially attractive commodity. Beaver felt hats were the rage in northern Europe and the traditional suppliers, Russia and Poland, could not meet the growing demand. While the VOC showed little interest in Hudson's report of plentiful furs and friendly Natives, other independent traders noticed. The result was a sharper focus on where furs could be obtained successfully and within a few years several ships sailed intentionally for Hudson's river.[7]

Not all these entrepreneurial ventures were strictly "Dutch." For example, in June 1611, Arnout Vogels, an Amsterdam fur trader, entered into partnership with two Norman merchants from Rouen. The ships they sent to Canada sailed from the Seine.[8] By 1613 a fierce, even violent rivalry existed among the small companies trying to exploit this new market. The squabbling was temporarily suppressed by the creation of the New Netherland Company in 1614. This new consortium of merchants from Amsterdam, Hoorn and other towns was established by the States General, the Republic's legislature, and given a three-year monopoly over the trade.[9]

Under the New Netherland Company, trading became more regular. Most significant was the construction of a small, fortified trading house on Castle Island near the mouth of the Normanskill. Fort Nassau, as it was known, provided both a year-round base for resident traders and a clear destination for Native people, Mahican or Mohawk, interested in trade. From here, the most enterprising traders, known as *bosloopers*, ventured farther inland to scout for precious metals and better understand the Native peoples who lived in this vast new land. Among those known to have been stationed in this isolated outpost were Jan Rodrigues, a "mulatto of Santo Domingo" who spent the winter of 1613–1614, and Jacob Eelkins, who later claimed to have "lived four years with" the local Native population.[10] While few operational details have survived, the New Netherland Company appears to have used much the same inventory of trade goods that Hudson and the other independent traders did to obtain furs – the increasingly standardized set of kettles, axes, knives and glass beads as well as anything else that appealed to a Native customer and could be spared.

By 1618, however, the New Netherland Company's monopoly had expired and the trade probably reverted back to its former chaotic state. Although many of the same merchants continued to control the trade, their efforts may not have been as effective. The resident traders did not return and the arrival of ships became irregular and unpredictable. Fort Nassau did not last either. Located next to the river, the fort was

cm

FIGURE 2.5
Above: Late 16th-century beaver hat, excavated from the Karperkill harbor, Hoorn, the Netherlands.
Courtesy of the Department of Archaeology of Hoorn.

FIGURE 2.6
Left: A merchant in a beaver hat and two seamen with exotic pets in the courtyard of the Amsterdam exchange, 1609.
Detail of a print by Boetius Adam Bolswert. Courtesy of the Municipal Archives, Amsterdam.

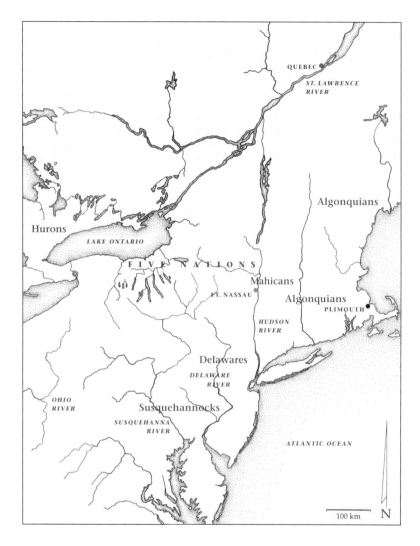

FIGURE 2.7
*Map of the
Northeast
in 1620. Orange
dot indicates
Dutch site, red
dot English and
blue is French.*
Map by Booth
Simpson

were killed during a surprise attack. A year later
even the renowned Jacques Eelkins was unable
to trade successfully and shifted his attention
to the South, or Delaware, River. While Dutch
traders were surprised by this lack of interest,
they largely had themselves to blame. Faced
with intense competition, some traders
resorted to strong-arm tactics. For example,
in 1622, Hans Jorisz Hontom, captain of the
Witte Duyf (White Dove), held a Mohawk chief
for ransom in order to guarantee the trade but
then castrated and killed his hostage anyway.[12]

Fierce competition existed on the Native
side as well. With a regular Dutch presence
after 1614, the river that had brought Mahican
and Mohawk people together for generations
became a source of controversy, then conten-
tion. Since the few Europeans present were not
knowledgeable or interested enough to record
this side of the story, little is known for certain.
However, the primary issues appear to have
been access to European traders and on whose
land the trade would occur. By 1624, the river
that had bound the region's Native people
together now functioned as a hostile border
with the Mahicans centered on the east side
and the Mohawks on the west. It would take
generations of intertribal warfare before this
dispute was finally resolved.

Important as these events were, they
were only small pieces in the greater scheme
of international trade and empire building.
In 1621, the twelve-year truce between the
Republic and Spain ended and warfare between
Catholics and Protestants again swept over
western Europe. It was a much stronger and
more aggressive Dutch Republic that resumed
the war. This martial spirit was reflected in the
chartering of a new company in 1621, one
focused on the riches of the Atlantic world –
West Africa, Brazil, the Caribbean and North
America. The establishment of the Dutch West
India Company, or WIC, marked the end of
private trading in the Western Hemisphere.
However, the West India Company was

frequently flooded and with the demise
of its parent company, there were no funds
for upkeep or repair. Still, as a known location
for trade, the site probably remained in use
from several more years until Fort Orange
was built in 1624.[11]

The trade may have faltered after 1618 for
many reasons. Aside from the demise of the
New Netherland Company, there was continued violence and an increased unwillingness
on the part of Native people to do business.
In the spring of 1619, Hendrick Christiaensen,
probably the most experienced trading captain
of the period, and the greater part of his crew

designed primarily as an instrument of war, not an engine of commerce. North America, though interesting, was viewed as the least of its priorities.[13] Not until 1624 was any serious effort made to establish a permanent settlement in New Netherland. Until then, the trade limped along much as it had after the collapse of the New Netherland Company.

Changes on the Land

How does the archaeological evidence help us see these dramatic events more clearly? In two ways, the first of which is by looking at the location of sites from the period. Where people choose to live says a great deal about what is most important to them. As discussed above, both Mahican and Mohawk people chose locations that gave them the best access to the resources they needed. The presence of Dutch traders, basically a new resource to be utilized, began to change the established patterns.

However, before discussing the Native sites further, more needs to be said about the primary factor that drove these changes– where the Dutch were located. Unfortunately, no Dutch archaeological sites from this period are known. In fact, only one site ever existed, Fort Nassau on Castle Island, and that location has never been found. Aside from Fort Nassau, most of the trading appears to have occurred either on board ship or along the shore wherever it was convenient. This means that, like Hudson's voyage, these early trading sites are essentially invisible in archaeological terms. What we do know comes primarily from the Mahican and Mohawk sites of this period.

Mahican Sites. At least seven Mahican sites have been identified that date between 1609 and 1624.[14] Although most of these sites were occupied over a long time span, all have produced artifacts, glass beads in particular, that are diagnostic of the Independent Traders period. In terms of location, these sites show little change from those of the preceding Protohistoric period. All are located along

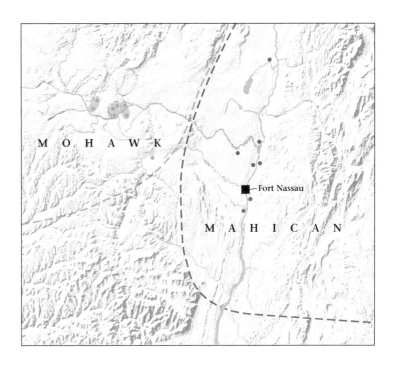

the banks of the Hudson River or its major tributaries, well within the traditional boundaries of Mahican territory. These Early Historic period Mahican sites are traditional in other ways as well. Though little archaeological research has been done on them, they appear to follow the earlier patterns of small size and seasonal occupation. There is no evidence to date that any of these sites were fortified. While it is difficult to say much about Mahican population given such slight evidence, it seems likely that it remained in the range of 2,000 to 3,000 people.

Mohawk Sites. At least seven Mohawk sites have produced artifact assemblages associated with the Independent Traders period.[15] Unlike the Mahicans, the Mohawks tended to occupy their villages for the specific period of time, perhaps ten years, then move to another location. This periodic change in location is especially helpful in seeing patterns of continuity and change in Mohawk culture during this period of intensified contact with the independent Dutch traders.

FIGURE 2.8
Map of Mahican and Mohawk sites and tribal lands during the Independent Traders period, 1609 to 1624. The Vanderwerken site, located in the Scholarie Valley, maybe a Mohawk site of this period.
Map by John Skiba and Booth Simpson.

Here too, the basic pattern remains the same. Most of these Mohawk sites were large, upland villages containing from six to eight longhouses and built in strong defensive locations. These sites appear to represent the movement of three different communities, each centered in a different drainage. While only limited archaeological work has been done on these sites, the evidence suggests that Mohawk population probably remained basically the same as during the preceding period, about 5,000 people.[16] However, there are hints of change. These sites were located closer to the Mohawk River and, in one case (Cromwell), have actually moved to the south side of it. Better access to the Dutch at Castle Island is one explanation for this shift.

Two other important changes occur by the end of the Independent Traders period, although they are less evident on the map. By 1624, the Hudson River had become a hostile boundary between the Mahicans, located primarily on the east side, and the Mohawks who increasingly dominated the west side. It is also likely that this is when the Mohawks begin to play their traditional role as keepers of the "the eastern door" in a more powerful way. During the 17th-century, the Iroquois Confederacy was often portrayed as a great longhouse that stretched across what is now upstate New York. The Senecas were the keepers of the western door, the Mohawks guarded the eastern door and the Onondagas tended the Council fire at its center. As the Dutch began to establish themselves along the upper Hudson, the Mohawks were in an increasingly strong position, one that controlled the access of the rest of the Five Nations to this new source of material wealth and power.

Tools of the Trade

Just as site locations help us visualize where people were during this period, the artifactual evidence gives us a much more detailed picture of what was being traded, by whom and when. As with the documents, there is considerable evidence but lots of holes as well. Take Henry Hudson's voyage as an example. While the historical significance of this event was enormous, the documentary evidence is slight and the archaeological evidence non-existent. Yet, although Hudson's voyage remains archaeologically invisible, the period of Independent Trading it initiated is one of the most dramatic phases in the region's 13,000 year-long archaeology record.

To piece together the archaeological side of this story, we again start in the Dutch Republic. Much of the best archaeological evidence comes from Amsterdam. In 1972, the City Council established an Archaeological Research Department to work jointly with the Department of Public Works and the Amsterdam Historical Museum. Under the direction of Jan Baart, and now Jerzy Garwonski, the Department has recorded information and conducted excavations throughout the city for more than thirty years. This evidence has allowed archaeologists to reconstruct much of the city's development in detail, especially its rapid growth, increasing wealth and economic specialization.[17]

By the early decades of the 17th-century, Amsterdam was a wealthy and cosmopolitan city. With the expansion of overseas trade, new commodities flowed into the city from around the world. These ranged from the pepper and spices from the East Indies to the fish and furs of *Terra Nova*. Along with these commodities came new consumer goods – porcelain from China, elegant rugs from Turkey and fine tableware from Italy and Portugal. The artifactual residue of this global economy has been well documented in the Amsterdam excavations.

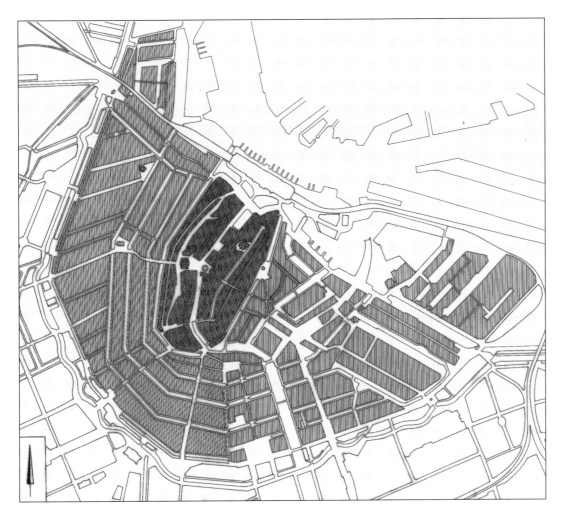

FIGURE 2.9
Map of Amsterdam showing the 15th century city core and areas added during the late 16th and early 17th-century.
Photo by Wiard Krook, afdeling Archeologie, BMA

Archaeology also provides good evidence for the increase in specialized production that supplied Amsterdam's growing population and provided goods for new foreign markets. When Dutch vessels sailed for distant shores, they took with them a diverse set of locally produced goods that could be used for trade or exchanged for supplies. Inventories from the period list a bewildering array of merchandise including blankets, glassware, axes and adzes, mirrors, armor and beads as well as many kinds of linen and woolen cloth. Whether the destination was Africa, Asia or America, it is likely that these early cargos were similarly eclectic.[18]

Henry Hudson probably carried just such a speculative cargo. We know from Robert Juet's account that "beads, knives and hatchets" were exchanged for food and furs. Although we will probably never learn more about *de Halve Maen's* cargo, information from an earlier VOC expedition to the Indies gives us a more complete idea of what she may have carried. In 1596, Willem Barentz attempted the northern passage to the Indies. Stopped by bad weather, then frozen in pack ice, Barentz had his men build a shelter where they successfully spent the winter. The following spring they built new boats from the ice-crushed remnants of their

cm

FIGURE 2.10
*A Dutch copper
kettle* (NM-7652)
and broad axe
(NM-7784)
*recovered from
the site of
Willem Barentz'
1596 camp on
Nova Zembla.*
*Courtesy of the
Rijksmuseum, Amsterdam.*

cm

original vessels and sailed back to Amsterdam. Archaeological investigation of Barentz' camp in *Nova Zembla* has provided a remarkable view of what was brought for the voyage. In addition to the usual ship supplies, tools and hardware, a wide assortment of clothing, shoes, personal possessions, even books and engraved prints were recovered from this cold, dry arctic site. Since Barentz' expedition occurred only thirteen years before Hudson's, and each had the same destination, the materials recovered provide some hint of how *de Halve Maen* may have been outfitted. Interestingly, this included very little that we would consider as "trade goods." No glass beads were found. Some woolen broadcloth, with lead seals still attached, and possibly some of the knives might fit into this category. However, the axes and copper kettles recovered were all typical Dutch domestic forms and quite different from those intended as trade goods.[19]

Some of these trade goods, such as glass beads, have been well documented in the Amsterdam excavations. Prior to 1600, most of the drinking vessels and other glassware used in Amsterdam were imported from Venice. By the early decades of the 17th-century several glass works had been established in Amsterdam to produce table glass, mirrors and beads. The first of these known to produce beads was owned by Jan Jansz Carel, a director of the VOC, and managed by his son-in-law Jan Schryver Soop from 1601 to the mid-1620s. Given that Hudson sailed under VOC auspices, it is quite likely that the glass beads he took along came from Soop's glass house. During the 1970s and early 1980s, construction projects in Amsterdam uncovered several deposits of glass beads and associated production waste. Some of these deposits were quite large and contained thousands of complete and partially made beads. Recent excavations along the Kloveniersburgwal have revealed a portion of the actual glasshouse along with production waste for drinking glasses and beads. Many

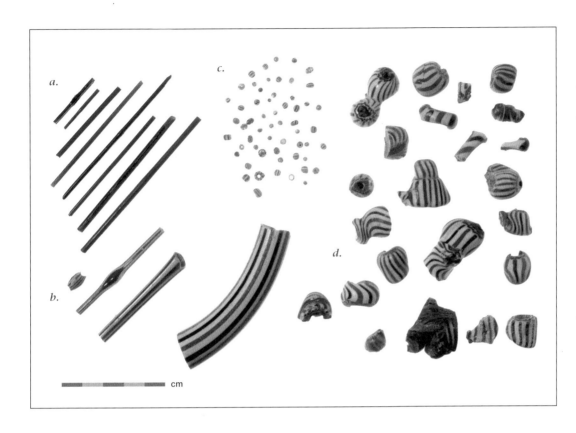

FIGURE 2.11

Sample of beads and production waste from KG10, Amsterdam.

a. Blue and red glass rods used to make stripes on beads and beakers.

b. Production tubes from which individual beads were made.

c. Small finished beads (predominantly Kidd IVb16 and related styles).

d. Production waste and discarded examples of large polychrome beads (Kidd IVnn4).

Courtesy of the AHM/BMA. Photo by Wiard Krook, afdeling Archeologie.

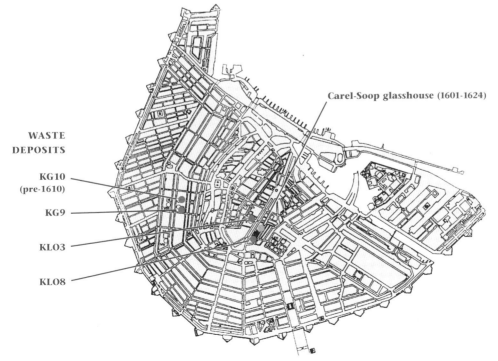

Carel-Soop glasshouse (1601-1624)

WASTE DEPOSITS

KG10 (pre-1610)

KG9

KLO3

KLO8

FIGURE 2.12

Left: Map of Amsterdam with the location of the Carel-Soop glass house and related waste deposits.

Photo by Wiard Krook, afdeling Archeologie, BMA.

Glass Beads: Styles and Seriation

Archaeologists value glass beads for several reasons. Since the styles that Europeans chose for the fur trade changed frequently, beads provide a good indication of when a particular site was occupied. Recent discoveries in Amsterdam have made clearer where and when many of these beads were made, though not necessarily who traded them.

Beads are also common on most 17th century sites. This means that archaeologists can usually get a large enough sample to make useful comparisons among sites. One technique for comparison is called seriation or tracking how a trait changes over time. For example, one can follow when a particular bead style is introduced, when it becomes most common, and when it disappears from the archaeological record. Bead frequencies can also be used to determine what sites may be of the same time period. Such observations formed the basis for defining the Canadian Glass Bead Periods in Canada and a similar set of Glass Bead Horizons for Mohawk and Mahican sites (*See Table 2.1*).

For such comparisons to work, standard descriptions are essential. Most archaeologists in the Northeast use the system developed by Ken and Martha Kidd to describe glass beads. The Kidd system classifies beads in terms of their method of manufacture, complexity and color.

Both Europeans and Natives valued glass beads but for different reasons. For Europeans, beads were a predictable and successful commodity, even if they were an expensive item to purchase. For Native people, the brightness and vivid colors of glass beads had strong associations with the traditional substances of power. Like many of the fur trade's other signature artifacts, glass beads worked because they made sense on both sides on the cultural border.[20]

TABLE 2.1 Glass Bead Horizons on Mahican and eastern Five Nations sites: 1600 – 1665						
Glass Bead Horizons	**Mahican Sites**	**Mohawk Sites, Eastern**	**Mohawk Sites, Central**	**Mohawk Sites, Western**	**Oneida Sites**	**Onondaga Sites**
Canadian GBP2 Beads (Kidd # Ia5, Ia19, IIa15, IIa55-7) ca. 1600–1614	?	Barker	England's Woods	Dewandelaer	Diable	Chase
Polychrome Beads (Kidd # IVk3/4, IVb29-36, IIbb1, IIb15) ca. 1614–1624	Mechanicville Rd., Lansingburgh	Martin	Rice's Woods, Coleman-Van Duesen	Wagner's Hollow	Cameron	Pompey Center
Seed Beads (Kidd# IIa7, IIa12, IVa11/13, IVa19) ca. 1624–1635	Lansingburgh, Menands Bridge	Briggs Run, Yates I	Swart-Farley	Crouse ?, Sand Hill	Wilson, Blowers	Pratts Falls
Round Blue Beads (Kidd # IIa40, IIb56) ca. 1635–1645	Lansingburgh	Bauder	Rumrill-Naylor, Van Evera-Mckinney	Failing ?, Oak Hill	Thurston, Marshall	Shurtleff
Tubular Blue Beads, unfinished ends (Kidd # IIIa12) ca. 1645–1650	Lansingburgh, Riverside, Rip van Winkle	Yates II	Mitchell	Lipe II	Quarry	Carley
Tubular Blue and Red Beads, unfinished ends (Kidd # IIIa12, IIIa1-3) ca. 1650–1657	Lansingburgh	Printup	Fiske	?	Quarry	Lot 18
Short tubular Red and striped beads, finished ends (Kidd # IIIa3, Ib3, Ib12) ca. 1657–1665	Lansingburgh, Four Mile Point	Freeman	Brown, Allen	Ft. Plain Cemetery	Dungey	Indian Castle

Drawings by Ellen Chase

FIGURE 2.13
*"The Combmaker"
(De kammemaker).
From Het Menselicjk
Bedrijf, Amsterdam
1704.*
Courtesy of the Museum
Boyman-Van Beuningen,
Rotterdam.

dise with them, hoping that something would appeal to potential customers. Based on the successful experiences of the earlier Basque and Norman traders, it was clear what the Native people of northeastern North America wanted. By the time the New Netherland Company was established, trade goods meant an increasingly standardized set of objects that included brass kettles, iron axes, knives and awls as well as simple monochrome beads and small brass bells. These are the most commonly occurring European artifacts on Native sites of this period. As the trade grew, these were supplemented with new products made in Amsterdam specifically for export, although not necessarily for the New Netherland fur trade. Among these were more expensive polychrome glass beads, woolen broadcloth and ivory combs.[22]

The interests of Native people were not necessarily limited to what Europeans brought for trade. Whether the exchange took place on land or on shipboard, a wide range of novel items ended up in Native hands – as gifts, as part of a deal, or otherwise. These more exotic objects fall into three broad categories: expedition equipment, personal possessions and "trash" (or "curiosities," depending on one's point of view). Expedition equipment included objects such as iron hardware (nails, spikes and other fittings), tools (scissors and adzes), and weapons, especially swords. Among the personal possessions that ended up on Native sites of the period were small coins, pewter spoons, clasp knives and articles of clothing (as evidenced by buttons and other fasteners). Of particular interest are those objects that were probably considered trash by Europeans but were still highly valued by Native people. Examples include broken tools and implements (especially scissors and sword blades), fragments of European dishes and bottles, and an occasional gun part or musket ball. Odd as these choices may seem to us, it is not difficult to understand Native peoples'

of these beads are identical to those recovered from the Mahican and Mohawk sites in the Capital region.[21]

Moving beyond the sites in Europe, the most important archaeological evidence for the Independent Traders period comes from the Mohawk and Mahican sites of the Capital region. If Amsterdam was the source of production, these Native sites were certainly one of the destinations where much of the material ended up. While the historical documents make only brief mention of the beads, kettles and other "trifles" used by Europeans, the archaeological record fills in the details.

One of the important developments of the Independent Traders period was a clearer definition of "trade goods." As discussed above, most expeditions took a grab bag of merchan-

interest in such objects. They had little experience with firearms and the aura of power surrounding these weapons was undoubtedly still strong. As we will see below, even broken iron tools had great potential for reuse. In terms of broken dishes, it is less clear. Eating and drinking were an important part of these early encounters, as Hudson's account makes clear. It may be that a brightly glazed fragment of a Weser ware dish or the pewter top of a case bottle were tangible reminders of these encounters and had a value far beyond their superficial appearance. Whatever the reason, these discardable items were eagerly sought by the region's Native people. Whether it was practical use or symbolic value, one man's trash certainly could become another man's treasure.[23]

Defining Assemblages for the Independent Traders. Between 1609 and 1624 the nature of the trade, as well as what was being traded, changed quickly. From Hudson's unexpected arrival through the ups and downs of the Independent Traders period to the establishment of Fort Orange, the definition of trade goods became more precise and more inclusive. Archaeological evidence from Mohawk and Mahican sites suggests that three artifact assemblages can be identified that correspond to these rapid shifts.

The first assemblage comes from Mohawk sites such as England's Woods and Cromwell, and reflects the activity of Independent Traders up to the establishment of the New Netherland Company in 1614. These sites have only a small amount of European material, much of which is similar to that used by the Norman traders. These include brass kettles, axes and knives as well as glass beads of the GBP2 style. This is no surprise since several of these early trading companies, such as that of Lambert van Tweenhuysen, were joint Norman-Dutch ventures.[24] What makes this assemblage distinctive is the marked increase

a.

◼▬▬▬◼ cm

b.

◼▬▬▬◼ cm

FIGURE 2.14
Werra and Weser ware dishes.

a. A Werra "cavalier" dish dated 1597, found in Delft (F 3235).

b. A Weser dish with wavy bands, found in Amsterdam (F 3767).

Courtesy of the Museum Boymans-Van Beuningen, Rotterdam.

45

in European material, compared with previous sites, and the presence of new items such as high-quality polychrome beads.[25] This assemblage appears to represent to activities of merchants like van Tweenhuysen and Arnout Vogels, who drew on traditional sources for some of their merchandise and on new producers in Amsterdam for the rest. These were the merchants who provisioned Adriaen Block and other early traders.

A somewhat different assemblage comes from Mohawk sites such as Martin, Rice's Woods and Wagner's Hollow. These sites appear to be slightly later in time and produce dramatically more European objects. Most distinctive are polychrome glass beads. This increase has prompted some scholars to call to this time period the Polychrome Bead Horizon.[26] However, more is present in this assemblage than just beads, kettles and axes. Also included are pewter spoons, glass buttons and ivory combs.[27] These objects probably originated in Amsterdam. Nails, spikes and other kinds of hardware are more common as are sword fragments and exotic objects such as the serpentine from a matchlock musket and coins of small denomination.[28]

FIGURE 2.15
The pewter top from glass case bottle (NM-7724) and a pewter spoon (NM-7681-3) recovered from the site of Willem Barentz's 1596 camp on Nova Zembla.
Courtesy of the Rijksmuseum, Amsterdam.

Of particular interest are many fragments of European ceramics, especially German Werra and Weser ware, plus some evidence of glass case bottles.[29] This assemblage probably represents the extended contact that occurred under the New Netherland Company, 1614 to 1618, and reflects the activities of men like Jacob Eelkins and Hendrick Christiaensen, each of whom served as commander at Fort Nassau, and were among the most experienced Dutch traders.[30]

A final assemblage comes from sites like Coleman-Van Duesen and appears to represent the period from the end of the New Netherland Company in 1618 to the establishment of Fort Orange in 1624.[31] This period of transition is not well documented, either in the documentary or archaeological record. However, it appears that the trade was considerably more variable and this is reflected in the artifacts. The overall quantity of European material lessens and new styles of beads begin to occur as well as other objects such as lead cloth seals and iron mouth harps.[32] This assemblage probably reflects the trading activities of men such as the notorious Hans Jorisz Hontom and his competitor Lambert van Tweenhuysen, who continued to sponsor trading voyages to the Hudson until 1623.[33]

Tradition and Innovation

What did the region's Native people make of this flood of new, exotic material? What did they think was going on and how did they respond? Since little from their point of view survives in the written accounts, we must try to infer answers from the archaeological record.

Several things are evident. As their acquaintance with Europeans grew, it became clear that these strange beings were not manitous, but men, albeit strange ones with very different technology and considerable material wealth. It is also certain that Native people were exposed to a much broader range of European material culture than the small trickle of objects that had percolated into the interior during the preceding Protohistoric period. It is hard to know how long the aura of power clung to Europeans and their things; however, objects such as firearms and iron tools must have still retained the ability to impress, even awe, those unfamiliar with them for some period of time.

Once Europeans were seen as men, the Native attitude toward them became markedly more pragmatic. Native people were remarkable for their ability to adapt and utilize whatever resources were available. As the presence of Europeans became predictable, they became one more resource to exploit on a seasonal basis. And if the "price" was too high, as it apparently was between 1618 and 1624, then Native people simply did not show up to trade. It is also important to remember that Native people and Europeans approached "trading" from very different points of view. For Europeans, the fur trade was a business, a way of making money. In Native culture, where money did not exist, the exchange of goods was as part of a social system based on kinship and mutual obligation. From a Native point of view, there was no reason to deal with Europeans when their behavior turned ugly.

How do the artifact assemblages from Mahican and Mohawk sites bear these ideas out? Most striking is how little the artifacts from these sites differ from those of the previous ones. Traditional objects and materials – pottery vessels as well as tools and utensils of chert, bone, antler and wood – continue to dominate the assemblages. Certainly there are differences. Face and full-figure effigies begin to adorn ceramic pots, although it is not clear why. Given their earlier abundance, clay smoking pipes are surprisingly scarce, perhaps because metal tools made it easier to carve pipes from wood and stone. Chert arrow points remain common, outnumbering those made from copper or brass by more than 10 to 1. Although the evidence of contact is increasingly pervasive on these sites, the Native response continued to be selective and conservative, one in which European objects and materials were incorporated, and often modified, to meet traditional needs.

The Many Lives of an Iron Axe

FIGURE 2.16
For Europeans, an iron axe was a simple and straightforward tool. Drawing from Gerrit de Veer, Diarium Nauticum, 1598, figure 13 (NG-1982-1).
Courtesy of the Rijksmuseum, Amsterdam.

Iron axes were one of the most common items that Europeans brought to northeastern North America for trade. These early 17th-century axes were simple implements averaging about 20cm (8 inches) in length and weighing about 1.5kg (3 pounds). Many were produced in the Basque region of southern France and adjacent Spain. These were not the same kind of axe that Europeans fashioned for themselves. Rather, these "trade axes" were made from wrought iron and were of inexpensive, one-piece construction. These were tools with a limited life expectancy, an item to be traded, used, then discarded. From a European point of view, the appeal of an axe was straightforward and it was assumed that Native people would use them much as Europeans did. However, as one early account indicates, this was not the case.

After their first encounter with Indian people, the Europeans went away... and returned in the following season, when both parties were much rejoiced to see each other; but the whites laughed at the Indians, seeing that they knew not the use of the axes and hoes they had given them the year before, for they had these hanging to their breasts as ornaments.[34]

It has been argued that once Indian people figured out what iron axes were for – they already had perfectly good lithic ones – European ones were sought because they were "superior." However, the archaeological evidence indicates something different occurred. As with copper kettles, there is considerable evidence that complete axes were deliberately and systematically dismembered, and the pieces converted into celts, scrapers and other traditional tool forms. Axes, it seems, were viewed primarily as a source of raw material from which Native people could make their own implements.

An iron trade axe could be dismantled in several ways. The two most common are illustrated here. One was to remove triangular sections from the blade through scoring and abrasion. These pieces were then ground down further into celts, the traditional form for a Native axe. A second method focused on the thinner strip of iron that formed the axe's socket. When cut open and hammered flat, a wide range of knives, scrapers and other implements could be produced. Native-made tools such as these, as well as pieces of recycled axes, are common artifacts on Native sites dating from the first quarter of the 17th-century.

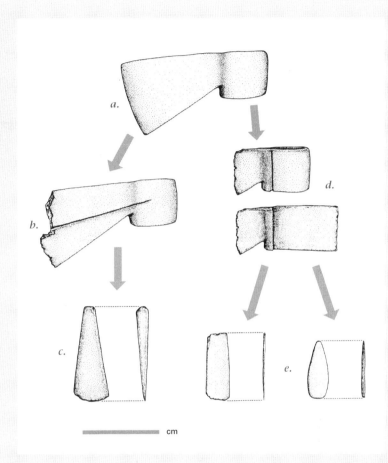

FIGURE 2.17

For Native people, an iron axe was an opportunity to make traditional tools from a new material. As with a copper or brass kettle, an iron axe frequently served as the source of material from which other tools were made. An axe (a) could be re-used in two ways.

One was to score the blade (b) removing triangular sections that were further processed in iron celts (c). The second was to score, then cut open the socket (d) and use the resulting large flat piece of iron as a blank from which several forms of scrapers, knives and other implements could be made (e).

After Bradley 2005:147, Figure 16.

FIGURE 2.18

Examples of re-used European knives.

a. A knife blade re-worked into a harpoon.

b. A knife blade re-worked into a carving (crooked?) knife, side and top views.

From Rice's Woods, see note 35.

Drawing by Ellen Chase.

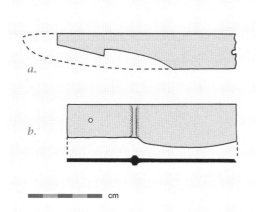

FIGURE 2.19

Re-using a sword blade.

a. The hilt portion of the blade from a typical late-16th-century German rapier was often re-worked into an efficient scraper. Note that the broken end has been re-ground and beveled.

b. Two sword blade fragments from the Martin site.

One (A2002.10AZ.20.02) is unmodified; the other (A2002.10AZ.02.03) has been re-worked into a beveled scraper.

Courtesy of the NYSM.

Drawing by Ellen Chase.

Photo by Ted Beblowski.

One thing is certain, Native people were not passive in their acceptance or use of European things. In fact, what characterizes this period is the intense and often experimental way in which European objects were processed into traditional Native forms. For example, the recycling of brass kettles into a wide variety of ornamental and utilitarian forms is much more widespread than on earlier sites. This metal working was done through traditional means, such as scoring and abrasion, as well as with newly available iron knives and scissors. The results were tubular beads of several sizes,

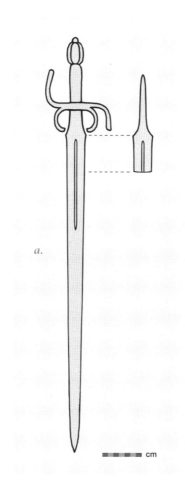

FIGURE 2.20
A wooden ladle with an effigy handle (5005/102), from the Seneca Factory Hollow site.
From Sempowski and Saunders 2001 II:567, figure 7-253.
Courtesy of the RMSC.

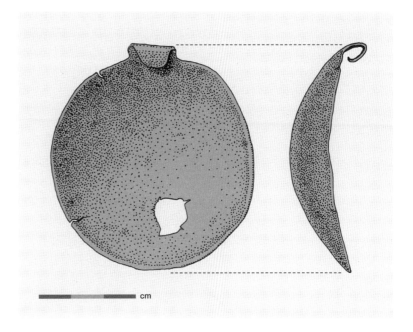

cm

pendants (both circular and effigy-shaped) and an increasingly diverse array of knives, scrapers, projectile points and other tools. It is also worth noting that nearly all the discarded "scraps" of brass from sites of this period show cut marks or other evidence of these fabrication processes.

Brass was not the only metal Native people learned to use. The same metal-working processes were applied to iron. Axes in particular were cut up and converted into celts, the ungrooved axes used by the Native people of the region. Other iron implements were recycled as well. For example, knives were frequently converted to harpoons as well as other forms while sword blade fragments were systematically converted into scrapers.[35]

The process of transforming European objects into Native ones extended beyond the utilitarian. Many of the brass beads and pendants were probably used for ritual, not just ornamental, purposes. Even the fragments of European ceramics were often converted into traditional Native forms such as gaming pieces and pendants.[36] If Europeans laughed

FIGURE 2.21
A Native-made brass spoon, front and side views, from the Wagner's Hollow site.
Courtesy of Wayne Lenig.
Drawing by Ellen Chase.

Combs and Cultural Boundries

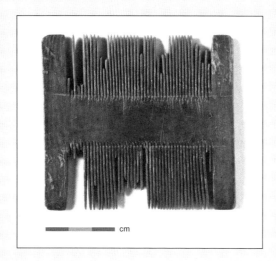

FIGURE 2.22
*A Dutch bone comb
from Amsterdam.*
Courtesy of the Amsterdam
Historisch Museum/Bureau
Monumenten & Archeologie.
Photo by Wiard Krook, afdeling
Archeologie, BMA.

Ivory combs were one of the European objects that had an immediate and highly visible impact on Native culture. Antler combs had been a part of Native material culture for thousands of years. These combs usually had a small number of long, widely spaced teeth and may have functioned more as hair pins than combs. However, combs could also play an important role in ritual activities. For example, during the formation of the Iroquois Confederacy, the Peace Maker was able to comb 'the snakes of discord' out of the hair of Tadodaho, an Onondaga chief who opposed his plan.

Combs served a dual purpose in Europe as well. On the practical level, their fine teeth made it easier to remove lice and fleas. This made combs a popular consumer item and, by the early 17th-century, Amsterdam was the center of their production. But here too, combs could symbolize many kinds of cleansing. "A high ranking officer of a country is not unlike a comb, cleaning the land of harmful crooks..." observed one contemporary source. "Purgat et ornate" [It purifies and beautifies] declared another.[37]

While such symbolic subtleties may have been lost in the process of trading, the functional value of a comb certainly was not. Ivory combs were among the first European object to receive the highest form of flattery – Native artisans immediately began to copy them. On Mohawk sites, European ivory combs or antler replicas occur at Rice's Woods, Martin and Wagner's Hollow – the sites of the Polychrome Bead Horizon.

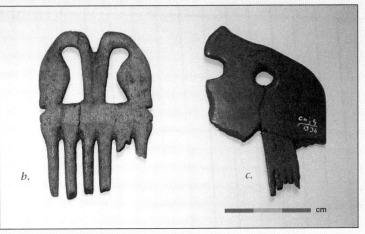

a.

b.

c.

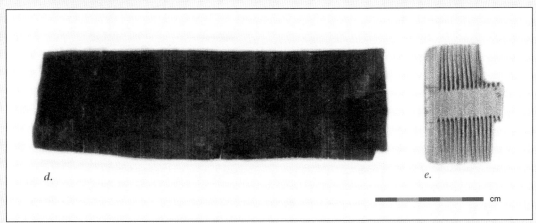

d.

e.

FIGURE 2.23
Mohawk antler combs.

a. A partially sawn comb blank.

b. An effigy comb with old style, widely spaced teeth.

c. An effigy comb with sawn teeth.

All three are from the Wagner's Hollow site.

d. A Native-made brass saw (10AZ.99.38).

e. A Mohawk antler copy of a Dutch comb (10AZ.02.04).

Both are from the Martin site.

Wagner's Hollow combs courtesy of Wayne Lenig; the Martin artifacts are from the Swart collection, NYSM. Photo by Ted Beblowski.

This ability to reproduce European-style combs was made possible by another piece of Native ingenuity. By taking a piece of sheet brass and nicking the edge, Native craftsmen produced small saws capable of cutting much finer teeth.

The advent of European combs did more than inspire copies; it initiated an artistic explosion. More than thirty antler combs, complete or in process have been recovered from Mohawk and Mahican sites of this period. Styles range from geometric shapes to elaborate human and animal effigies.[38]

about the naïvete of Native people as they tried to figure out how to use European objects, there was, undoubtedly, plenty of laughter the other way as Native craftsmen put European objects, and even "trash," to a variety of uses.

Other changes are more subtle but equally significant. One was the impact of new shapes. European combs provide a good example. While antler combs had been a part of Native material culture for thousands of years, European combs inspired a sudden increase in comb making, imitating European forms as well as initiating a whole range of new effigy and geometric styles. Pewter spoons are another case in point. Here again, this type of utensil was not new. Native people in the Northeast had made ladles of antler and wood long before the arrival of Europeans. But once pewter spoons begin to occur on Mohawk sites, so do Native copies made from kettle fragments.[39] In addition, the shape of European spoons begins to influence the traditional form of antler and wooden ladles, just as European combs reshaped Native ones. These changes are evident not only on Mahican and Mohawk sites, they occur across Iroquoia as far west as the Seneca sites in the Genesee Valley.[40]

While novel European forms influenced the shape of traditional utensils, European metal provided the means to make a new generation of tools capable of producing these more stylish and sophisticated objects. In addition to the knives and other cutting or perforating tools that could be made from nails or other iron objects, these included some implements new to Native tool kits. Most significant are small saws made from brass that could be used to cut the teeth for antler combs and crooked knives for carving wooden ladles and bowls. The latter were made from regular European

knives with the blades modified for carving.[41] These new tools, hybrids of European material and Native ingenuity, brought about a renaissance in traditional carving skills, one that would continue throughout the remainder of the 17th-century.

All this underscores a fundamental aspect of the Native response to European contact, one that has been frequently overlooked. In addition to being selective and conservative, it was amazingly creative. When Native people sought out the brass kettles and iron axes offered by Independent Traders, it was not because these objects were superior, but because they offered new ways to strengthen traditional Native culture. There was a price however. Just as there can be no innovation without tradition, tradition itself is subject to change and revision. Even when the intent was conservative, the increasing acceptance and use of European materials began to reshape Native culture in fundamental ways.

Summing Up

The increased contact with Dutch traders had implications far beyond the Hudson and Mohawk valleys. As the archaeological record from other Five Nations sites of this period demonstrates, the changes visible in Mohawk material culture rolled across Iroquoia like shock waves. On the political side the results were equally powerful. It would not take long before novel European items became necessities and soon access to Europeans and their wares would become a driving factor in tribal politics. Mahican and Mohawk people responded to the independent traders with remarkable flexibility and creativity. However, this ability to adapt to changing conditions would be tested even further as Europeans came not just to trade, but to settle.

CHAPTER THREE: Starting Up, 1624–1640

FIGURE 3.1
*Fortuna,
an early 17th-
century gable
stone from
Amsterdam
by Hendrick
de Keyser
(BK-NM-10513).*
Courtesy of the
Rijksmuseum,
Amsterdam.

By 1621, the truce between Spain and the Dutch Republic, so carefully negotiated twelve years earlier, had outlived its usefulness and war resumed. The peace had been very good for the Dutch providing a period of unparalleled stability and prosperity at home and commercial growth abroad. Dutch merchants fully exploited the opportunities that the peace presented. Overseas trade grew at a phenomenal rate, expanding into the Far East at the expense of the Portuguese. Now those entrepreneurial eyes turned to the Western Hemisphere. With the creation of the West India Company (WIC), the means were established to bring the riches of the Atlantic World into Dutch hands.

The WIC was a strange creature, one built on a combination of patriotic zeal and the desire for quick profits. As outlined in its charter, the goal was to bring the entire trade of the Western Hemisphere under Company control. Formation of the WIC also marked the end of private trading since the Company was given a monopoly over all trade for the next twenty-four years. The plan was as impractical as it was grandiose and ignored the realities of distance, international affairs and the Company's financial strength. It also meant that colonization was not a priority. New colonies seldom provided a speedy return on investment. Worse, colonies were expensive to establish and maintain. The Company's only real hope for rapid wealth lay in war and privateering.[1]

It was not until the summer of 1624 that four new settlements were finally begun in New Netherland. The first was established on the South (Delaware) River and designated to be center of Company operations. Other settlements were built in the lower Connecticut River Valley, staking out the

province's eastern boundary, and at the mouth of the Hudson River. The last settlement was located far up the Hudson near the traditional location for fur trading. Here a small fort with four bastions was constructed and named Fort Orange in honor of the Republic's stadholder, or chief executive, Prince Maurice of the House of Orange. After a few dwellings had been erected and crops sown successfully, the Company vessel sailed back to the Republic, leaving the small contingent of soldiers and settlers to fend for themselves.[2]

As Dutch settlement finally got underway, important political changes were occurring back in the Republic, ones that would have a profound influence on the future direction of New Netherland. In 1625, Kiliaen van Rensselaer, a wealthy Amsterdam businessman, became one of the Nineteen, as directors of the West India Company were known. A shrewd and self-made man, Van Rensselaer quickly became New Netherland's most passionate and persistent advocate, often to the annoyance of his fellow directors. Over the next two decades, Van Rensselaer would take a special interest in the problems and potential of New Netherland, and his vision would shape its growth more than that of any other person.[3]

The international scene was changing as well. In the Republic, Prince Maurice had died and was succeeded by his half-brother Fredrik Hendrick. Across the channel, England also had a new king as Charles I replaced his father James I. The relationship between these two Protestant allies remained cordial and both leaders signed a treaty of ongoing cooperation against their traditional Catholic enemies. However, economic competition, especially between the VOC and the English East India Company in the Far East, began to strain the friendship and would soon send events on a very different trajectory.[4]

New Neighbors

Back on Hudson's River, it was a rough start for the settlers of Fort Orange. Although the three-month voyage across the Atlantic had hardened them to cold, wet conditions, they were not prepared for the more extreme climate of their new home. This was a surprise since Fort Orange was located on nearly the same latitude as Rome and the expectation was for more moderate weather, like that of the new English settlements in Virginia. As it turned out, it was also near the peak of the Little Ice Age and weather conditions were more variable and extreme than usual.

Initially, relations between the newcomers and their Native neighbors were good. As one early settler recalled, the "Indians were as quiet as lambs"[5] and the trade for furs was brisk. This was no surprise, given the Company's monopoly, and during the first few years thousands of otter and beaver skins were shipped back to Amsterdam. However, with little structure to guide it, trading often degenerated into a

free-for-all. As individuals tried to outbid each other, the settlers frequently exchanged their utensils, food, anything that Native traders wanted, until there was literally nothing left.[6]

Although centered on the nearby Mahicans and Mohawks, the trade at Fort Orange quickly grew into a larger, more complex system, one that included the rest of the Five Nations and northern Algonquian tribes or "French Indians." Within this network, furs moved to Fort Orange while iron tools, woolen blankets and wampum went the other way. The Company's plan was as simple as it was naïve – to minimize hostilities among these groups and keep all these Native tribes "devoted to us."[7]

Even when the trade went well, the new colonists faced serious problems. They were at the edge of the frontier, far away from other Europeans. There were no roads and it was a long day's sail down the Hudson River to Manhattan under the best of conditions. During the winter when the river froze, the settlers were completely isolated. They were

FIGURES 3.2 & 3.3

Top: WIC House in Amsterdam. Courtesy of the Municipal Archives, Amsterdam.

Above: The Geoctroyeerde Westindische Compagnie (GWC) or Dutch West India Company monogram.

also caught between two increasingly hostile groups of Native people. This meant tough choices. On an abstract level, how should Native people be treated, and more practically, which side should the new settlers take if the Mahicans and Mohawks went to war?

From the beginning, Dutch traders had dealt with Native people in two very different ways. Men such as Hans Jorisz Hontom and Wilhem Verhulst, the provisional director of New Netherland, typified one approach. They saw Native people as little more than commodities to be used in making money; and had no qualms about mistreating them. Official WIC policy, on the other hand, was quite different. For all its martial and mercantile intent, the Company also stood for the Dutch values of tolerance and due process. In its instructions to Verhulst, the WIC directors made clear that Native people were to be treated fairly, and that Company employees not take sides in their disputes. This view was reinforced when the Company's secretary, Issac de Rasiere, visited New Netherland in 1626 and empha-sized that the Natives must be "well treated."[8] There was nothing softheaded or idealistic about this policy. Fairness and evenhanded treatment were just good business practice.

For the Dutch settlers at Fort Orange, these issues were far less abstract. Treating their Native neighbors well was a matter of survival, literally and economically. They also could not afford to offend either the Mahicans, on whose land they lived, or the Mohawks, who supplied most of the furs. Nor were they in control of events.

Sometime between 1625 and 1626, the long simmering dispute between the Mahicans and Mohawks boiled over into hostilities. Initially the Mahicans appeared to have the upper hand, attacking one of the easternmost Mohawk villages. This raid may have caused the Mohawks to relocate most of their villages to the south side of the Mohawk River. The Dutch at Fort Orange had little idea what

was happening around them. Since few of them spoke the Native languages, it was easy to miscalculate. One such error was made by Daniel van Krieckenbeeck, the fort's commander, early in 1626 when he decided to assist the Mahicans in an attack on the Mohawks. Instead, they were ambushed and Krieckenbeeck killed along with several of his men. When the Dutch inquired why this had happened, the Mohawks expressed their regrets and asked in turn why the Dutch had meddled in their affairs. The Company representative quickly distanced himself from this "reckless adventure" and re-emphasized the WIC's policy of not taking sides.[9] Shortly after, the remaining settlers were removed to Manhattan leaving only a small garrison at Fort Orange and the trade at a standstill.

By late 1628 the first Mahican–Mohawk war was over and significant changes had occurred on the landscape. The victorious Mohawks now claimed the right to trade at Fort Orange as well as the Mahican land on the west side of the Hudson River around the fort. While the Mahicans still controlled the east side of the river, they began to shift their sites farther away from the troublesome Dutch, north toward Troy and the Hoosic River, and south toward Stockport Creek and present-day Hudson. They also began to think about Dutch requests to sell pieces of land, something they had not considered earlier.[10]

The Mahican–Mohawk war also underscored the Company's problems with the trade. While its approach was sound, the Company did not expend the effort or resources required to put the fur trade on a sound business footing. Trade practices, good on paper, were seldom enforced. For example, trade goods, though well chosen, were often in short supply or of poor quality.[11] The war also proved it was naïve to assume that the Dutch and neighbor-ing tribes could all trade together peacefully. One could no more trade with all parties than be everyone's ally in war. Finally, the war revealed how quickly the trade network based at Ft. Orange was encroaching upon those of other Europeans, especially the French along the St. Lawrence and the English in New England. The political implications of living with these new neighbors would soon become evident.

By 1628, New Netherland itself was in serious trouble. Costs continued to mount and the province's population was small and unhappy. Of the original four settlements, two had failed completely. Only New Amsterdam on Manhattan and Fort Orange upriver continued to struggle on. After its initial success, the fur trade was stagnant. The capture of a Spanish treasure fleet by Piet Heyn made the situation look even worse. Compared with millions of guilders in gold and silver, the profits from peltry were paltry and much of the Nineteen's time was consumed by disputes over the province's future.[12]

The strongest voice for saving New Netherland was that of Kiliaen van Rensselaer. For several years he had promoted a plan to revive the floundering province with private capital. By allowing individual investors to purchase land and set up their own colonies under the Company's auspices, Van Rensselaer believed that New Netherland could be successful. Although controversial, Van Rensselaer's plan was approved in June 1629 and he immediately began to implement plans for Rensselaerswijck, his own personal colony.[13]

The first step was to purchase land and Van Rensselaer knew exactly what he wanted. In January 1630 he instructed his agent to buy a large tract from the Mahicans "above and below Fort Orange on both sides of the river" for his colony. Since Company policy required that such land purchases be formal and legal, papers transferring title were signed in August. In exchange for an unspecified amount of merchandise, Van Rensselaer now owned most of what we consider Albany and Rensselaer counties.[14]

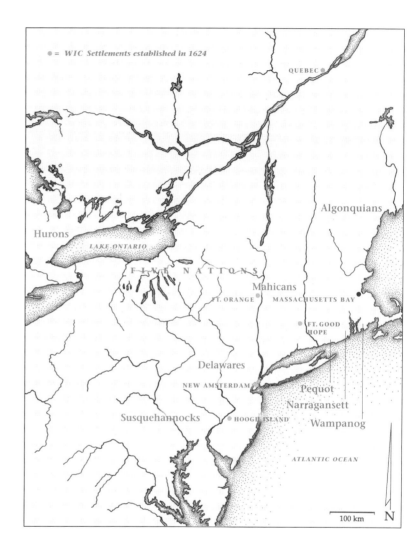

● = WIC Settlements established in 1624

Van Rensselaer had very specific ideas for his colony. Since the Company controlled the fur trade, he planned to build an agricultural colony on the rich alluvial soils of the upper Hudson River. Here his tenants would grow grain that could be exchanged for valuable commodities, sugar from Brazil and tobacco from Virginia, that would be sent back to Europe. The initial plan was to establish a series of farms along the river terraces and islands with a small administrative and milling center located on the east side opposite Fort Orange. The Colonie, as it soon became known, was also to be set up with

FIGURE 3.4
Map of the Northeast, 1624 to 1630.
Map by Booth Simpson

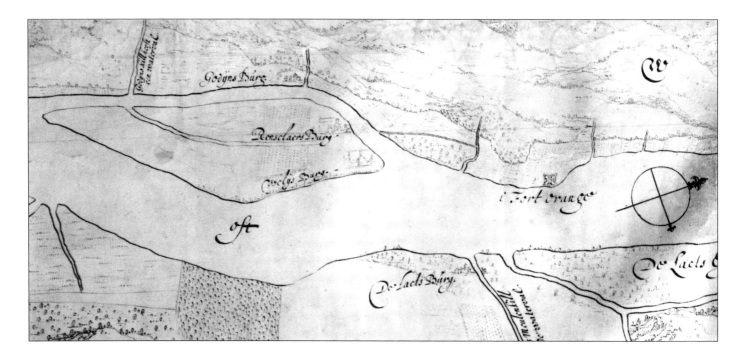

FIGURE 3.5
*A section of
the 1632 Van
Scheyndel map of
Rensselaerswijck
showing Fort Orange,
De Laetsburg and
three of the early
farms on Castle
Island and the
west side of the
Hudson River.*
Courtesy of the New York
State Library, Manuscripts
and Special Collections.
Photo by Ted Beblowski.

the appropriate Dutch institutions. This meant a court and judicial officers of its own and the promise of a church and minister. Following good Dutch practices, Van Rensselaer also had a map of his colony drawn showing the location of planned farms and settlements.[15]

By 1634, the great experiment was underway. The patroon (or patron) had signed contracts with several dozen men and shipped them to the Colonie along with cargoes of building material, farm supplies and livestock. A few "fine farms" had been established on each side of the Hudson and successful crops of wheat, rye and oats produced.[16] It was certainly an attractive country with plenty of fish in the river and game in the woods. But life was hard on these isolated farms, the first attempt to settle beyond Fort Orange, and the patroon found it difficult to keep reliable tenants.

The situation at Fort Orange had not improved either. The trade remained sluggish and the Company's decision to appoint the difficult and violent Hans Jorissen Hontom

as commander in 1632 was spectacularly ill timed. The situation became so desperate that in December 1634 a small party was sent out to visit the Mohawks and find out why the "trade was going very badly." It did not take long to find out. The polite reply was that, too often, there were no goods available, annoying for those who had traveled great distances to trade. The more direct response "derided us as scoundrels, and said that we were worthless because we gave them so little for their furs."[17] That was lesson number one. Lesson number two was that French traders gave them a much better deal, came to their villages and brought a wide range of better-quality merchandise with them.

These, and other observations recorded by Harmen van den Bogart during the trip, provide the first detailed descriptions of Mohawk villages and cultural practices. Although Van den Bogart's primary concerns were economic, his remarkable journal also hints at the forces that were beginning to transform Native life – the pervasiveness of

European materials, the presence of new diseases, and the ever increasing hostilities among Native peoples as trade networks expanded.

It was not just the Native way of life that was being transformed. In 1632, King Charles of England did the unthinkable, signing a peace treaty with Catholic Spain and ending English support for the Dutch Republic. When pressed by the Dutch ambassador, it became clear that this was part of a larger problem, one in which economic competition had replaced the old bonds of Protestant allegiance. In addition, Charles let it be known that the English now disputed Dutch claims along Hudson's River, suggesting that those lands belonged to England by right of prior discovery.[18] Such a threat may have seemed foolish, since the Dutch Republic was at the height of its power; however, circumstances were changing quickly and in very tangible ways. In 1636, English settlers from Massachusetts Bay built a new settlement called Hartford on the Connecticut River near the site of an earlier WIC trading house.[19] Two years later, William Pynchon established a trading post farther upriver at Springfield and began to compete directly for furs. These actions not only deflected furs away from Fort Orange; they threatened to cut off Dutch access to wampum. These small white-and-purple shell beads, produced primarily by the Narragansett and Pequot people who lived along Long Island Sound, had become a mainstay of the trade. Hostile English intent was no longer an insignificant matter.

Affairs in neighboring New England threatened to spill over into New Netherland in other ways. In October 1636, Massachusetts Bay sent a military expedition to punish the Pequot for a series of alleged offenses. The Puritans' short but brutal campaign virtually destroyed the Pequot and left the wampum trade in the hands of the Narragansett, allies of the English. A few small bands of survivors managed to hide with neighboring tribes. One group of Pequot even sought refuge among the Mohawk. For Native people across the region, the lessons of the Pequot War were frighteningly clear: Europeans could not be trusted, their methods of warfare were without scruple or mercy, and obtaining firearms was a necessity.[20]

Reviving the Trade

By 1639, New Netherland was on the verge of collapse. A series of inept governors had done little to revitalize the economy or attract new settlers. The fur trade remained stalled. With the exception of Rensselaerswijck, the patroonship experiment had failed. Back in the Republic, the WIC was not in much better shape. Virtually bankrupt, the Company was forced to acknowledge that its attempts to control the fur trade had failed. In January 1639, the Nineteen made the decision to abandon their monopoly and announced that the trade would now be open to all Dutch citizens.[21]

Amsterdam's merchants had eagerly awaited this decision. Free trade meant great new opportunities and none was more prepared than Kiliaen van Rensselaer. Throughout the 1630s he had continued to pour money and material into the Colonie, purchasing additional land from the Mahicans in 1637 and establishing a series of new farms along the east side of the Hudson in the Papscansee Island area.[22] However, farming for export had not proved as successful as Van Rensselaer had hoped. It was far easier, and more profitable, for his tenants to acquire furs whether it was legal or not. Free trade meant that the patroon could now, legitimately, tap this potential as well.

Van Rensselaer had long suspected that it was not a lack of furs that stifled the trade but Company mismanagement, particularly the failure to supply adequate quantities of good quality merchandise. He planned to solve this problem in two ways – by making sure the right kinds of trade goods were available, and by sending someone reliable to oversee the trade. As usual, Van Rensselaer threw himself into the details. Wool blankets were one of the commodities Native people wanted and throughout 1639 and 1640 the patroon corresponded with his suppliers in Leiden and Campen over the size, color and weave of the cloth to be sent.[23] As the new decade began, Van Rensselaer felt that these efforts were paying off. "The fur trade begins gradually to get into our hands" he wrote to his Leiden agent.[24]

The patroon also had a solution in mind for the other half of the problem. In late 1637 he sent his grandnephew Arent van Curler to New Netherland to serve as an assistant to the Colonie's commissary. Although only eighteen, Van Curler learned fast, and by the fall of 1639 he was not only the secretary and bookkeeper for the Colonie, but acting *commis* (or business agent) as well. This put Van Curler in charge of all the Colonie's supplies, everything from farming equipment and building materials to the food, clothing and personal items needed by settlers. It also made Van Curler the point person for the patroon's plans to expand the trade. Van Rensselaer could not have made a better choice. With his deep interest in and respect for the region's Native people, Van Curler was the perfect person to implement the patroon's plans.[25]

While the new decade may have looked promising for Van Rensselaer, the prospects seemed grim elsewhere. Tensions were still high between the Mahicans and Mohawks. The Mohawks themselves seemed divided, some choosing to court French traders and even the occasional Jesuit missionary, while most remained staunchly for the Dutch. The situation was no better down the Hudson River. Like the neighboring Puritans, Willem Kieft, the new governor-general of New Netherland, believed that military suppression was preferable to negotiation and open war between the Dutch and the local Native

population was imminent. Although Kieft attempted to calm the situation by banning the sale of firearms to the Indians "on pain of death," the Company no longer had the ability to enforce such rules. Meanwhile the trade in contraband flourished. The new decade promised to be a difficult one.

Changes on the Land

The establishment of Fort Orange, small and ineffectual as it often was, produced big changes on the landscape. From a Native point of view, this European outpost was a new fixed point on their map of regional resources. As the first long-term European settlement in the area, Fort Orange was the center from which Dutch materials and influence would spread increasingly throughout the Hudson Valley and beyond.

Fort Orange. What do we really know about this site? Contemporary accounts say little more than "a small fort with four bastions." Paul Huey has been able to fill in some of the details based on his excavation of a small portion of the site in 1971. He has also done extensive research on other Fort Oranges built around the world. Huey sees the initial fort as a modest affair with walls built of horizontally stacked, hewn logs. The bastions may have been more substantial, possibly built of brick and filled with earth. This may be the reason why the bastions survived periodic flooding better than the walls did. Huey also believes that, even though this was a small fort on the far frontier, it was an official facility and built, as much as possible, to impress. The fort's main entrance was probably ornate, perhaps even emblazoned with the Company's monogram.

We know less about what was inside the walls. For example, it is unclear what the first dwellings looked like. Caterina Trico's recollection of "hutts of bark" may actually have been a kind of semi-subterranean cellar house. Basically these were wood-lined cellars

FIGURE 3.6.
Kiliaen van Rensselaer's shipping monogram.
After Van Laer 1980: 399.

with a roof of thatch, bark or whatever else was available above them. Though not luxurious, such dwellings provided an expedient yet efficient shelter, one that could be improved later by jacking up the roof and adding a framed structure over the cellar. In terms of more substantial buildings, Huey found some evidence that a brick guardhouse was built just inside the main entrance. Beyond these fragmentary hints, we know little about the original fort.[26]

It was not until 1635 that improvements were made. Most important was the construction of a large elegant building in the center of the fort that served as the Company's trading house and main storage facility. With its flat roof, balustrade and lattice work, this was a structure designed to impress visitors. Eight smaller buildings were also constructed to house the garrison's soldiers. By 1635, garden plots and a few houses had also been built outside the fort. In spite of these efforts, Fort Orange appears to have remained a small and marginal place. It certainly did not impress the French Jesuit Issac Jogues, who described it a few years later as "a wretched little fort… built of logs."[27]

Archaeology provides some additional and important information. While most of the levels that Huey excavated at Fort Orange date from later periods, one component (96c) may relate to the fort's initial construction and occupation. This was a large trash pit located just inside the fort's main gate. The lowest level of this pit contained considerable evidence of construction activities especially masonry (brick fragments, stone chips and mortar) and carpentry (wood shavings, split lathe and nails). Directly adjacent to this trash pit was the remnant of a red brick foundation wall that had been braced with river cobbles on both sides. Although Huey initially identified this as part of Jean Labatie's 1647 brewery, he now believes this was the original 1624 guard house and that the

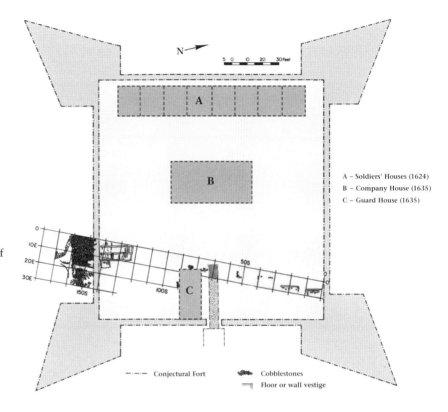

A – Soldiers' Houses (1624)
B – Company House (1635)
C – Guard House (1635)

--- Conjectural Fort
⬟ Cobblestones
⌐ Floor or wall vestige

debris in component 96c was a by product of its construction.[28]

Other archaeological evidence for Fort Orange and its buildings prior to 1640 is limited. Unfortunately, Huey's excavation found no evidence of the 1635 period Company house or soldiers' dwellings. However it is clear from the evidence recovered that Fort Orange contained a combination of wood frame and brick structures. A considerable amount of imported brick was used, both red brick from the Vecht valley south of Amsterdam and yellow brick from farther south or east. At least some of the buildings had whitewashed walls, roofs of imported red clay pantile and glass windows while the fort's forge produced the necessary nails, hinges, latches and other hardware. While the accommodations in Fort Orange may not have been luxurious, they were probably not as grim as some descriptions have suggested.

FIGURE 3.7
Huey's excavation plan of Fort Orange with conjectural location of buildings in 1635.
After Huey 1988:728, figure 106. Drawing by G.Y. Gillette.

FIGURE 3.8
*Sketch of a Dutch
sloep or small open
sailing vessel.*
Courtesy of L.F. Tantillo.

Rensselaerswijck. If we know little about Fort Orange, we know less about Rensselaerswijck. The best information comes from Van Rensselaer's own account prepared in July 1634. This is a remarkable document and provides real insight into the meticulous way that Van Rensselaer worked. It contains a detailed description of the lands "formerly inhabited by and belonging to the free, rich and well known nation named the Mahikans" as well as the names of the chiefs who sold the land. In some cases, the merchandise used to pay for the land is also noted – wampum, duffels (a type of coarse woolen cloth), axes, knives and other goods. Of equal interest are the lists of settlers, livestock and supplies that Van Rensselaer sent to establish his tenant farms. By 1632, two "fine farms" had been built, one south of Fort Orange on Castle Island, the other across the river in an area known first as de Laetsburgh and later as Greenbush, or the pine woods. These were substantial farms. Each had a large brick building that served as both dwelling and barn as well as hay barracks, sheepcotes and other smaller structures. Van Rensselaer also notes that each "house was furnished with all kinds of farm implements and necessaries" for "the comfort and support" of the animals and the people.[29]

In addition to farms, the patroon sent millstones and "all kinds of ironwork… for the erection of a saw and grist-mill" to serve the needs of Fort Orange and the country around it. He also provided sailing vessels so that the settlers could move about freely in a land without roads. By 1635 a few additional farms had been established on the east side of the Hudson and, after the purchase of Papscanee in 1637, another set of farms was built. Still, Dutch settlement beyond Fort Orange was limited and the patroon's dream of producing large quantities of grain and tobacco for export remained unrealized. In terms of archaeology, it would be fascinating to examine sites from this period; however, none have been found to date.[30]

Mahican Sites. It is difficult to see Mahican people clearly during this time of warfare and initial land sales. It is likely that they had lost population both from their war with the Mohawks and exposure to European diseases, but there are no reliable figures from the period. As a result of their defeat by the Mohawks, Mahican sites begin to concentrate on the east side of the Hudson. While they appear to have given up the land around Fort Orange (from Cohoes to Bethlehem), the Mahicans did not abandon the west side entirely. At present, four sites are known that have artifact assemblages from this period.[31] All these sites occur in areas that Mahican people had used for generations. Two are located on the west side of the Hudson River while the remaining two sites are located on the east side.

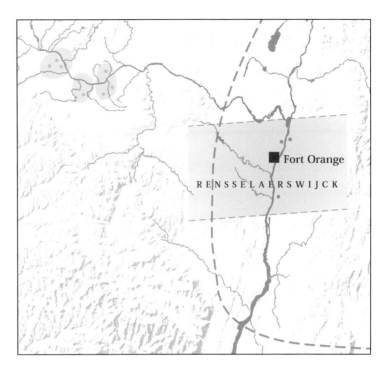

A few fortified sites are reported in the contemporary documents of this period, particularly the Rensselaerswijck map of 1632. These include "Monemin's castle," possibly on Peebles' Island, and "Unuwat's castle" located near what is now Hoosic Street in north Troy.[32] No archaeological evidence of these sites has survived.

In general, the Mahicans and Dutch got along well together and learned to live side by side. However, in spite of this cordial start, being quiet neighbors was not a long-term option. Like their Algonquian kin in New England, Mahican people found themselves faced with the same set of limited choices – they could accommodate, fight back or move on. In keeping with their tradition of political autonomy, not all Mahican groups made the same decision. However, as tracts of land were sold and Rensselaerswijck farms began to fill in the landscape, Mahican people started to leave the central portion of their traditional territory, moving south to Schodack and beyond or north into Lansingburgh.[33]

FIGURE 3.9
Left: Detailed sketches of three farms depicted on the 1632 Van Scheyndel map of Rensselaerswijck.
Courtesy of L.F. Tantillo.

FIGURE 3.10
Above: Map of Dutch, Mahican and Mohawk sites, 1624 to 1640.
Map by John Skiba and Booth Simpson.

FIGURE 3.11
A conjectural reconstruction of a Mohawk village, the Briggs Run site
Courtesy of the NYSM.

Mohawk Sites. As during the preceding periods, it is much easier to find the Mohawks, with their large palisaded village sites and extensive middens, planted solidly in the middle of their valley. Even so, it is more difficult to follow them during this period. One reason is that, with the near collapse of the fur trade, these sites have less European material than those that preceded them. As a result, several of these sites have been assumed to date from earlier periods.[34] A second reason for confusion is that these sites are less well documented than those of the previous periods.

At least six Mohawk sites are known that produce artifact assemblages associated with the West India Company period, or between 1624 and 1635. Four additional sites appear to date from the mid-1630s into the 1640s, the period when Kiliaen van Rensselaer began to revive the fur trade. With one exception (Briggs Run), these sites are located on the south side of the Mohawk River where they were more protected from Mahican and other adversaries to the north. All fall within the three traditional areas of Mohawk settlement.[35] Formal archaeological excavations have been

carried out on some of sites. SUNY Albany conducted field schools at the Rumrill-Naylor and Oak Hill sites in 1984. However, most of our knowledge comes from private investigations and collections.

In general, these sites are located close to the Mohawk River in traditional settings – easily defended hilltops or terraces above the river plain. Most appear to be in the same size range as earlier sites, one to three acres in extent, and to share the same basic characteristics – a series of longhouses enclosed by a palisade. In addition to archaeological evidence, we also have a contemporary description. Van den Bogart noted that the Mohawks had many villages. These included four large ones, which he called castles, and four smaller ones. Here is how he described the first one he visited:

We came into their first castle that stood on a high hill. These were only 36 houses, row on row in the manner of streets, so that we easily could pass through. These houses are constructed and covered with bark of trees… Some are 100, 90 or 80 steps long, and 22 or 23 feet high… These houses were full of grain… In some we also saw ironwork: hinges, chains, bolts, harrow teeth, hoops, and spikes which they steal when they are away from

here… The principal chief lived one quarter mile away in a small cabin because many of the Indians here in the castle had died of smallpox.[36]

Van den Bogart's account with its wealth of detail has intrigued archaeologists for decades. Still, the details don't always fit. For example, Van den Bogart reports thirty-six houses while the archaeological evidence indicates that Mohawk villages rarely had as many as a dozen. While several attempts have been made to identify the villages he visited in terms of the archaeological sites known from of this period, a convincing case has yet to be made.[37]

Van den Bogart's journal makes clear that new diseases had begun to have an effect on the Mohawks but provides little information on the size of the population. Snow has argued that the Mohawk population grew dramatically during the second and third decades of the 17th-century to over 7,000, then fell by more than sixty percent as a result of disease and warfare.[38] These estimates are hard to verify and seem out of line with an overall pattern of settlement that differs little from that which preceded it. My sense is that the Mohawk population, like site size and location, remained much more stable during this period.

Tools of the Trade

As the Dutch began to come to New Netherland to live, not just trade, they brought with them all the supplies and material goods needed to re-create the kind of life they had known back in the Republic. This included the bricks, roofing tiles, window glass and other items needed to construct buildings as well as

FIGURE 3.12
Winter in the Mohawk Valley, ca. 1634.
Courtesy of
L.F. Tantillo.

the tools and stock for carpentry, iron working and all the other essential crafts. For Rensselaerswijck, the inventory of necessary goods also meant the implements needed to raise, harvest and store crops, from shovels and scythes to plows and wagons. In addition, there were the domestic utensils and equipment required to maintain households plus personal possessions. Whether they were soldiers, traders or farmers, the new settlers had to eat, have sufficient clothing and

desire for European goods other than kettles, axes and knives would radically re-define the standard trade-good assemblage.

Defining a Dutch domestic assemblage. Still, much of what the Dutch brought with them was too exotic to be useful to Native people since it reflected European tastes and technologies. For the Dutch, these customs and practices were the links to home and they maintained them as much as possible given the demands of a new and different environ-

FIGURE 3.13
A typical assemblage of early 17th-century Dutch cooking and serving dishes. All recovered from a single trash pit in Amsterdam.
(courtesy of the AHM/BMA. Photo by Wiard Krook, afdeling Archeologie).

something to do in their spare time. Taken together, it was a huge and diverse inventory that the Dutch brought with them.

Just as the materials used for everyday life differed from those that the Dutch brought for the fur trade, so archaeologists draw a distinction between a Dutch domestic assemblage and a fur trade assemblage. However, one of the most important dynamics of this period was a blurring of these categories as Native people saw new objects, such as scissors, fish hooks, files and firearms, and added them to their shopping list. By 1650, this exposure to and

ment. How does the archaeological evidence help us visualize this?

Let's return to Huey's excavation at Fort Orange and the artifacts from component 96c, possibly the earliest period of the fort's existence. In addition to the building materials discussed above, the lower level of this trash pit documents much about the food preferences and personal possessions of the fort's first occupations.

Food remains indicate that, like Native people, Dutch settlers quickly learned to rely on local resources. In addition to deer,

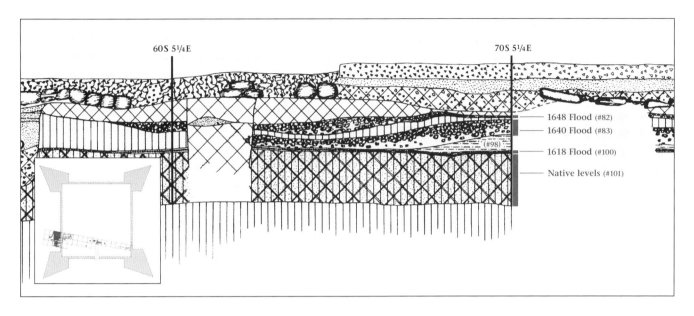

60S 5¼E

70S 5¼E

1648 Flood (#82)
1640 Flood (#83)
(#98)
1618 Flood (#100)

Native levels (#101)

sturgeon and other fish bones were recovered as well as the remains of birds, possibly cranes and ducks. Mixed with these were bones from some of the pigs the settlers brought with them – a small taste of home. If the food was a little unusual, the utensils used to prepare and serve it were not. Typical Dutch vessels of buff and red earthenware were used for storage and cooking. On the table were glass case bottles for spirits as well as *roemers* and beakers for drinking beer and wine. Food was served on Dutch-made majolica platters decorated with motifs copied from Italian styles or Chinese porcelain, tableware that differed little from that used back in the Republic. Personal possessions tell much the same story. A brass clothing buckle, fragments of a bone comb and several pieces of white clay tobacco pipes are all typical objects from Dutch domestic life.[39]

Huey's excavation also documented other levels that date before the end of this period. These include the upper portions of the trash pit described above (component 96a and b) and two buried A horizons, or old ground surfaces, that occurred beneath the level of the April 1640 flood (components 98 and 99).[40] These deposits provide a larger artifact sample

and give us a better idea of what the Dutch occupants of Fort Orange used on an everyday basis prior to the Company's abandonment of its monopoly in 1639.

Food remains from these levels show the same heavy reliance on deer, birds, fish, oysters and other local resources. As Huey has pointed out, this actually was a curious reversal of the situation back home where only nobility could afford to eat game. Life may have been hard in New Netherland but it was still a land of plenty. With a larger sample, the artifacts used for food preparation and serving show even stronger connections with home. While typical Dutch utilitarian red and buff earthenwares continue to be used for cooking, more expensive German stoneware is also present. Dutch majolica and faience still predominate in terms of serving vessels but are now accompanied by other stylish wares from northern Europe. Roemers and beakers are more common as are glass case bottles.[41]

Personal possessions are also more plentiful. The first occurrence of clay marbles, iron mouth harps, and whistles made from pipe stems reflect common Dutch pastimes as does the large quantity of discarded smoking pipes.

FIGURE 3.14
A section of profile A, Fort Orange. Components 82, 83, and 100 show three of the major early 17th-century flood levels recorded at the site.
Huey 1988:756.

FIGURE 3.15

Pre-1640 Dutch tableware from Fort Orange.

a. and b. Examples of a roemer and a beaker from Amsterdam. Fragments of identical vessels were recovered at Fort Orange.
Courtesy of the AHM/BMA. Photo by Wiard Krook, afdeling Archeologie.

c. Dutch majolica dish decorated in the Italian (Montelupo) style.
Courtesy of the AIHA, 1983.5.8.
Fragments from Fort Orange.
Courtesy of Paul Huey and OPRHP.

d. Dutch majolica dish decorated in the Chinese (Wan-Li) style.
Courtesy of the AIHA, 1983.5.3
Fragments from Fort Orange.
Courtesy of Paul Huey and OPRHP).

a.

b.

c.

d.

These pipes are typical of those found in the Republic during this period. There are examples of "Baroque" pipes with molded stems as well as the more common plain varieties. Several have maker's marks and two of these represent expatriate English pipe makers who lived in Amsterdam: TM, probably the mark of Thomas Michiels, who worked between 1629 and 1642, and a crowned rose with the initials BC, probably the mark of Benjamin Chapman who worked between 1637 and 1651/2.[42]

Not surprisingly, there was also some indication of Company armaments in these early deposits. While Huey recovered only a few gun parts, there was considerable evidence for casting musket balls and shot. He also found a complete bar of lead, the stock from which these were made. By the end of the period, fragments of these twelve-inch-long, five-pound lead bars often ended up on Native sites, even though it was illegal to trade them. At the large bore end of the spectrum, a three-pound cannon ball was recovered. This would have fit the surviving brass cannon, dated 1630 and marked with the Company's monogram that probably served as part of Fort Orange's defenses.[43]

Defining the WIC Trade Assemblage, 1624-1635. Material goods for the fur trade were an essential part of the supplies that Company settlers brought with them. The fur trade was, after all, the primary reason for Fort Orange's existence. While no inventories of this merchandise have survived, Issac de Rasiere's letters of 1626 provide a useful summary. Many of the trade items he mentions are familiar – the kettles, axes, knives and awls that had become standard components of the fur trade. De Rasiere also requested more glass beads, but these were to be small white and black beads, not the fancy polychrome varieties used by the Independent Traders. He also specified several other types of merchandise that Native people wanted – better-quality

FIGURE 3.16
Five different pipe makers' marks from pre-1640 components at Fort Orange.
Huey 1988:739, Figure 114.

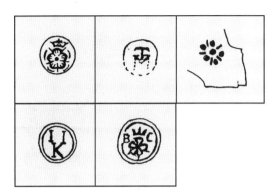

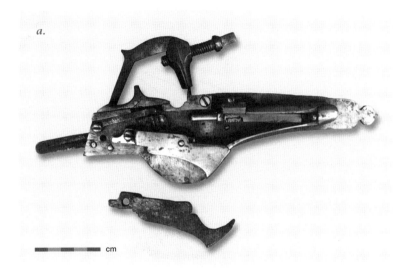

a.

FIGURE 3.17
WIC armaments.
a. Above: A complete Dutch wheel lock and an excavated fragment (bridle) from Fort Orange.
Courtesy of Paul Huey and OPRHP).

b. Right: A bronze cannon, dated 1630, probably from Fort Orange (H-1937.41).
Courtesy of the NYSM.

b.

ARTIFACT
PROFILE 6

European Smoking Pipes

White clay pipes for smoking tobacco
are one of the clearest indications of
Native American influence on the
culture of early 17th-century Europe.
Tobacco was indigenous to the Americas
and had been used by Native peoples
long before Europeans arrived. However,
once tobacco was introduced into northern Europe, pipe smoking became very
fashionable. As one observer noted "the
smell of the Dutch Republic was the
smell of tobacco."[44]

FIGURE 3.18

"The Smokers,"
Adriaen Brouwer.
Courtesy of the
Metropolitan Museum
of Art, Michael
Friedsam Collection,
(32.100.21).

Smoking became popular in England
during the 1580s when Sir Walter
Raleigh and others introduced it from
Virginia. As tobacco use became common, a guild of English pipe makers
quickly grew up to provide clay pipes
for this new market. These pipes were
often highly ornamented and had small
bulbous bowls, a reflection of tobacco's
scarcity and high price.

Many of the English pipe makers
were Protestants and after James I, who
had Catholic sympathies, became king
in 1603, several moved to the Dutch
Republic. The majority settled in
Amsterdam and by the 1630s the city was
a thriving center of pipe production. While
pipes were also made in Gouda and other
cities, Amsterdam was the largest producer
of pipes on the Continent by 1650. English
expatriates formed the heart of the pipe-
making community. These included men such
as Thomas Michiels, John Plumber, Walter
Smith and Benjamin Chapman, all of whom
married Dutch women, settled down and
raised families. They also made pipes similar
to those they had made in England.

Pipes were produced at several levels of
quality. The cheaper ones were unmarked
while better quality pipes were finely finished
and stamped with identifying marks. These
usually included the maker's initials and other
devices such as the lily (fleur de lis) and rose.
Some scholars have suggested that the rose was
used by English expatriates because of its association with the Tudor family. Others believe
that the lily and rose were used as generic
marks of quality during the early 17th-century
and had no particular symbolic meaning.[45]

Initially, these early 17th-century Dutch pipes resembled their English predecessors. While many were plain, others were more elaborate with molded floral motifs or depictions of biblical characters such as Jonah and the whale. Many examples of these "Baroque" style pipes have been recovered in Amsterdam. Notice that pipe bowl size also grew larger as tobacco became more popular and available.

Although clay pipes are not specified in the inventories of goods shipped to New Netherland during the 1620s and 1630s, either by the WIC or to Rensselaerswijck, they were certainly there. Pipes were too popular an item to leave behind. Besides, the archaeological evidence confirms their presence. Numerous pipe fragments were recovered from the 1624 to 1640 period components at Fort Orange. Not surprisingly, these represent typical Dutch domestic pipes. Most have small bulbous bowls and are marked with the maker's initials, the rose or a combination of both. A few examples of the more elaborate Baroque style were also recovered. In general, however, the impression is that these pipes were mid-level quality and that few of the fancy, more expensive pipes reached frontier outposts such as Fort Orange.

Although not common, a few examples of these Dutch domestic pipes have been found on Native sites. Although most are fragmentary and unmarked, two examples may date prior to 1640. One group of pipes are marked on the heel with a stylized IP, the mark of John Plummer, an Amsterdam maker who died in 1637. The second example is a nearly complete pipe from the Oneida Blowers site. This pipe, marked MTS on the heel, was probably made by Matthias Stafford, another of the English pipe makers who lived in Amsterdam during the 1620s.[46]

It seems surprising that European pipes would appeal to Native Americans who certainly had smoking pipes of their own. Nonetheless, these small white pipes were sought after. Whether the reason – novelty, prestige or their striking white color – these pipes, designed for Europeans, appealed to Native tastes as well. They first appear on Native sites during the 1630s and by the 1640s had become a staple item of trade. As a result, pipes began to be made specifically for that purpose and one more Dutch domestic object became part of an evolving collection of "trade goods." This transition is explored further in Chapter 4.

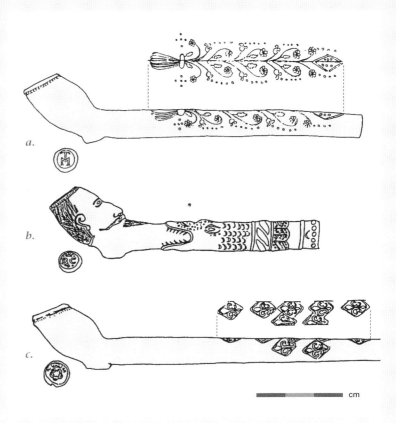

FIGURE 3.19

Early 17th-century Amsterdam pipes.

a. A simple Baroque pipe with leaves and flowers molded on the stem.

b. An elaborate Baroque pipe molded in the shape of Jonah and the whale.

c. A short bulbous bowl pipe with fleur de lis stamped on the stem.

After De Haan and Krook 1988:32 (#102), 35 (#125) and 37 (#147).

kettles, hoes to be used for spring planting and, most important, two new commodities – a coarse woolen cloth usually referred to as duffel, and wampum. Both were in high demand and not only by the Mohawks and Mahicans. The French Indians "come to us for no other reason than to get wampum." As De Rasiere observed, if the Company would "supply me continually with duffels, I know how to get wampum and to stock Fort Orange in such a way that the French Indians will never again come there in vain." [47]

De Rasiere's letters make it clear that Native demand drove the trade and that the Company had a difficult time supplying the products that Native people wanted. Things hadn't improved when Van den Bogart visited the Mohawks and Oneidas eight years later. At the end of his journal, Van den Bogart attached a list of commonly used words in both Dutch and Mohawk. This list includes all the standard items of trade – kettles, axes, knives, awls, cloth, wampum and beads. More interesting, it also contains words for many new items, things the Mohawks had seen and now wanted. Among these were adzes, spoons, swords, looking glasses, scissors, combs, bells and scrapers. [48] Since Van den Bogart and his party had not brought any of these desirable items with them, it is no wonder they received such rough treatment. All they could offer as gifts or to purchase food were a few knives and awls. Van den Bogart's word list is also important for what it does *not* include. There is no mention of firearms, alcohol or European clay pipes. All these would become staples of the trade within the next five to ten years.

In sum, the WIC trading assemblage was basically an extension of what the earlier Independent Traders had used so successfully, with a few key substitutions (especially in glass bead styles) and additions (woolen cloth and wampum). Beyond this, the big difference was the wide range of European materials, not traditionally considered trade goods, that

could be obtained. Just as the Independent Traders had discovered, personal possessions and even trash could be used for exchange. Now that the Dutch had begun to settle, more of both was available.

What does the archaeological evidence tell us about the Company's trade during this period? The artifacts from Fort Orange and the Mohawk sites confirm the changes indicated by the documents. Some of the standard trade goods are different, especially the beads. Huey's excavations indicate that polychrome beads are gone, replaced by smaller, less expensive white, black and dark blue ones. Though not very impressive, it is these small "seed" beads that dominate the assemblages on Mohawk sites from this period, more than eighty percent at Briggs Run and Yates I. In fact, this Seed Bead Horizon defines the WIC period just as the preceding Independent Traders period is defined by the prevalence of polychrome beads. [49]

The archaeological record also confirms the growing importance of wampum. All the early deposits at Fort Orange contained wampum beads as well as glass ones. This is also the case on Native sites. Though not as common as they would be in another decade, wampum beads and other forms of marine shell are more abundant, not just on Mohawk sites but across eastern Iroquoia. [50]

Other classes of artifacts are harder to see. In some cases, such as duffels, there is little archaeological evidence to find, only the rare fragment of a lead cloth seal. [51] However, very few trade goods were recovered from Fort Orange and while this isn't surprising – most of the trade goods had gone out the door – it is the paucity of material on Native sites that is telling. If the archaeological record from this period indicates anything, it is that this was an impoverished trade, especially when compared with the Independent Traders period.

On Mohawk sites such as Briggs Run and Yates I, European material is not only less common, it has a different character.

cm

FIGURE 3.20
*Apostle spoon
from the
Briggs Run site.
See note 52.*

demand these items. Other objects such as iron mouth harps and European pipes may have been novelties but quickly became part of the inventory of material goods that Native people expected. In addition to the kinds of hardware noted by Van den Bogart, the broader range of European tools occurs on these sites – a hammer, a piece of file or an iron fish hook. There were the new items Native people wanted, the gifts that Van den Bogart had not brought, and though not plentiful, they were slowly becoming more available.

Reviving the Trade, after 1635. During the late 1630s, many changes were underway. We will focus on two – the increasing influence of the French, and Kiliaen van Rensselaer's growing interest in the fur trade.

As Van den Bogart learned, the French were busy exploring Iroquois country and making friends during the 1630s. While these were primarily traders, an occasional Jesuit mission-ary may have visited as well. During these years, Jesuit concern was focused on new missions among the Huron and other tribes farther west. Conversion efforts directed toward the Mohawks and the rest of Five Nations tribes would come a decade or two later. Though focused on spiritual matters, the Jesuits were very savvy about earthly affairs, especially how to make themselves welcome. In 1637, as part of their instructions for traveling among Native people, Father Superior Paul Le Jeune advised that "each one should be provided with a half a gross of awls, two or three dozen small knives called *jabettes,* a hundred fishhooks, and some beads." These would serve as "the money with which they will buy their food, wood, bark house, and other necessaries."[53]

Archaeologically, a distinctive set of iron artifacts on Mohawk sites such as Bauder, Rumrill-Naylor and Oak Hill reflects this French influence. These include small folding knife blades, distinctive tools for scraping

Everything appears to have been used more intensively. The axes and knives are frequently worn out, reduced to fragments. The same intense re-use occurs with kettles. Very few large pieces of un-utilized metal are found on these sites. On the other hand, nails and spikes occur much more frequently along with other items that Dutch settlers may have considered trash – pieces of chain, bits of lead casting waste, fragments of European ceramics and glassware.

Although Dutch personal possessions form the smallest part of the European goods found on Native sites between 1624 and 1635, they best indicate the changing nature of the trade. Some of these desirable items were not totally new. Native people had seen, and occasionally obtained, spoons, combs and scissors from the Independent Traders. Now they began to

Wampum and Its Relations

Few artifacts evoke the complexities of the early fur trade better than wampum. Known to the Dutch as sewan, these small tubular beads were made from shell by the tribes of southern New England, especially the Pequots and Narragansetts. White beads were made from the columella or central core of whelks while the more valuable purple beads were produced from hard-shell clam.

Wampum's most remarkable quality was its ability to work across cultural boundaries. These beads could be used in many ways. For the Dutch, small strings of beads were used to buy food and other necessities, serving as cash when little coinage was available. Larger quantities were used to pay for furs, buy supplies and purchase land. From a Native point of view, wampum had other essential purposes. Individual beads were often set into wooden pipes, war clubs and bowls as well as used for personal adornment. More important, small strings of beads and larger belts were used to communicate messages and mark ritual activities. As relations between Native people and Europeans grew more complex during the 17th-century, wampum belts became the Native means to record treaties and document agreements.[54]

Although shell beads had been an important part of Native culture for thousands of years, the form we call wampum rarely occurs prior to European contact. It remains unclear exactly how the wampum trade began. One possibility revolves around Jaques Eelkins, the same trader who had commanded Fort Nassau in 1615. In 1622, Eelkins received a huge amount of wampum from the Pequots in exchange for a hostage. Although the Company disavowed

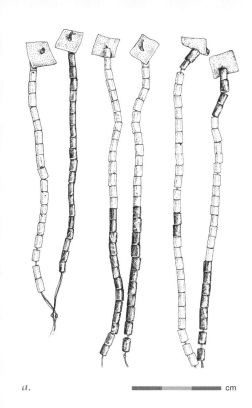

a.   cm

this kind of activity, the discovery of wampum's value to Native people was duly noted. By 1626, wampum was the most valuable trade commodity at Fort Orange. There is no evidence that the Dutch made wampum themselves until much later.[55]

The discovery of wampum's value by the Dutch also had a profound effect on the tribes who produced it. "Strange it was to see the great alteration it made in a few years among the Indians themselves," William Bradford observed in 1628. The wampum trade has made them "rich and powerful, and also proud...."[56]

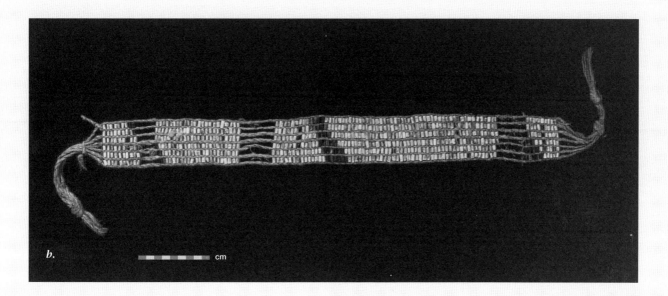

b.

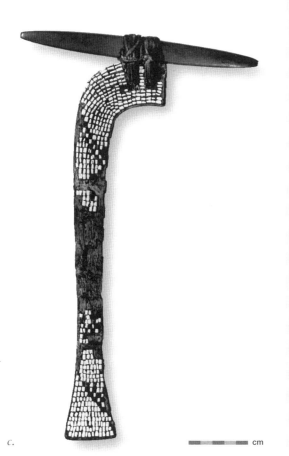

c.

FIGURE 3.21

Some of wampum's many uses.

a. Strings of beads for conveying specific messages.
After Trigger, ed. 1978:439.
Courtesy Smithsonian Institution.

b. The "Esopus" Belt, a mid 17th-century wampum belt.
Courtesy of the County Clerk's office, Ulster County, NY.

c. An early 17th-century war club with stone bar celt and inlaid with wampum beads.
Ehb 26. Courtesy of the National Museum of Denmark.

a.

cm

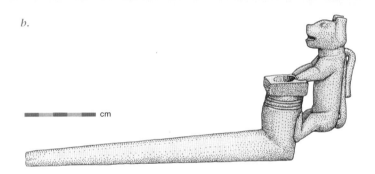

b.

cm

c.

Another class of artifacts also expressed this new sense of power and identity – elaborate stone pipes. As Roger Williams noted in 1643, "they make such great pipes, both of wood and stone, that they are two feet long, with men or beasts carved [on them], so big… that a man may be hurt mortally by one of them." Several examples of these large ornate pipes have been found on Narragansett and Wampanoag sites. William's commentary then takes a curious twist as he adds "these [great pipes] commonly come from the *Mauquauwogs,* or Man Eaters, three or four hundred miles from us."[57] Interestingly, fragments of similar, even identical, stone pipes have been found on several Mohawk sites of the 1630 to 1650 period.[58] While it remains unclear at present exactly who made these spectacular objects, they clearly reflect the wampum trade and the complex alliances and agreements that underpinned it.

FIGURE 3.22
Early 17th-century stone pipes.

a. Fragment of a stone effigy pipe from the Mohawk Fiske site (NYSM #A-38381).
Photo by Ted Beblowski.

b. A nearly identical example from the Burr's Hill site, Warren, RI.
After Gibson 1980:43. Drawing by Ellen Chase.

c. A Mohawk (Maquaes) Indian with his pipe. From the pamphlet by Johannes Megapolensis, "A Short Account of the Mohawk Indians," published 1644.
Courtesy of the Municipal Archives, Amsterdam.

skins, iron projectile points with a long cylindrical tang, and offset awls.[59] In addition to these utilitarian objects, the presence of an occasional religious ring or medal, even a pilgrim badge, confirms the presence of French Catholics rather than Dutch Protestants.[60]

More significant than the French presence was the growing influence of private Dutch traders, those who skirted the Company's monopoly to take advantage of the fur trade. As the population of New Netherland grew, so did the number of people who sought to profit from trading. With the effective declaration of free trade in 1639, few controls remained in place and trading quickly returned to the free-for-all it had been prior to the establishment of the WIC. There were certainly many private traders but none had the resources or the connections that Kiliaen Van Rensselaer did. Through his buying power with suppliers in the Republic and extensive clientele in New Netherland, van Rensselaer's ability to reshape the trade was significant.

Whatever the source, the results were dramatic. By 1640, much more European material was flowing out of Dutch settlements and into Native hands. These changes are most evident on Mohawk sites such as Bauder, Rumrill-Naylor and Oak Hill. Not only are the stock trade goods much more evident; many of the new objects that Native people wanted now occur more frequently. These include a wider range of tools and hardware as well as pewter spoons, iron mouth harps and other domestic items such as combs, scissors and thimbles. Other hallmarks of this expanded trade include a greater variety of white clay pipes from Gouda as well as Amsterdam,[61] and a different set of glass beads, especially round blue beads with or without white stripes (Kidd #IIa40 and IIb56). In fact, some researchers have termed this the Blue Bead Horizon.[62]

Two other artifact groups reflect the magnitude of change. The first are lead cloth seals. These seals were attached to bolts of cloth by

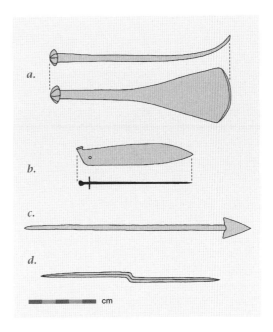

FIGURE 3.23
French-related artifacts from the 1635 to 1645 period.

a. An iron scraper, side and top views.

b. A folding knife blade, side and top views.

c. An iron point with a long tang.

d. An offset iron awl.

Drawings by Ellen Chase.

the guilds that produced them and the town inspectors who checked them for quality. Most come from important textile-producing towns such as Campen or Leiden and probably reflect Van Rensselaer's efforts to import the products that Native consumers wanted. Since these seals often can be dated, they provide a valuable record of when these commodities were made and used.[63] Firearms are the other significant change. On Mohawk sites such as Bauder, Rumrill-Naylor and Oak Hill, it is clear that guns are present, if in limited number.[64] It is hard to track the trade in firearms. Since they were contraband, the historical documents tell us little. Archaeologically, it appears that by 1640, the Mohawks were getting guns, but exactly from whom remains unclear. We will look at the firearms trade in more detail in the next chapter.

By 1640, the quantity of European material in Native hands had increased dramatically, exceeding even the amounts received during the Independent Traders period. For the Mohawks, most of this material came through trade usually in exchange for furs. However there was also a practical, everyday side to the

FIGURE 3.24
*Two lead cloth seals
from Campen.*

*a. A tubular seal
from Amsterdam
(MWE5-88).*
Courtesy of the AHM/BMA.
Photo by Wiard Krook,
afdeling Archeologie.

*b. A similar
tubular seal from
the Bauder site
(A2002.13AE.99.38).*
Rumrill collection, NYSM.
Photo by Ted Beblowski.

trade and Dutch settlers often used these goods to obtain food, guide services or other necessities.[65] Although Mahican people obtained the same kinds of merchandise in the same ways, they also received large amounts of trade goods in payment for the sale of land. Whatever the source, this rising tide of European material had an increasingly powerful effect on traditional Native culture, and not always in predictable ways.

Adapting and Adopting

If the artifacts from Mohawk and Mahican sites show the growing influence of new materials and technologies, they also indicate that Native people strove to maintain their traditional ways. Corn was still ground into meal with stone mullers and notched pebbles continued to anchor fishing nets. In many ways, continuity marks this period as much as change does.

Native ceramics are a good example. On sites of this period, Native-made pottery is still prevalent although vessels tend to be smaller and less elaborately decorated. Instead of the oblique lines and opposed triangles that characterized Garoga horizon pots, bands of horizontal lines are the primary decorative motif. Effigy figures often occur on these vessels as well. Yet the evidence of a changing world is here too. Fragments of a different

style of Native pottery, one more typical of southern New England, have also been recovered from the Briggs Run and Yates I sites.[66] While it is not clear whether these fragments of Shantok-related pottery indicate marriage alliances, the presence of refugees or captives, they certainly link the Mohawks with the growth of the wampum trade.

Exotic styles of Native pottery also point to the other arena of Iroquois interest. On sites such as Rumrill-Naylor and Oak Hill, the frequency of Huron-related pottery is greater than on previous sites, a reflection of the growing intensity of the Mohawk and Huron conflict.[67] As the Mohawks lost population through warfare and disease during these decades, it became increasingly important to rebuild their numbers through a deliberate strategy of capturing other people.[68] These exotic ceramics are the material evidence for how the Mohawks adapted and adopted in order to survive.

Native-made ceramic pipes, though not common, occur more frequently than on the preceding Protohistoric sites. While the exotic white pipes brought by the Dutch were also attractive, it seems clear that many of the Mohawks preferred to smoke their own. My sense is that most of the European pipes found on Mohawk and other Iroquois sites post-date the establishment of free trade of 1639.

The story is similar with stone and bone tools. Traditional triangular projectile points were still made of local chert although points cut from sheet brass rapidly replace them. On sites such as Briggs Run and Yates, the ratio of stone to metal points is in the range of 1 to 1; on later sites like Bauder, Rumrill-Naylor and Oak Hill, the ratio swiftly shifts toward 1 to 10. A similar process of replacement occurs with other traditional tool forms. Although small chert scrapers and knives, as well as bone awls and antler harpoons still occur, European implements and a variety of Native-made tools of iron and brass were increasingly used

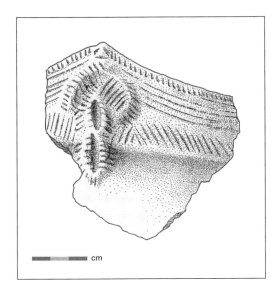

indicate, not only that flintlock muskets had become a significant part of the Mohawk arsenal, but that the traditional technology for making stone tools had been adapted to fill a new need. By 1640 these Native-made gunflints are a common occurance on Mohawk sites.

The dramatic increase in metal tools had profound effect on the material culture of Mohawk and Mahican people. Metal tools encouraged and enabled more technically difficult, artistically elaborate work in stone, wood, antler and other traditional materials. For example, there is a significant increase in the occurrence of stone pipes during this period. These come in many forms from effigy styles to vasiform shapes to those that copy European pipes. By 1640, there is also more evidence of wooden pipes, antler combs and ladles. These artifacts hint at a richness of Native material culture that survives only rarely in the archaeological record. It is primarily through Van den Bogart's description that we can glimpse the elaborately carved and painted sculptures, masks, staffs and other regalia that were an essential part of Native life.

Metal tools also meant a greater ability to work metal. Sites of this period produce evidence of hammers, files, even small anvils. With these tools, it is not surprising that Mohawk craftsmen began to produce more sophisticated metal objects. The simple conical liners for pipe bowls as well as the more elaborate liners for wooden pipes that became common during this period are a case in point.[69] While some have argued that Europeans made these copper and brass liners as trade goods, there is no reason why Native people could not have produced them. Technically, they are no more complex than the Native-made spirals of the early Contact Period and, with better tools, they were not difficult to make.

By 1640 Mohawk and Mahican people were also beginning to experiment with another metal – lead. While the impetus came from

FIGURE 3.25

Left above: Fragment of a 1630s Mohawk pot from the Failing site. Note the full figure effigy and the change in collar motif.
Courtesy of Wayne Lenig. Drawing by Ellen Chase.

FIGURE 3.26

Left below: Fragments of a Shantock-related pot from the Briggs Run site (A2002.10AC.13.2).
Swart collection, NYSM. Photo by Ted Beblowski.

instead. These include the sword blade scrapers, brass knives, kettle handle awls and harpoons made from knives discussed in the previous chapter.

This process of replacement is dramatic, but it is important not to oversimplify its implications. An object's material could change, yet its form and function remain the same. A brass point was as effective in hunting as a chert one. Nor were traditional skills necessarily lost as changes in material preferences took place. Making stone tools is a good example. As the frequency of chert points decreases, there is a corresponding increase in the occurrence of chert gunflints. These

FIGURE 3.27

Right: An early 17th-century wood pipe (Edc16) collected prior to 1650. Note that this panther effigy has brass eyes, insets that appear to represent tattooing, and a conical bowl liner.

Courtesy of the National Museum of Demark.

FIGURE 3.28

Below: Copper and brass liners from early 17th-century Mohawk wooden pipes.

a. A conical liner from the Coleman-Van Duesen site (A2002.10AJ.2.30).

b. A conical liner from the Rumrill-Naylor site (A2005.13BM.99.31).

c. An extended liner from the Rumrill-Naylor site (A2005.13BM.99.31).

d. An extended liner from the Briggs Run site (A2002.10.AC.S.1).

b. and c.– Rumrill collection; a. and d.– Swart collection, NYSM. Photo by Ted Beblowski).

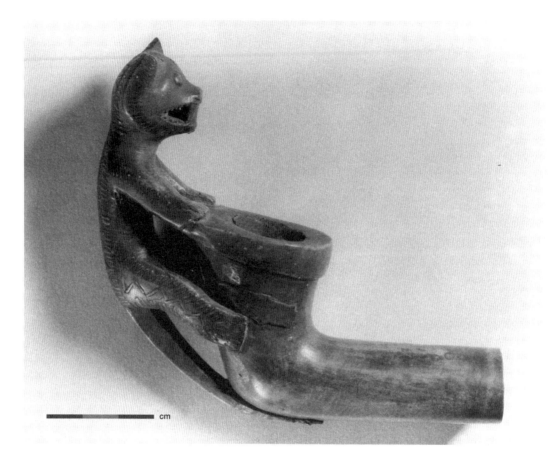

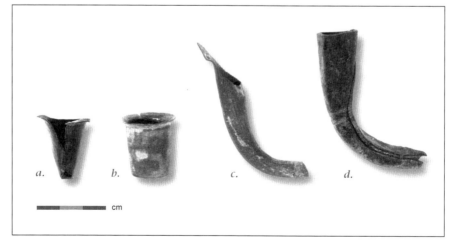

a.   b.   c.   d.

cm

cm

producing musket balls and shot, small-scale casting was a common domestic activity among the Dutch and it is likely that Native people of the region saw buckles, buttons and other small items made this way. The first lead figures from Mohawk sites appear to be made from sheet lead, perhaps a flattened musket ball or piece of casting waste. These are simple figures, usually showing an animal in profile. In shape, they often mimic earlier forms that were cut from sheet brass or, before that, made from bone and antler.[70] It is unclear whether Native people had begun to cast objects by 1640 but, as we will see in the next chapter, they quickly began to experiment with this technology during the new decade.

Summing Up

By 1640, the dynamics that would fundamentally reshape the Capital Region were well underway. Dutch settlement was a significant factor in these processes. The once ephemeral Europeans were now a permanent feature on the land and the impact of their presence was visible in several ways. One was an increase in competition. More people meant a greater demand for the same, often scarce, resources – food, furs, the land itself. The political and military stakes were also higher. Greater competition meant that allies were essential. In this rapidly changing world, one's friends and enemies were increasingly defined by who controlled key commodities such as wampum and firearms. Just as the economic implications of the fur trade now extended far beyond Fort Orange, so did the scale of potential hostility and risk.

For the Dutch, the issue was whether these fragile new settlements could survive. For Native people, it was a matter of maintaining their traditional ways against an onslaught of new materials and foreign ideas such as land ownership and Christianity. The new decade would see an acceleration of the forces that drove both concerns.

FIGURE 3.29
Native-made lead effigy figures.

a. Lead bear from the Bauder site (A2005.13BM.99.136).

b. Lead deer (?) from the Rumrill-Naylor site (A2005.13BM.99.137).

Rumrill collection, NYSM. Photo by Ted Beblowski.

CHAPTER FOUR: Settling In, 1640 to 1652

Inauspicious from the beginning, the 1640s proved to be a decade of difficult yet surprising events. In Europe, the Thirty Years' War continued to ravage much of Germany and the Low Countries, although the original religious reasons for hostility had become progressively more dynastic and nationalistic. Across the Channel, the bitter dispute over authority between Charles I and Parliament had ended first in stalemate and then, by 1642, in civil war. However, this internal struggle provided no reduction in English hostility toward the Dutch. In fact, tensions over trade and territory between New England and New Netherland grew more heated throughout the decade.

Things were already not very good in New Netherland. In 1640, the population was small, probably less than one thousand people, and the economic situation fragile. Instead of using the Company's decision to open up the fur trade to his advantage, the new director, Willem Kieft, chose a campaign of intimidation against the Algonquian peoples of the lower Hudson Valley and Long Island. The unsurprising result was Governor Kieft's War, several years of intermittent hostility that stifled immigration and depleted the province's strained resources even further.[1]

Upriver, the situation was a little better. The new decade started, much as the old one had ended, with floods and poor crops. In April, high water inundated Castle Island and even forced a temporary evacuation of Fort Orange.[2] The fur trade was still a mess, and while Mohawk and Mahican people were beset by new diseases and lingering antagonisms, at least there was no open hostility within the region. It is against this backdrop

that the importance of Arent van Curler and his actions is best seen.

Van Curler's significance lies in three inter-connected accomplishments, all of which were critical in reviving the fur trade. This, in turn, provided the economic base that would allow stable Dutch communities such as Beverwijck to emerge. It was Van Curler who understood how to work with the Native people of the region. This meant both the Mahicans, who still controlled most of the land needed by Dutch settlers, and the Mohawks, who controlled much of the fur trade. Since tensions between these former friends and neighbors remained high, this was no small feat and Van Curler had to strike a fine balance to work with both – one based on personal knowledge, respect and trust. Van Curler was also the one who took Kiliaen van Rensselaer's ideas for strengthening the fur trade and translated them into an economic reality. Finally, it was Van Curler who understood the importance of the west side of the Hudson River and took active steps to move the Colonie's operations there.

Connecting Threads

By 1640, Van Curler had been in the Colonie for two years. He held several important appointments and it is clear from his great uncle's frequent and detailed letters of instruction that much was expected of him. Van Curler's primary responsibility was to oversee the administration and business of the Colonie. This meant a great deal of paperwork, especially keeping accounts and reporting them back to the patroon – pretty dreary stuff for an ambitious and energetic twenty-year-old. It is small wonder then that Kiliaen's letters often reflect impatience. "I hear that you spend too much time in the woods… you must stick to writing and never again neglect to copy your papers and accounts but always have some ready to send [to me] when there is an opportunity."[3]

In spite of such complaints, the job was not all paperwork. Among the patroon's early requests was a directive to construct a church, plus houses for a minister and sexton, on the east side of the Hudson River opposite Castle Island. Others were encouraged to build their houses nearby, making this the nucleus of the Colonie's settlement. There were also leases to monitor, debts to collect and ordinances to enforce. If New Amsterdam was a tough company town full of hard drinking, hard living men and women, Rensselaerswijck was the wild edge of the frontier and Van Curler's responsibilities were as much those of a policeman and judge as a bureaucrat.[4]

Aside from running the Colonie, Van Curler's chief responsibility was to revive the fur trade. This was a complex problem, one that required solutions at several levels. Most important were good relations with the region's Native people. By spending "time in the woods," Van Curler, like other *bosloopers*, became well acquainted with the country and people beyond the area of Dutch settlement. However, it was Van Curler's attitude toward Native people that made him so different from many of his predecessors and contemporaries. Unlike Hontom or Kieft, Van Curler treated Native people as intelligent adults instead of wayward children. As a result he was able to build a series of personal relationships that would become the basis for new economic and political agreements.

There was another aspect to the problem of rebuilding the fur trade – establishing some level of control over his fellow Europeans. The problem was that, with deregulation, unauthorized private traders or "residents" now controlled most of the trade. As he wrote

to Van Rensselaer in early 1643, "Neither I nor the Company have had any trade this year [although] I believe that the residents have shipped fully 3,000 to 4,000 skins." The potential for the trade to be "very profitable" was great, he continued, but only if the private traders were forbidden to operate within the

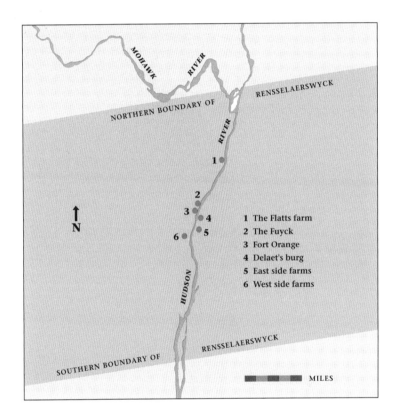

1 The Flatts farm
2 The Fuyck
3 Fort Orange
4 Delaet's burg
5 East side farms
6 West side farms

Colonie. The real problem was that no one enforced the existing ordinances. As with any trade in contraband, it was dangerous and there was too much money to be made.[5]

Van Curler's solution to this seemingly impossible problem was actually quite simple – establish good relations with the customer, have the best quality merchandise available in quantity and control the key points of access. While these may sound like common sense to us, they were novel ideas at the time. They would also change the course of Dutch settlement in the region.

FIGURE 4.1
Map of Dutch settlement during the 1640s.
After Huey 1984:64. Map by Booth Simpson.

FIGURE 4.2
The last page of Arent van Curler's letter to the Patroon, June 16, 1643. Damaged in the State Capitol fire of 1911.
Courtesy of the New York State Library, Manuscripts and Special Collections. Photo by Ted Beblowski.

Building good relationships with the Mohawks was essential and by 1643, Van Curler had emerged as the key personality on the Dutch side. That spring he traveled by horse with two other traders to visit the three major Mohawk villages, bringing presents and requesting a continuation of trade and peaceful relations. As Van Curler reported to the patroon, they were received with "great joy" and entertained generously wherever they went, quite a different response than Van den Bogart had received nine years earlier. The only disappointment was that the Mohawks refused to ransom three French prisoners including the Jesuit Isaac Jogues.[6] Both the Dutch and Mohawks would later recall this visit as a major turning point in their evolving relationship.

The second part of Van Curler's plan, providing quality merchandise in quantity, came directly from the patroon. While Van Rensselaer could negotiate the details with suppliers back in the Republic, it was Van Curler who actually found out what Native people wanted. No one was in a better position to do so. As secretary and bookkeeper, Van Curler had a thorough knowledge of all the material goods that came into the Colonie. With his personal contacts among both the Mahicans and Mohawks, he also knew which of those items most appealed to Native tastes. His job was to get that information back to the patroon.

The most visible part of Van Curler's plan was to move the Colonie's center from the east side of the Hudson River, where the patroon wanted it, to the west side. To be successful in the trade, one had to have ready access to the Native traders who brought the furs. Van Curler took a first step in this direction in 1640/41 when he built a new house for the patroon on the west side of the Hudson just north of Fort Orange. He also made this house his personal residence.[7] But things were changing quickly, and by 1642 his thinking had evolved in a different direction.

Disgusted with the chaotic conditions around Fort Orange, Van Curler planned to leapfrog around them and establish a new base for the trade. That location was the patroon's farm at the Flatts (*de Vlackte*) four miles north of Fort Orange.

Many of the details of Van Curler's thinking are laid out in a letter to the patroon dated June 16, 1643. This is a remarkable document, and one of the few pieces of Van Curler's own writing that has survived. It is clear that Van Curler had already started to implement his plan. He reports that during the previous year, he had a house built at the Flatts and kept a trader there over the winter. He also reviews his plans for the current year including construction of another, larger farmhouse and the purchase of additional land from the nearby Mahicans. Most interesting, he makes several personal requests. One is for permission to return to the Republic and "make good to the patroon whatever shall fall short in the accounts." Van Curler also requests the lease of the Flatts farm for himself and states his willingness to "share the expenses" for developing it further. He ends by announcing his plans to marry and his desire to keep "my residence in your Honor's Colonie for a good many years to come." It is clear that Van Curler had mapped out a strategy for himself as well as the Colonie and was anxious to have the patroon's full approval.[8]

The Flatts were central to this plan. This would be Van Curler's base of operations, both as a farm and as a new base for the fur trade. Yet as enticing as the Flatts were, Van Curler was already thinking beyond them. "Hardly half a day's journey from the Colonie," he wrote to the patroon, "lies the most beautiful land that the eye may wish to see…". Though this stretch of the Mohawk Valley could not be reached by boat, "it may be possible to reach it with wagons." Though not fully developed, the idea that would become Schenectady was already forming in Van Curler's mind.[9]

Van Curler did not wait for the patroon's reply. He proceeded with the construction of the new farmhouse at the Flatts, a combination house and barn (*hallehuis*) 120 feet long and 28 feet wide.[10] As Van Curler settled in, the Flatts increasingly became the scene of important activity. Visits from Mohawk traders were common and, during the summer of 1643, one such party brought a prisoner with them, the French Jesuit Isaac Jogues, whom Van Curler had tried to ransom the year before. This time, Van Curler helped Jogues escape. It was also about this time that the first "treaty of friendship and brotherhood" between the Dutch and Mohawks was concluded.[11] Few details of this treaty and how it came to pass have survived, but it is likely that Arent van Curler was involved.

Although the patroon's response to Van Curler's June 1643 letter has not survived, Van Rensselaer confirmed his grand nephew's re-appointment as *commis* in September.[12] All seemed to be fine until Kiliaen van Rensselaer died in October and his son Johannes became patroon. Van Curler proceeded with his plans in spite of Kiliaen's death. He married Anthonia Slachboom, the widow of Jonas Bronck, in 1644 and also hired several additional hands to work at the Flatts farm. By October, however, he was ready to leave for the Republic both to fulfill his promise to the previous patroon and make the acquaintance of the new one.

Allies and Adversaries

With Kiliaen van Rensselaer's death, the course of New Netherland changed. Its strongest advocate was gone and it was unclear how the void in leadership would be filled. Other changes were also underway. In December 1644 the directors of the WIC voted to recall Kieft for mismanagement of the province and his ill-considered war on the Native population. The following spring, Petrus Stuyvesant,

recently governor of Curacao, was appointed as his replacement. Stuyvesant's commission from the States General ordered him to maintain and improve the trade as well as safeguard the province from encroachment by its pushy European neighbors. A dedicated Company man and experienced soldier, Stuyvesant was one who took his orders seriously.

Van Curler departed for the Republic in October 1644, leaving his assistant Anthony de Hooges as *commis*. Although he did not take his new wife with him initially, he decided to extend his stay and sent for her to join him. There were many reasons to prolong his visit, the most important of which were the decisions the new patroon and his guardians would make about the Colonie's future. In November 1646, Brant van Slichtenhorst, a prominent Gelderland tobacco grower, was appointed as director of the Colonie.[13] While the records are largely silent on how this decision was made, it is likely that Van Curler, one of the few people with direct experience in the Colonie, was a participant. Another important decision was also made – to build a new settlement on the west side of the Hudson and shift the Colonie's center there. This was a radical departure from what Kiliaen van Rensselaer had envisioned, a plan much more indicative of Van Curler's ideas.

Whatever role Van Curler played in re-thinking the Colonie, he certainly used the time back in the Republic to solidify his own base of operations. In September 1647, he finally received a six-year lease for the farm at the Flatts. There can be little doubt that Van Curler and his wife used this opportunity to select building materials and furnishings to take back home. It is also likely that Van Curler used this time to make direct contact with the suppliers of important trade goods, just as his great uncle had done earlier. These included not just the usual woolens from Campen and Leiden, but a series of new products made for the trade and based on Van Curler's experience.

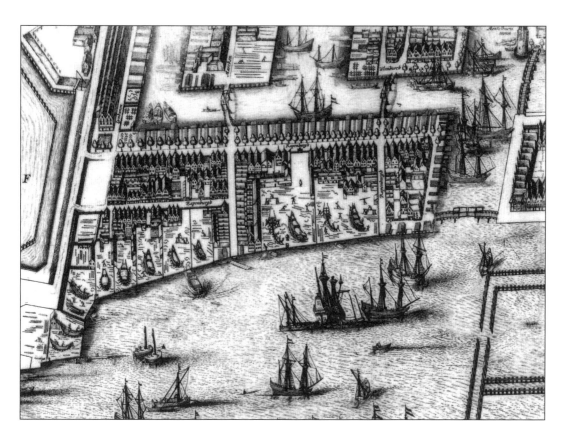

FIGURE 4.3
Amsterdam waterfront, ca. 1650. Detail from map by Balthasar Florisz van Berckenrode.
Courtesy of the Amsterdam Municipal Archives.

Van Curler returned to New Netherland with Van Slichtenhorst, arriving in March 1648. Much had happened since Van Curler's departure nearly four years earlier. In 1644 the WIC had closed its "house of commerce" in Fort Orange, acknowledging what Van Curler had already determined, that the Company had lost control of the fur trade. Private traders still operated in and around the fort but virtually without regulation. This changed with Stuyvesant's arrival in May 1647. The new director-general was a whirlwind of activity. He quickly cracked down on the unauthorized trade that had so frustrated Van Curler. He also made a brief visit to inspect Fort Orange, found it in "bad condition" and authorized new construction to remedy the situation. This included the construction of a brewery, the first of several ventures designed to raise funds for repair by privatizing portions of the fort.[14] Under Stuyvesant, the political landscape was very different and the old policy of laissez-faire was over.

Much had also changed on the Native side while Van Curler was away. The Mohawk raids along the St. Lawrence and west into Huronia that had begun in 1640 had increased to a nearly year-round state of siege. Although Kieft had managed to negotiate a treaty with the Mohawks and Mahicans at Fort Orange during the summer of 1645, it had done nothing to dampen the spiraling scale of warfare among Native people. Nor were Europeans exempt from these conflicts, as the Jesuits soon learned. After escaping three years earlier, Isaac Jogues elected to return to the Mohawks during the summer of 1646. His goal was to establish a mission; by October, he had been killed. Meanwhile, the war against the Hurons raged on until 1649, when virtually all their villages

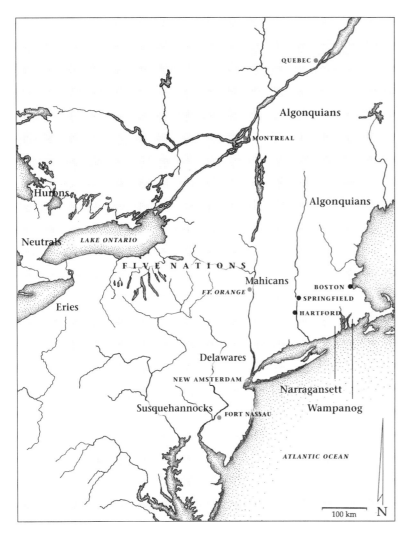

FIGURE 4.4
*Map of the
Northeast,
1640 to 1652.*
Map by Booth Simpson.

him into conflict with Stuyvesant. Stuyvesant's concern was defense. An exceptionally strong spring flood in 1648 had washed much of Fort Orange away and Stuyvesant immediately began an ambitious program of rebuilding. Stuyvesant worried that settlement so close to the fort would further weaken its defensive capabilities and ordered all new construction stopped. Van Slichtenhorst refused. This disagreement quickly escalated into a fundamental dispute over authority between the Colonie and the West India Company. This feud grew increasingly heated until Stuyvesant ended the matter in April 1652 by removing the area around Fort Orange from the jurisdiction of the patroon and establishing a new settlement named Beverwijck under the Company's authority. When Van Slichtenhorst protested, he was arrested and taken to Manhattan.[16]

Arent van Curler stayed out of the political feuding. Now twenty-nine and married, he focused on improving the Flatts farm. In November 1649, he was granted a living allowance for the laborers engaged "in building or otherwise working at the Flatts." This suggests that renovations and even substantial changes were made in the farm after the Van Curlers' return from the Republic. He also began to purchase the land described to Kiliaen in 1643, buying two islands from the Mahicans in 1650 and the third the following year. In addition to putting more prime land under cultivation, Van Curler concentrated on raising horses. It is no surprise that by 1651, the Flatts was listed as "the best farm" in the Colonie.[17]

Though less obvious, Van Curler's participation in the fur trade was equally important. This meant good relations with the Mohawks, never an easy task. In September 1650, Van Curler was appointed as a commissioner and asked to "renew the former alliance and bond of friendship" with the Mohawks. There may have been a personal side to this as well. Things were not going well at home. His

had been destroyed or abandoned.[15] While the survivors scattered in several directions, many chose refuge among victorious Mohawks.

Although they had returned together, Van Slichtenhorst and Van Curler took very different paths once they were back in the Colonie. For Van Slichtenhorst there was much to be done. Almost immediately, he began to implement the plan for a new settlement on the west side of the river. By late summer several houses had been built north of Fort Orange. An autocratic, hot-tempered man, Van Slichtenhorst's aggressive actions soon brought

marriage to Anthonia proved childless, and increasingly Van Curler was away from the Flatts on business. In 1652, he fathered a Mohawk daughter suggesting that he had, again, been spending "time in the woods."[18]

At the grand scale, the board had also changed. The Peace of Westphalia, signed in October 1648, finally brought an end to the Thirty Years' War. Although the treaty did little to solve the political and economic problems that plagued northern Europe, at least it brought an end to the fighting. Across the Channel, things were less happy. In January 1649, Charles I was tried, condemned and executed by the Puritan radicals under Oliver Cromwell, an action that sent shock waves across Europe. With the monarchy out of the way, Cromwell could turn his attention to the Dutch. The Navigation Act, passed by Cromwell's Parliament in 1651, was a perfect piece of protectionist legislation. It forbade the importation of goods into England or its colonies by Dutch ships. Designed to provoke a fight, it was successful and within a year the two old Protestant allies were at war with one another.

Changes on the Land

During the 1640s, the Dutch became a permanent presence on the landscape. No longer restricted to Fort Orange and a few isolated farms, they increasingly spread out along the Hudson River in a series of farms, mills and small settlements. This meant that interactions between the Dutch and Native people occurred in a much broader range of settings and that their influences on each other were more subtle and complex.

Fort Orange. By the mid-1640s, Fort Orange had begun to diminish in importance. With the end of the Company's monopoly, it was no longer the exclusive location for trade and, after two decades, it was beginning to show its age. Little had been done to keep things up.

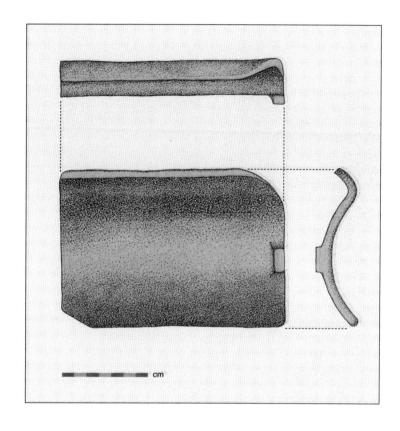

As the Company's fortunes diminished, so did the willingness to reinvest in its facilities. It was not until Stuyvesant's arrival that any effort was made to repair or modernize.

This period of slow decline is represented by component 83 in Huey's excavations. A level of dark brown alluvium and occupational debris, this level formed between the flood of 1640, which appears to have destroyed the 1624 guard house, and the construction of Labatie's brewery in the same general location seven years later. While no building foundations were uncovered, component 83 contained a great deal of building material, especially fragments of imported red and yellow brick as well as pieces of mortar and plaster. These, plus remnants of red clay roofing tiles, white delft wall tiles and leaded glass windows, provide hints of what the buildings of this period looked like.[19]

FIGURE 4.5
Drawing of an imported red clay roofing tile, commonly called a "pan tile."
Courtesy of Paul Huey.
Drawing by Gwen Gillette.

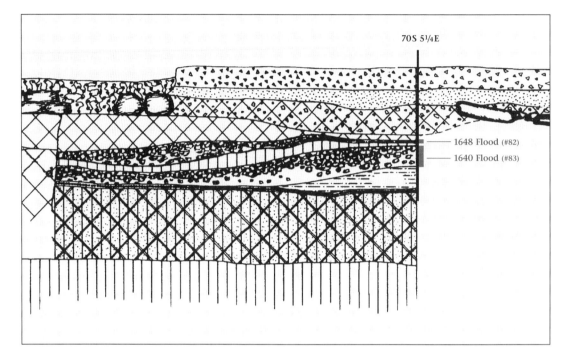

70S 5¼E

1648 Flood (#82)
1640 Flood (#83)

FIGURE 4.6
Profile of excavations at Fort Orange showing flood levels (components 83 and 82).
After Huey 1988:756

Directly above component 83 was another deposit of dark brown sandy soil mixed with brick fragments, oyster shell and charcoal. Huey labeled this level as component 82 and identified it as the fort's ground surface between the floods of 1648 and 1654.[20] Just as the events of 1648 reshaped the direction of Dutch settlement in the region, the flood of 1648 provides a clear reference point in the complex archaeological record of Fort Orange. Below it is the chaotic era of Kieft's administration; above is the rebuilding that occurred under Stuyvesant's direction.

The most significant architectural remains from the period are Stuyvesant's improvements to the fort itself. These included the construction of a more extensive moat lined with river cobbles and a small, freestanding bastion of quarried stone outside the fort's south wall. Known as a ravelin, this defensive structure was designed to strengthen the fort at its most likely point of attack, from enemy vessels sailing upriver.[21] Clearly, Stuyvesant

considered the threats from neighboring New England to be serious.

Huey also uncovered evidence of Stuyvesant's plan to revitalize the fort through privatization. In August 1648, the governor-general signed a resolution that encouraged private traders and other artisans to build houses at their own expense within the fort. While these buildings would be privately owned and could be sold, the ground on which they stood remained the property of the Company. In addition to Labatie's brewery, Huey located portions of two other buildings constructed between 1648 and 1651, the house of Abraham Staats (which may also have been a blacksmith shop) and the house of Hendrick Andriessen van Doesburgh, a gunstock maker. These were substantial buildings. Each had an excavated cellar with wood plank walls that extended 4 feet below ground level. In the Staats house, the cellar floor was made of packed brick fragments while the Van Doesburgh cellar had a wooden floor supported by wooden joists.[22]

Although Huey's excavations were limited to a narrow swath across the fort's eastern side, his meticulous recording gives us a clear view of how Fort Orange changed physically under Stuyvesant's administration. It was changing in other ways as well. By 1650 Fort Orange had grown obsolete. Too old and too close to the river with its periodic floods, the fort would soon be eclipsed by the new, rapidly growing settlement that spread just beyond its walls.

Beyond Fort Orange – The *bijeenwoninge* and the Fuyck. With the Company's decision to open up the trade to all residents in 1639, settlement beyond Fort Orange was inevitable. While there was some activity to the south, farms on Castle Island and Pieter Cornelisen's mill on the Normanskill, it was north of the fort where things happened. Among the early buildings located just beyond the fort were the patroon's storehouse (*pakhuis*), probably built in 1639/40, and past that, the patroon's house where Van Curler lived, built the following year. A sense of the emerging community can be gleaned from Isaac Jogues' rather dismissive description made during the summer of 1643. "This colony is composed of about one hundred persons, who live in 25 or 30 houses built along the River… All their houses are merely boards, and are covered with thatch. There is as yet no masonry, except in the chimneys." Court sessions were held in the Company house within the fort and the patroon's storehouse served as the church.[23] No, it wasn't much of a community, yet.

By 1648 things were quite different. Soon after his arrival, Van Slichtenhorst began to implement the plans for a new settlement. In March there were only four houses, including the patroon's, standing near the fort. By August eight more had been constructed. When the great dispute with Stuyvesant came to a head in April 1652, Slichtenhorst claimed to have built nearly one hundred new houses although the actual number was probably

closer to forty.[24] But even forty new buildings near the fort was a startling change. It is no wonder Stuyvesant objected, claimed jurisdiction of all property within a cannon shot of the fort, and ordered the buildings within that range to be demolished.

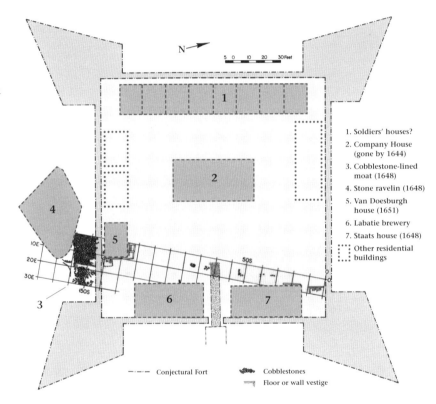

1. Soldiers' houses?
2. Company House (gone by 1644)
3. Cobblestone-lined moat (1648)
4. Stone ravelin (1648)
5. Van Doesburgh house (1651)
6. Labatie brewery
7. Staats house (1648)
- - - - Other residential buildings

---·--- Conjectural Fort   Cobblestones   Floor or wall vestige

In spite of the political wrangling, a new community was emerging. Slichtenhorst referred to it as a *bijeenwoninge* or a place for "living together." As Venema notes, he did not use the term *dorp* or village and this may indicate that a planned town was the objective. By 1648 another term had come into use. The Fuyck, as the new settlement was known, got its name from a funnel-like shape, reminiscent of a fish net.[25]

Here is another instance where archaeology helps us visualize things when the written record is vague and incomplete. Two recently

FIGURE 4.7
Plan view of Fort Orange with structures from the 1640 to 1652 period. The structures shown are known from the historical record. The fort was probably much more crowded with buildings than is illustrated here.
After Huey 1988:728. Map by Booth Simpson

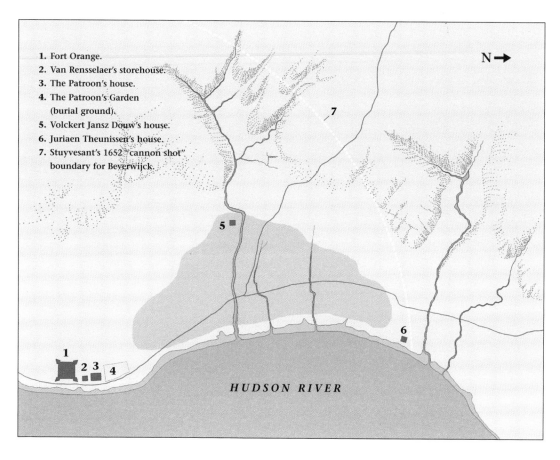

1. Fort Orange.
2. Van Rensselaer's storehouse.
3. The Patroon's house.
4. The Patroon's Garden (burial ground).
5. Volckert Jansz Douw's house.
6. Juriaen Theunissen's house.
7. Stuyvesant's 1652 "cannon shot" boundary for Beverwijck.

N➤

5 ◼

7

6 ◼

1
2 3 4

HUDSON RIVER

FIGURE 4.8
Dutch settlement beyond Fort Orange – the Fuyck, ca. 1648.
After the Romer map 1698. Map by Ellen Chase.

excavated sites suggest that settlement may have already spread far north of Fort Orange even before Slichtenhorst's arrival. One site was discovered during excavations at the KeyCorp site. The second was found during archaeological fieldwork prior to construction of the new DEC headquarters.

The first house was located on higher land along the Rutten Kill not far from the "path to the Maquaes" or present-day State Street, an excellent place to intercept Native traders on their way to Fort Orange.[26] It was built by Volckert Jansz Douw, a Lutheran immigrant and aspiring trader. Although granted this lot by Stuyvesant in 1652, Douw may have lived here as early as 1647 when he began to pay taxes on the property. The site itself revealed a complex history with elements of Douw's house as well as the subsequent almshouse

that occupied the site after 1686. Once again, only a portion of the cellar survived. In contrast to the earth-fast cellars at Fort Orange, Douw's house appears to have had a cellar with stone walls and a wooden floor on irregularly spaced joists.[27]

The second house was also located north of Fort Orange in an excellent spot for trading, on the west bank of the Hudson River just south of the Vossen Kill. This structure was probably built by Juriaen Theunissen who, like Douw, received official permission to occupy the land in 1652. He continued to live there, working as a tavern keeper and a glazier, until he sold the property after 1657. It is not known when Theunissen arrived in the Colonie or how he was initially employed. Here again, only a portion of a collapsed cellar survived. The remainder of the structure appears to have been washed away, probably by the same 1648 flood that devastated Fort Orange. There was no evidence of rebuilding after the flood and the abandoned cellar hole gradually filled with soil and garbage until buried by the flood of 1654.

The archaeologist who excavated the site has interpreted it as an illicit trader's house.[28] This seems basically correct to me, although it is more likely that the prospect of future floods rather than any restriction by Stuyvesant caused Theunissen to rebuild farther from the river, where excavators found a fragment of his 1650s house. The earlier structure also seems more substantial than a hut or wigwam. In terms of its construction, the cellar with its wood plank walls and floor was very similar to the Van Doesburgh house. Here, however, the vertical supports had been mortised into a sill suggesting that there was a substantial frame structure overhead. With its riverside location, Theunissen's house could easily have functioned as a warehouse and tavern as well as a residence.

What makes these sites so important is that they are what archaeologists call sealed deposits. This means that, with the exception of the later buildings that capped them, they remained undisturbed until excavated. Even though the number of artifacts from these sites is not large, they are among the best-controlled mid 17th-century samples yet found in the Beverwijck area.

By 1652, the emerging settlement of Beverwijck was well on its way to becoming a stable Dutch community. It could provide all the services that held a community together: those of the court, church, school and poor-house. Equally important, there was enough wheat to make bread and enough oats to brew beer. With a growing population and an ever-greater number of trades, from tavern keepers to brick makers, bakers to gun stock makers, there was no longer any question as to whether the Dutch were here to stay.

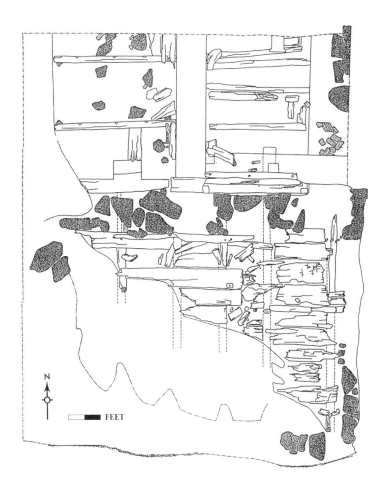

Rensselaerswijck. Outside the rapidly growing community that would become Beverwijck, Dutch farmers were also settling in. Although Van Rensselaer had established a series of farms on the east side of the river after the Papscanee purchase of 1637, few of these really got going until the early 1640s. Through the documentary research of Shirley Dunn and Paul Huey, we know a great deal about these early farms, who lived on them and the often difficult relationships with the patroon and their neighbors.[29] Most of these farms were of modest size, fifty to sixty acres, and had a standard set of buildings invariably described as "a house, barn and hay barracks." This suggests that the people and animals lived in separate buildings in contrast to a "large farmhouse" (or *hallehuis*) were everyone lived

FIGURE 4.9
Plan view of Volckert Jansz Douw's cellar walls and floor, KeyCorp site, Albany.
After Huey 1987:20, Figure 5.

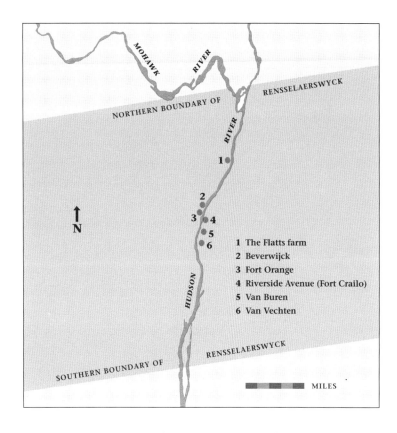

FIGURE 4.10

*Map of archaeo-
logical sites in
Rensselaerswijck,
1640 to 1652.*
*After Huey 1984:64.
Map by Booth Simpson.*

1 The Flatts farm
2 Beverwijck
3 Fort Orange
4 Riverside Avenue (Fort Crailo)
5 Van Buren
6 Van Vechten

together under one big roof. This style of
farmhouse is described in more detail below.

While none of these early farms have been
thoroughly excavated, archaeologists have
examined two sites in a preliminary way. The
first, known as the Van Buren site, was discovered by Art Johnson in 1973. After extensive
research in the documentary records, Huey
concluded that this was probably the farm of

Cornelis van Buren, who lived there from
1637 until he and his wife were drowned in
the flood of 1648. This is a large and complex
site, scattered over several acres. To date, little
excavation has been done and the site is
known primarily from surface evidence. This
site has several distinct loci, or concentrations
of artifacts. Each locus probably represents
a specific building and preliminary study
suggests that this farm changed significantly
in size and layout over time. A small portion
of the site, tested recently by Hartgen
Archaeological Associates, Inc., confirms the
presence of deeply buried deposits. In addition
to evidence that Mahican people had lived in
this area for hundreds of years, the archaeologists uncovered remnants of a European-style
structure buried by a flood deposit. These
included portions of a wood-lined earthen
cellar and several large flat stones that probably
served as footings for a framed building.
The artifacts recovered were consistent with
those found in 1640s contexts at Fort Orange.
However, this was not the whole story. Above
the flood level, and a little farther south,
was evidence of another structure. Here the
artifacts dated from the 1650s indicating that
the site had been reoccupied after the flood
and a new series of buildings built.

It remains unclear which of the early
Rensselaerswijck farms is represented at
the Van Buren site. Shirley Dunn's research
indicates this may have been the farm

FIGURE 4.11

*Profile of Trench 3,
the Van Buren site.*
*After Huey and Luscier
2004:71, Figure 9.*

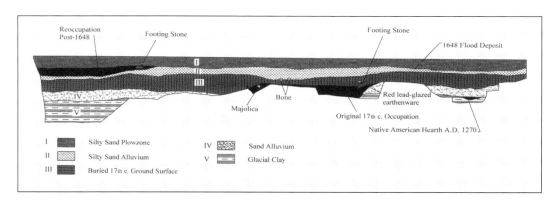

occupied by Symon Walichsen in 1637, who gave up the lease to Edward Pels in 1647 and left for Manhattan. Pels stayed only two years, transferring the farm with a "new house and barns" to Juriaen Bestval in March 1649.[30] Could it be that Pels was unlucky enough to obtain this farm, only to lose it in the 1648 flood? Only careful archaeological investigation can answer such a question. Until then, sites like Van Buren are public treasures that need to be protected and preserved.

The second early farm site to be identified is that of Teunis Dirckse van Vechten. Like several of his neighbors, Van Vechten came from the Gooi region east of Amsterdam along the Vecht River. He received the right to establish a farm from the patroon in 1639 and lived there until his death in 1685. On the surface, the Van Vechten site seems very much like Van Buren, a scatter of mid 17th-century artifacts from a modest farm. However, appearances are often deceptive and this is

certainly the case with Teunis Dircksen. Like most of his contemporaries, Teunis Dircksen was an entrepreneur first and a farmer second. In addition to running a successful farm, he was also a trader who dabbled in other ventures. In 1648 he purchased a half interest in the brewery located upriver in Greenbush, not surprising for someone who produced large quantities of oats. He also bought a half-share of the yacht *Het Zeepaert* (The Seahorse) in 1651. Known for his violent temper, Teunis Dircksen was often in court, argued frequently with Van Slictenhorst and even threatened the Dutch Reformed minister, Domine Megapolennsis.[31] Since the Van Vechten site is still unexcavated, archaeology tells us less about this contentious man and his surroundings than the historical documents do. However, the potential to visualize this early farm and understand its story in much greater detail still lies buried in the ground.

FIGURE 4.12
"Homeport."
A conjectural view of Teunis Dirckse van Vechten's farm, ca. 1650.
Courtesy of L. F. Tantillo.

FIGURE 4.13
A sketch of the Flatts farm, ca. 1644, with Van Curler's "new bark."
Courtesy of L. F. Tantillo.

Although Rensselaerswijck extended on both sides of the Hudson River, we know less about the farms on the west side, now in the Town of Bethlehem. Here too the patroon established farms beginning in May 1641. During the 1980s, the Bethlehem Archaeology Group under the direction of Floyd Brewer conducted excavations around the ca. 1730 Nicoll-Sill house. One of the features they encountered was a badly disturbed "stone foundation" that contained mid-17th-century artifacts. At present, it is unclear whether this was an earth-fast cellar with stone footings similar to the Van Buren site or if the site actually had a stone foundation. Brewer identified it as the house of Cornelis van Nes who owned a farm between 1642 and 1650.[32] However, it is equally possible that this site is related to one of the other early settlers along the Vlomankill.

The Flatts. Of all the Rensselaerswijck farms, none were as large or significant as the patroon's own farm at the Flatts (*de Vlackte*). Located four miles north of Fort Orange in what is now the Town of Colonie, the Flatts was situated on some of the best soils in the region. We know several details about the farm from Van Curler's letter to the patroon in June 1643. Although more than twenty acres had been planted, primarily with oats and wheat, the emphasis was still on clearing the land and buying additional property from the nearby Mahicans. Livestock was an important component of farm operations and Van Curler reports that he has at least twenty draft horses and fourteen "milch cows." Unfortunately, most of the sheep had died, in part due to wolves, and there was no way to account for the hogs which tended to "stray into the woods." In terms of buildings, there was the house 30 feet long with a tile roof that Van Curler had built the year before for "the carpenters and farmhands to live in" and there were plans for the new, large farmhouse to be built that year. Unlike the descriptions of other Rensselaerswyck farm buildings, this was clearly a *hallehuis,* or combination house and barn. This would be a big structure – 120 feet long with the first 40 feet set aside as the dwelling area and the remaining 80 feet serving as the barn. A cellar would be dug beneath the dwelling portion while the barn would include a sleeping chamber for the servants as well as box stalls and stabling for the animals.[33] Although these are the only buildings Van Curler mentioned in his letter, there were undoubtedly others. Hay barracks would have been essential, especially with all

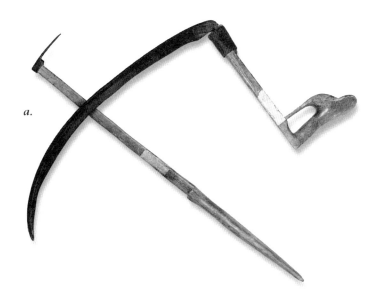

a.

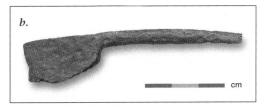

b.

c.

FIGURE 4.14
Dutch harvesting tools.

a. An early 19th century mathook and sith.
Courtesy of the Schoharie County Historical Society.

b. A mathook excavated from cellar #1, the Flatts farm.

c. Two imported Norwegian whetstones from cellar #2, the Flatts farm.
Courtesy Paul Huey and Bobby Brustle. Photos by Joe McEvoy.

that livestock, and some sort of docking facility was likely given that Van Curler used "new bark" to transport livestock and other merchandise to Virginia and beyond. Even at this early date, the Flatts was not a small or simple farm.

After Van Curler and his wife returned from the Republic in early 1648, the pace of activity at the Flatts picked up dramatically. Now that he held the lease, Van Curler made substantial changes, purchasing additional land and

FIGURE 4.15
Above left: Summer landscape with reapers at work (detail). Esaias van de Velde, ca. 1629. Private collection. Note the use of mathooks and siths for harvesting.

The Flatts, 1643–1652

Two excavations have occurred at the Flatts. Between 1971 and 1974, Paul Huey excavated the remains of an L-shaped cellar while investigating the area around the late 17th-century Schuyler House. The cellar was 14 feet long on the northwest side, 19 feet long on the southeast side and 29 feet wide facing southwest. It was 6 feet deep and contained evidence of stairs to an outside entrance, floor joists and footings for vertical posts. The cellar also contained a wide range of artifacts dating from

Cellar #2 was located north of cellar #1. It had similar dimensions but a different orientation. Like cellar #1, this cellar also contained internal features – stairs in the southwest corner and a section of brick wall. Brustle also uncovered other features related to these cellars. These included additional brick and cobblestone footings and a pavement of yellow brick.

The archaeological evidence indicates that the two cellars had very different histories of use. Cellar #1 was extremely clean; very

FIGURE 4.16
*Profile
of cellar #1,
the Flatts farm.*
*After Huey 1984:78,
Figure 7.*

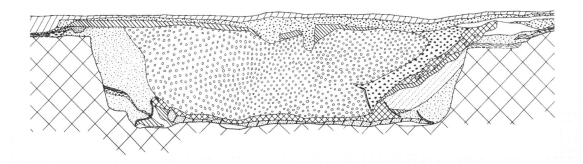

the 1640s to 1660s and appeared to have been filled with coarse yellow gravel between 1672 and ca. 1690.[34] In addition to the cellar, Huey also identified other features related to a mid 17th-century occupation including brick footings for the above ground structure, a horseshoe pit and a section of palisade or fence line. Between 1981 and 1982, a second cellar was discovered and excavated by Bobby Brustle.

little debris was present on floor level. This suggests that the cellar had been periodically cleaned and the plank walls repaired or replaced. Any accumulated refuse was thrown behind them as backfill. In contrast, cellar #2 had a layer of trash roughly 1 foot deep. This level appears to date to Van Curler's occupation of the site. Above this was a layer of demolition debris containing brick, cobbles, tile fragments, window glass and hardware. This material had been thrown into the cellar from the west side and probably was deposited during Jeremias van Rensselaer's rebuilding of the house in 1669.

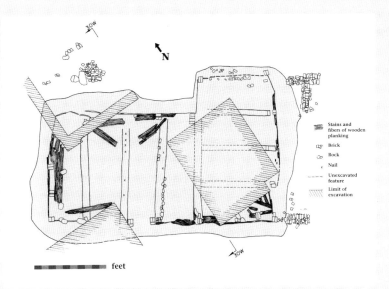

FIGURE 4.17
Plan view of cellar #1, the Flatts farm.
After Huey 1987:15, Figure 1.

Both cellars, and the other related features, appear to relate to the "large farmhouse" Van Curler planned to build in 1643. This structure was 120 feet long and had 40 feet set aside for dwelling purposes leaving 80 feet for the *bouwhuys* or barn. This plan fits the description of an aisled-house or *hallehuis*, the style of farmstead with the widest geographical distribution in the Netherlands.[35] These large farm buildings had several distinctive characteristics. Most distinctive is an H-shaped frame, often referred to as bents, set in several bays. These frames were set on stone or brick footings rather than into a sill, and created a large, undivided open space that could be used for dwelling quarters, stalls for animals and work areas such as a threshing floor. Usually the dwelling area was located at one end while large double doors for animals and wagons were set at the other. The dwelling area had an open hearth with a smoke hole in the roof instead of a chimney. In the Republic, wattle and daub was often used for the exterior walls and thatch for the roof. In New Netherland, with its abundance of lumber, the exterior was probably clapboard.

In the Netherlands, these late medieval-style farm buildings were often improved during the late 16th and early 17th centuries as families became wealthier. Typical modifications included the addition of a brick firewall and chimney between the dwelling and barn, other interior partition walls and a more stylish brick façade.[36] Van Curler probably made a series of similar improvements after he returned from the Republic in 1648.

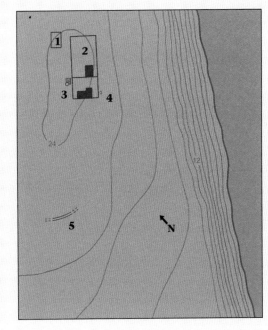

FIGURE 4.18
A reconstruction plan of the Flatts farm ca. 1644, based on archaeological excavation.
Map by Ellen Chase

1 1642 workmens' house.
2 1643 *hallehuis* with two cellars.
3 Yellow brick courtyard and cistern.
4 Horseshoe pit.
5 Fragment of palisade fence.

improving the buildings. By 1651, he had added nearly fifty acres of prime land, more than doubling the size of the farm. Van Curler also concentrated on raising horses, buying and selling them both locally and as far away as the West Indies. It is no surprise that in the 1651 inventory of Rensselaerswijck farms, the Flatts was described as "being the best."

Today, most of the Flatts farm has been destroyed, primarily by the commercial development and extensive re-grading that occurred during the 1970s and 1980s. Fortunately, a portion of the site survives as a Town of Colonie park. Two episodes of archaeological work have preserved much of the site's story. These excavations confirm much of what the documents indicate. Indeed, the dimensions of the large cellar found by Paul Huey fit Van Curler's dimensions remarkably well. However, the evidence also indicates that Van Curler may have changed his plans and constructed something slightly different than he proposed. The excavations indicate that the Flatts farmhouse had two cellars, one under the dwelling area as planned and a second within the barn portion, probably beneath a kitchen area. Just to the west of the house was a pavement of yellow brick and cistern that served as a courtyard for washing and food preparation. The main entrance was probably located on the east side of the house facing the river. In general, the layout of the Flatts was similar to that of many prosperous farms back in the Republic.[37]

Many of the artifacts recovered during these excavations document life at the Flatts farm. These included horseshoes and bits, wagon hardware and a range of the carpenter's tools needed on a busy farm such as framing chisels, auger bits and claw hammers. While no evidence of a forge was found, iron was clearly being worked at the Flatts. Smithing tools such as cross peen hammers, pincers and files, were found along with partially worked and discarded pieces. It is likely that most of the hardware, nails and many of the everyday objects recovered, from chain to ice creepers, were made at the Flatts.

While most of the farm-related implements found are fairly generic (a small hoe, a pitchfork, splitting wedges), some are more distinctive. One clear indication that this was a Dutch farm was the recovery of a mat hook and several small whetstones used for sharpening a sith. Among Dutch farmers, these were the preferred tools for harvesting wheat, oats and other grains. The whetstones themselves are a micaeous schist of Norwegian origin.[38]

De Laet's burg/Greenbush. Although farms predominated in Rensselaerswijck, the Colonie had two emerging areas of settlement on the east side of the Hudson River. The oldest, known as De Laet's burg was situated south of Mill Creek across the Hudson River from Fort Orange. The location of one of the earliest Rensselaerswijck farms, it also had a gristmill by 1632 and a sawmill before 1636. By the 1640s other craftsmen had built houses along the riverbank and a small community, often referred to as Greenbush (since it was near a pine grove or *t'greynen bosch*), had grown up.

Slightly south of De Laet's burg, a second cluster of houses began to form in 1642 when Van Rensselaer sent the long-promised minister to establish "a church neighborhood." This was the place, opposite Castle Island, where Van Curler had been directed to build a church, residence and palisade three years earlier. In his June 1642 instructions to the new minister, Johannes Megapolensis, the patroon made it clear that this was to be the Colonie's center, the place where the houses "of all the mechanics must hereafter be built."[39] To encourage this, Van Rensselaer also made it the location for a new brewery (and tavern) as well as the ferry across the Hudson to Fort Orange.

While most of De Laet's burg and Greenbush have disappeared beneath the City of Rensselaer, at least one important site has survived. In 1663, Jeremias van Rensselaer, one of Kiliaen's sons by his second wife, built a substantial new brick house on his Greenbush farm. Named Crailo after the family's farm back in the Republic, this building survives as a New York State Historic Site. An archaeological investigation of the property, conducted by Paul Huey and Lois Feister during the 1970s and 1980s, revealed much about this site including evidence of an earlier building that had been demolished. It is likely that this was the house Van Curler had built for the new minister and his family, and where Megapolensis lived from late summer 1642 until he departed for Manhattan in 1649. It is difficult to reconstruct what this house may have looked like, given the fragmentary nature of the evidence. However, like most of the other Rensselaerswijck houses, it appears to have been a frame structure built over a cellar with a chimney of imported yellow bricks and a pan tile roof. Fragments of decorated delft wall tiles, lead glazed floor or hearth tiles and leaded glass windows suggest a typical if slightly upscale Dutch interior. Most intriguing is a piece of broken, roughly squared stone built into Crailo's foundation. With the letters APOLENSIS carefully carved on one side, it could be a reused remnant of the original house. The authenticity of a second stone, inscribed "KVR 1642, Anno Domini" seems more doubtful.[40]

As Fort Orange slowed down during the 1640s, Rensselaerswijck was increasingly the scene of activity. Much of this occurred around the farms and emerging settlements on the east side of the Hudson, the clear focus of the patroon's plan. But with Kiliaen van Rensselaer's death in 1643 and a major rethinking of the Colonie's direction, the plan changed. Although the farms and small settlements on the east side would remain important, the heart of the Colonie would shift to the west side of the Hudson and the new community of Beverwijck.

Mahican Sites. As Dutch settlement grew, so did the contact with Native people. Whether in town or on the farm, daily interactions were the rule, not the exception. "They are very friendly to us," Megapolensis observed, "They sleep by us, too… I have had eight at once lying and sleeping upon the floor near my bed." Not everyone was so patient. As Van Slichtentenhorst grumbled, "I can honestly say that [during] the first three years we have, not even for half a day, been free from Indians." One result of these increased interactions was that Dutch accounts begin to record more details about the Mahicans, their customs and way of life. Some were simple observations such as De Vries' remark about Native fields on the "lowlands along the Kats-kil." Others are more detailed and personal. The most thoughtful account was made by Johannes Megapolensis whose duties as the Colonie's minister included preaching to Native people.[41] Taken together, these accounts provide many insights as to how the Mahicans were responding to their new neighbors.

One surprise is that the sale of Mahican land proceeded slowly. No land was sold between the Papscanee purchase of 1637 and 1648 when Van Slichtenhorst began to buy large tracts in what is now Greene and Columbia counties. However, with the rapid growth of settlement after 1648, the demand for land increased and by 1652, several additional tracts in what are now Albany and Rensselaer counties had been purchased. It is unclear whether the Mahicans understood what buying land meant to Europeans since Native people tended to think in terms of use rather than ownership. As one Dutch observer noted, they believe that "wind, stream, forest, field… and riverside are open and free to everyone."[42] From a Mahican point of view, there was still plenty of land for everyone.

But even when the Mahicans did decide to sell a piece of land, they were in no hurry to leave. The new owners provided too many

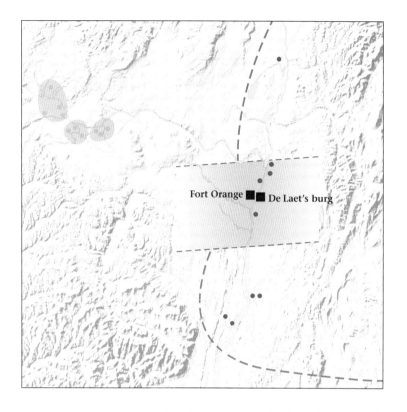

Fort Orange ■ ■ De Laet's burg

FIGURE 4.19
*Mahican and
Mohawk sites,
1640 to 1652.
Map by John Skiba
and Booth Simpson.*

wonderful opportunities for shrewd and experienced foragers to ignore. There were ongoing
occasions to trade. As Megapolensis observed,
settlers could usually get a deer or turkey in
exchange "for a loaf of bread, a knife or even
a tobacco pipe." The Mahicans could also continue to hunt and fish in their usual locations
since the Dutch were frequently slow to take
possession of their new holdings. In fact,
unless the Dutch actually occupied the land,
Mahicans were likely to believe that it was still
theirs. And sometimes this provided an excellent opportunity to sell the same piece of land
a second or even third time. On occasion,
there were even vacant farm buildings where
they could settle in, much to the annoyance
of Van Slichtenhorst, who complained bitterly
about Native people, their personal habits and
tendency to take anything that was not nailed
down. Best of all from a Native point of view
was the feasting and giving of presents that
occurred before, during and after each land

sale, a party that could continue for days.[43]
All this suggests that, even as land sales
progressed, there was limited movement of
Mahican people out of the traditional areas.

The archaeological evidence supports this.
At present, at least nine sites are known that
have components dating between 1640 and
1652.[44] While all these sites are located within
traditional Mahican core areas, some significant changes in their distribution have
occurred. By mid-century, the Mahicans had
split into two groups. Those located north
of the land sold to Van Rensselaer continued
to be known as Mahicans while those to the
south were increasingly known as Katskils.
While Mahican people were still very much
in evidence, their sites tended to be located
outside the boundaries of Rensselaerswijck by
mid-century. The one exception
is the Riverside site, located adjacent to
Megapolensis' house in the heart of the
Colonie. Here Huey excavated several refuse
pits that contained both Native and European
material confirming the Domine's comments
about living close together. It might also be that
this is where some Mahican people relocated
after the sale of Papscanee Island in 1637.[45]

Aside from this, much stayed the same.
Several of these sites – Winney's Rift,
Lansingburg and Leeds – were traditional
Mahican locations, ones that had been
occupied earlier and would continue to be
used for decades more. Mahican sites also
continue to occur on the west side of the
Hudson, especially to the north along Fish
Creek and south around Catskill, an indication
that Mahican people had not abandoned all
their territory to the Mohawks.

Unfortunately, there are no reliable estimates of Mahican population during this
period. However, the impression is that,
in spite of loss from disease, war and even
out-migration, the Mahicans remained a
substantial presence in the mid- and upper
Hudson Valley at mid-century.

Mohawk sites. The historical documents from this period have a great deal to say about the Mohawks. Megapolensis knew them well from their frequent visits and there are three other detailed accounts from the early 1650s. Two were made by Frenchmen who had been Mohawk captives – Father Joseph Poncet, a Jesuit, and Pierre Radisson, a trader who was adopted by a Mohawk family. The best information from a Dutch point of view is Adriaen van der Donck's *Description of New Netherland,* published in 1653.

While good relations with Mahican people were important to the Dutch, the Mohawks were "the principal nation… with which we have the most intercourse." This was not just a matter of the fur trade. The Mohawks had defeated the Mahicans after "a great war" and now "the conquered are obliged to bring a yearly contribution" as tribute to the victors. Since the Mohawks also claimed all Mahican land west of the Hudson by right of conquest, it was essential for the Dutch to keep the Mohawks as allies.[46]

If the 1640s had been difficult for the Dutch, they had been calamitous for the Mohawks. It had been a decade of unrelenting warfare – on the St. Lawrence, in Huronia, and then farther west. A serious epidemic swept through Mohawk villages in 1646–1647 followed by a bad harvest resulting in many deaths, including that of Isaac Jogues. A primary reason for the continued state of war, aside from vengeance, was to bring prisoners home for adoption replacing those who had been lost. As Jogues observed after his captivity in 1643, the intent was to capture the young and healthy prisoners, bring them back to Mohawk families and "to make them both but one people." This was exactly Radisson's experience ten years later. Not only was he captured and adopted for this reason; his Mohawk mother was an adopted Huron.[47] Clearly, the definition of who was Mohawk was changing.

Strained relations with other members of the Five Nations, especially the Onondagas, compounded these internal stresses. Throughout the 1640s, the Onondagas had made overtures to the French hoping to establish a new trading partner, one that did not require them to go through the Mohawks, who had become "unbearable even to their allies." The Mohawks, of course, saw things differently and strongly

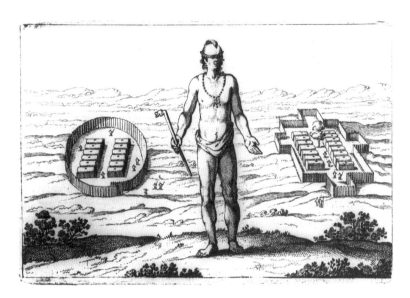

opposed any overtures to the French. Although the Five Nations and French signed a peace treaty in September 1653, the Mohawks were not happy and problems within the Five Nations remained far from resolved.[48]

By the end of the period, Mohawk relations with the Dutch were equally strained. During a meeting at the patroon's house, Van Slichtenhorst was curtly told by the Mohawk representatives that he "should supply them with every weapon… and every other necessary" they required, just as the French supplied their Indian allies. After all, it was the Mohawks who "allowed the Christians to live there" and if the Dutch didn't like it, they "might just as well cross the great water again." Meanwhile, if the Dutch weren't more cooperative, the Mohawks threatened to kill their animals.

FIGURE 4.20
Mohawk (Maquaes) Indian with two palisaded villages. From the pamphlet by Johannes Megapolensis, "A Short Account of the Mohawk Indians," published 1644.
Courtesy of the Municipal Archives, Amsterdam.

Radisson, who was there as a Mohawk, confirms this talk of war "against the Hollanders."[49]

However, from a Mohawk point of view, there was a good reason to be annoyed. They had played a key role in helping the Dutch end Governor Kieft's War a few years earlier and now felt that the Dutch were reneging on their promise of future assistance, just at a time when the Mohawks desperately needed it. The fact that a different Dutchman happened to be governor did not change the commitment his predecessor had made. Whatever the reasons, it is clear that by mid-century the Mohawks were prickly and demanding neighbors.

As during the earlier periods, the Mohawks continued to live in several settlements. Megapolensis describes three large fortified villages, which he calls "castles." Each was known by its dominant clan. The eastern most, which was also "the greatest and most prominent," was that of the Turtle. Next to them was the castle of the Bear, and farther west, the castle of the Wolf. In terms of the villages themselves, Van der Donck describes them in considerable detail. The large villages, or "castles," were usually located on a steep hill, often accessible on one side only, and were enclosed by a heavy wooden palisade. Within the stockade, twenty to thirty houses were built, often a hundred feet in length or more. Each housed sixteen to eighteen families depending on its size. In addition to these "castles," the Mohawk had other settlements "that lie in the open in the manner of villages" with "the woods on one side and their corn-fields on the other." There were also smaller settlements for fishing.[50]

The archaeological evidence bears out these contemporary descriptions. At least ten sites are known that date from the 1640 to 1652 period. Based on artifact assemblages, six of these appear to date from the 1635 to 1645 period and were discussed in part in the previous chapter. Another four sites have a slightly different artifact assemblage and appear to date

from the 1645 to 1652 period.[51] With one exception (Lipe), these sites continue to be located on the south side of the Mohawk River and fit well into the three established areas of settlement within the Mohawk Valley. Little professional excavation has been done on these sites and they are known primarily from private collecting and salvage efforts.

What do these sites indicate about Mohawk population? Certainly there was a shift in composition as captives were adopted in, but were there dramatic changes in size as well? Snow argues that, due to the combination of disease and war, Mohawk population dropped steeply during the late 1630s and early 1640s. Perhaps, but his estimate of a population of less than 2,000 people during this period seems too low to me, just as his estimate of nearly 8,000 for the previous period seems too high. One reason it is unlikely that Mohawk population dropped so dramatically is that the number and size of sites stays the same. As others have argued, the effects of disease, even when severe, were likely to be more gradual and Mohawk population probably remained in the range of 5,000 people throughout this period.[52]

New Ways in a New World

As the Dutch settled in, they became increasingly comfortable doing things in new ways. These shifts are visible across the whole spectrum of Dutch culture. As we saw above, building styles began to change both in response to the availability of different materials and the demands of a harsh, more variable climate. Similar shifts occurred in agriculture as native foods such as maize, pumpkins and beans were grown along with the traditional grains, peas and root vegetables. There was still a great deal of nostalgia for the Republic, and claims that the grapes or the butter of New Netherland were "as good as in Holland" were common. Things were still unquestionably Dutch, but they were also subtly different, on the way to becoming something new.

These changes in food preferences, a mix of new and familiar items, are clearly reflected in the archaeological record. At Fort Orange, the faunal remains from this period include a combination of pig and deer bones. Not only were deer plentiful, observed Megapolensis; in the autumn and early winter they were "as fat as any Holland cow." Deer also predominate in other reported assemblages with smaller amounts of cow, pig and sheep present plus the occasional bear, raccoon and dog. This strong reliance on local resources is also evident in the quantities of fish (sturgeon and catfish), bird (duck and crane) and shellfish (oysters and even freshwater mussels) recovered from Dutch sites of this period. Although plant remains are rare, they too tell the same story. From beneath the floor boards of Volckert Jansen Douw's cellar came not only lost trade goods but domestic trash that included pumpkin seeds, peach pits, butternut hulls, acorns and hazelnuts.[53]

Redefining Dutch Domestic Assemblages.

One thing that archaeological assemblages do well is to provide a basis for comparing continuity with change. By 1650, Dutch material culture was characterized by both. These trends can be seen in two groups of artifacts – the vessels used to prepare and serve food, and recreational items – what did these people do for fun?

While the food that Dutch settlers ate steadily diverged from that of the Republic, the ways in which it was stored, prepared and served remained steadfastly Dutch. Lead-glazed earthenware vessels remained the mainstay for cooking, especially three-legged cauldrons (*kookpots*), pipkins (*grapen*) and colanders of red earthenware. For serving and eating, tin-glazed earthenwares continued to dominate the table while beer and wine were drunk from fancy glass beakers and roemers. Yet even here, in this very stable portion of Dutch culture, changes are evident. Some reflect shifting

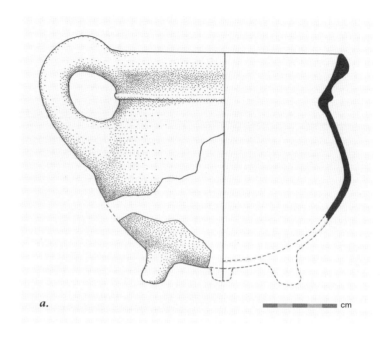

a.

a.

FIGURE 4.21
Typical Dutch vessels of the 1640 to 1652 period. Fragments of these vessels are common on most Dutch domestic sites and many Native sites of this period.

a. An earthenware kookpot, from cellar #2, the Flatts farm.
Courtesy of Bobby Brustle. Drawing by Ellen Chase.

b. A roemer with raspberry prunts from Amsterdam.
Courtesy of the AHM/BMA. Photo by Wiard Krook, afdeling Archeologie.

preferences back in the Republic, such as the increased use of red earthenware at the expense of the older white and buff bodied varieties. In a similar way, there was less majolica and more faience on the table, just as there was back home. The second quarter of the 17th-century was a time of dramatically increased ceramic production as Dutch potters in Delft and Haarlem replicated not just Chinese motifs, but vessels with the overall appearance of porcelain. This new variety of tin-glazed ware, known as "Dutch porcelain"

distinctive products were common not only in Amsterdam but in New Amsterdam and around Fort Orange as well. Another change was in glassware. While every Dutch household continued to use square glass case bottles to store brandy and other spirits, round-bodied wine bottles appear for the first time. These may be a reflection of new suppliers, or even new sources, of the wine that came to New Netherland, possibly from Bordeaux or Portugal. By 1640, Portugal had also won its independence from Spain (after being annexed

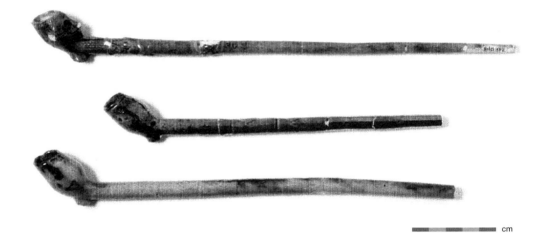

cm

(*Hollants Porceleyn*), was tin-glazed on both the front and back, and quickly replaced the previously popular majolica.[54] Instead of being known by its older Italian name, faience (after the town of Faenza where it was made), this new ware was increasingly referred to as delft.

The archaeological record also reflects the changing world of Dutch mercantile connections, networks that now stretched around the globe. For example, one result of the Peace of Westphalia was a dramatic increase in stoneware production by German potters of the Westerwald region. By 1650 these

in 1580) and while Portugal and the Dutch Republic remained economic competitors, they did maintain a truce between 1641 and 1652. It is during this period that the first evidence of Portuguese faience and earthenware occur on New Netherland sites.[55] Even events on the far side of the world had their impact. With the final collapse of the Ming Dynasty in 1644, shipments of Chinese porcelain to the West ceased. Although porcelain is rare on Company and Colonie sites, Chinese-inspired majolica and delft became more common and continued to be the most prestigious style of tableware.

Equally distinctive were the ways in which the Dutch amused themselves, aside from eating, drinking and other activities not visible in the archaeological record. As in the Republic, smoking was still the rage, a fact amply documented by the quantities of clay pipe fragments that occur on every Dutch site. Many of these show the signs of intensive use, even re-use, especially broken stems that have been reworked. As on earlier domestic sites, a wide range of makers is represented on these pipes. Huey recorded nearly thirty different marks from components 83 and 82 at Fort Orange.[56] This suggests that traders purchased their pipes from suppliers of their own choosing in Amsterdam and Gouda. There were other differences between the pipes the Dutch imported for themselves and those intended for trade with Native customers. As in the Republic, there was a continued fondness for fancy Baroque-style pipes, ones with molded decorations on the stem and bowl, and even occasionally finished with green glaze. Though never common, these distinctly Dutch pipes occur on domestic sites throughout this period.

Music and games are two other forms of entertainment that have left some archaeological trace. One simple but popular instrument was a whistle made from a clay pipe stem. Huey recovered more than thirty of these during excavations at Fort Orange and has argued that these were small homemade flutes or recorders, very much like the examples depicted in Dutch genre paintings of the period. Pieces of similar whistles have also been recovered from several of the Rensselaerswijck farms. Mouth harps (*mondharpen*), also known colloquially as Jew's harps, are the other common musical instrument found on Dutch sites. Used across northern Europe from the late 12th century on, these small iron-framed mouth harps are frequent finds on 17th-century sites on both sides of the Atlantic. By the mid-1640s,

FIGURE 4.23
Pipe stem whistles from Fort Orange.
After Huey 1974:105, Figure 1.

another style of mouth harp begins to occur on New Netherland sites. These are small, well-made brass-framed mouth harps, usually stamped R. While these also are found on Dutch domestic sites, they may have been a specialty item made for trade, and are discussed further below.[57]

Excavations in Amsterdam have provided evidence for many other 17th-century Dutch games and pastimes. Among these were chess pieces, dice and wooden tops. While none of these objects have been found on New Netherland sites to date, another game,

Being Dutch: Material Evidence of National Identity

FIGURE 4.24
*Brass mirror
box covers from
Iroquois sites.*

*a. Frederick Henry,
Prince of Orange,
Count of Nassau,
1634. Dann site
(Seneca), RMSC
#239/28.*

*b.Wilhem Frederick,
Prince of Orange.
Power House
site (Seneca),
RMSC #1348/24.*

*Courtesy of the RMSC.
Drawings by T. Miller.*

Few artifacts are more evocative than those
that convey our deepest beliefs and values.
For the mid 17th-century Dutch, such values
centered on a national identity built during
the successful revolt against Spain and but-
tressed by the Republic's astonishing economic
success. At its heart was the concept of *patria*,
a common homeland around which mutual
defense and assistance could be organized. In
material terms, the result was an iconography
of new national symbols that was quickly
distributed on coins and medals. Much of
this patriotic imagery focused on the House
of Orange, whose members had led the Revolt
and held the office of stadholder on a heredi-
tary basis throughout the period.[58]

By the 1640s, the Republic was again under
stress, this time from an increasingly adversar-
ial England, and expressions of patriotic zeal
again became fashionable. In addition to coins
and medals, small brass mirror box covers were
used to express patriotic sentiments. Since
mirrors were new and highly fashionable, these
small portable versions were the perfect place
for a political message. Although these mirror
boxes are surprisingly rare in the Republic,
several examples embossed with the image
of Prince Frederick Hendrick, stadholder from
1625 to 1647, are known from Native sites in
the Northeast.[59] By the mid 17th-century, these
emblems of Dutch nationalism had spread
from southern New England across Iroquoia to
the lower Susquehanna River Valley, effectively
defining the Dutch sphere of influence.

Demonstrations of patriotic zeal were also
found in Dutch households. During the 17th-
century, the hearth was literally the center of
the home – the primary source of heat and

a.

_____ cm

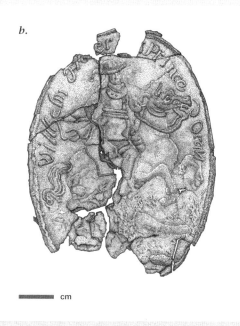

b.

_____ cm

cm

FIGURE 4.25
Fragment of a
Hollandia cast
iron fireback,
from cellar #1,
the Flatts farm.
Courtesy of Paul Huey
and OPRHP

FIGURE 4.26
A complete,
undated Hollandia
fireback.
Courtesy of Jan Baart.

light in a pre-electrical world. As a result, Dutch hearths were often decorated with tiles and a cast iron fireback that helped to protect the brickwork. Located at the heart of the household, a fireback was also emblematic of the owner's taste and values.

A fragment from such a fireback was found in cellar #1 at the Flatts. The device shows a seated figure holding a lance or pole. A complete example of this *Hollandia*-style fireback reveals the entire pattern, one that includes several well-known patriotic symbols of the period. Among these are a seated female figure holding a lance with a hat on its point, a crowned lion and a fenced enclosure representing "the Dutch Garden" (*de Hollands tuin*). Above are the words PRO PATRIA and HOLLANDIA. With such a fireback in one's home, there was no question as to where one's political allegiance lay.

cm

marbles, is well represented. Both redware and stoneware examples are known from Fort Orange and several of the Rensselaerswijck farms.[60]

Occasionally the archaeological record reveals something quite unexpected. The discovery of a horseshoe pit adjacent to the front door of Van Curler's house at the Flatts is just such a case. Horseshoes (*hoefijzerwerpen*), though not unknown in the Netherlands, is not usually considered a Dutch pastime. There are no depictions of pitching horseshoes

FIGURE 4.27
Horseshoe pit at the Flatts farm. The iron pin and ring are visible in the center of the photograph; the two horseshoes were found directly beneath them. The large, light-colored rock is from the level above and not related to the horseshoe pit.
Courtesy of Paul Huey and OPRHP.

in the genre paintings or on tiles, nor is it listed among 17th-century games. Yet here is a mid 17th-century Dutch horseshoe pit – a large iron stake in the center of a sandy depression with two horseshoes and an iron ring directly associated. How do we interpret this puzzle? The horseshoes themselves are no surprise, especially given the Flatts farm's reputation for raising horses. In this country, pitching horseshoes, also known as the game of quoits, is usually considered to be of English origin. However, Van Curler had been to Virginia and other British colonies. He could have easily watched others playing this game and brought the idea back to the Flatts. Perhaps, instead of a puzzle, this is that

rare instance of seeing how something different may have come about.

There is one other Dutch pastime, perhaps even a passion, that needs to be mentioned – the collecting of "curiosities." As the Dutch commercial activity expanded during the first quarter of the 17th-century, exotic wealth from all parts of the world poured into the Republic – Chinese porcelain, spices from the East Indies, fine carpets and tulips from Turkey, sugar and rare wood from Brazil. But more than marketable merchandise often caught the eye of Dutch traders or sailors. An odd animal, beautiful shells, the tools and weapons of strange new people were all brought back as additions to "cabinets of curiosities." Although these cabinets started out as actual pieces of furniture, they quickly evolved into the privately owned collections of royalty, nobility and gentlemen scholars. Those that have survived have become the foundation for many of Western Europe's greatest museums of natural and cultural history.[61]

Things were more modest in New Netherland of course, but the interest in "curiosities" was certainly there, and on both sides of the cultural divide. For the Dutch, there were many natural wonders in this new world. For example, pieces of coral have been recovered from several Dutch sites of this period. The fine quartz crystals known as "Herkimer diamonds" are another more local example. These occur throughout the Mohawk Valley and are common on many Mohawk sites where they were probably used both as tools and as ritual objects. However, several examples were also found around Juriaen Theunissen's house site. Perhaps these were these gifts from Mohawk visitors; perhaps Dutch adventurers had collected them. We don't know.

It is certain that gifts were exchanged, and that these were cultural items – a finely woven bag, a carved club or pipe – rather than natural history specimens. Pipes in particular were often used as presents or to seal agreements, and by mid-century, Native-made pipes begin to appear on Dutch sites. A good example is the finely made clay pipe with a face effigy found in component 83 at Fort Orange. Virtually identical examples of this style have been found on Oneida and Seneca sites of the same time period. Huey also recovered a second piece of effigy pipe from component 82.[62]

Curiosity and collecting went both ways. Even if Europeans and their things were less mysterious, there were still plenty of "curiosities" left as the occasional coin, apostle spoon or patriotically embossed mirror box found on a Native site indicates.[63] In fact, the line between Dutch domestic items and trade goods had blurred considerably by 1650. It would not stay this way for long.

Rise of the Private Traders

With the end of the Company's monopoly in 1639, private traders became the driving economic force in New Netherland. Up to this point, trade goods had been largely stock items purchased by the Company for "trading" in general. However, as the contacts between Native people and Dutch settlers grew, Native people saw and demanded a much wider range of merchandise, everything from better quality woolens to carpenters' tools, mouth harps to firearms. Increasingly, this demand, and the willingness of Dutch settlers to supply it, blurred the distinction between "trade goods" and what the Dutch imported for their own use. It also meant that virtually everyone could be a trader. As one visitor to Rensselaerswijck observed in 1643, every Dutchman was busy trying to outbid his companions, and satisfied if he could make a little profit.[64] This would soon change.

The man who understood the opportunity best was Kiliaen van Rensselaer. More than most, he knew why the fur trade had failed under the Company's management and what to do about it. As he wrote to a colleague in

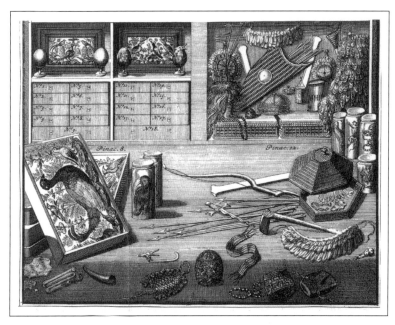

FIGURE 4.28
Top: Native-made effigy pipe from component 83, Fort Orange.
After Huey 1988:696, Figure 75.

FIGURE 4.29
Above: A Cabinet of Curiosities. From Levinus Vincent, Wondertooneel der Nature. Note the wampum belt in the middle foreground.
Courtesy of the Municipal Archives, Amsterdam.

June 1641, "If I now conduct the business on a somewhat large scale, this is done for the purpose of keeping others out and establishing ourselves."[65] While "others" meant primarily the French and English, it applied to private Dutch traders as well.

The man responsible for implementing the patroon's plan was Arent van Curler, the Colonie's business agent. Part of his job was to advise the patroon on what goods were needed, both by the settlers and for the fur trade. Another part was to enforce the ordinances that regulated the sale of merchandise. This meant making sure that the Colonie's settlers traded only with authorized traders, employees of the Company, and not with private "resident" traders. The trade was becoming freer but it wasn't free yet. The Company may have given up its monopoly but it was still in the business of making money and Van Rensselaer was a director. It was for this reason that the patroon had his trading storehouse (*pakhuis*), and later his own house, built adjacent to Fort Orange.

With Van Rensselaer's death in late 1643, everything changed. Although the trade and how to run it were left, temporarily, in Van Curler's hands, it was clear that the real decisions would be made back in the Republic. So that's where Van Curler went and stayed for the next three and a half years. During that time, much happened in New Netherland and many more entrepreneurs got into the business of becoming private traders.

What, exactly, did it mean to be a private trader, especially at a time when the rules were rapidly changing? While all could agree on the continued exclusion of the English and French, it got murky after that, especially in terms of what was allowed. A good example was the trouble that Volckert Jansz Douw got into in April 1649 when he received an order from the Rensselaerwijck court. "You have license to carry on lawful trade, but in no wise to carry on any illegitimate trade… You are hereby

warned and forbidden by the court to carry on such illegitimate trade, in violation of the ordinance." The documents do not make clear what differentiated "legal" from "illegitimate." Was it that he traded out of his house instead of at Fort Orange, or that he had not paid the appropriate duties? Perhaps, as the archaeology at the KeyCorp site suggests, it was because his inventory included firearms and lead when they were still, technically, contraband items. Whatever the problem, this early setback did not interfere with Douw's career. By the early 1650s, he was well on his way to becoming one of Beverwijck's most successful traders and a model citizen. With the establishment of Beverwijck in 1652, free trade finally became a reality. Once the town was under Company control, it was no longer possible for the patroon, his agents or anyone else to monopolize the trade.[66] All traders were now private traders. As Douw's career illustrates, those who succeeded did so because they were well connected, worked hard and were lucky.

While the definition of private trader was shifting in New Netherland, the sources of supply were changing back in the Republic. During the mid-1640s, several new kinds of merchandise began to be shipped to New Netherland. These included different styles of glass beads, smoking pipes and firearms designed specifically for Native customers, as well as a wide range of other consumer goods. Although the documentary record is silent on who ordered this merchandise, it is no coincidence that these changes occurred during the years when Van Curler was in the Republic. It was also not until after Van Curler's return in 1648 that these new trade goods began to occur in quantity on both Dutch and Native sites.

The development of merchandise specifically for Native customers changed the trade in fundamental ways. With trade goods increasingly specialized, the trade itself began to become a specialty instead of something that any farmer or townsman could do out the back door. Also, specialty goods were expensive and only available through certain suppliers. One needed a lot of connections and credit to get into and stay in the business. The result was a sorting-out process during the 1650s in which only a few individuals, Van Curler and Douw among them, were able to continue as major traders while most participants struggled to keep up.

Defining the Private Traders' Assemblage.
How does the archaeological evidence reflect these changes? Two trends document the fur trade's transformation between 1640 and 1652. First is the dramatic increase in the quantity and quality of trade goods that occurred as Kiliaen van Rensselaer geared up his efforts to take control. As discussed in Chapter Three, these changes are evident on Mohawk and Mahican sites of the late 1630s and early 1640s, and are represented by an assemblage that includes round turquoise blue beads, the first CAMPEN cloth seals, a wider range of European smoking pipes and more merchandise in general. When the patroon wrote to Van Curler in 1641 that "so much merchandise has been sent" that he should have no trouble obtaining furs, these appear to be the trade goods he meant.[67] Whether firearms were a part of this assemblage or not is unclear. The shift in merchandise that occurred when Van Curler took control after 1645 is the second change. Once again, there is a marked increase in the quantity of stock trade goods – kettles, axes, knives and awls. More significantly, a distinctly different assemblage begins to occur on Native sites, one characterized by dark blue tubular beads, "EB" pipes, first-class firearms and a wide array of small consumer items. By 1652 these new materials dominate artifacts assemblages not only on Native sites but on the house sites of the major traders as well.

Let's look at some of these items in more detail, especially those that appear to have been produced specifically for Native customers.

cm

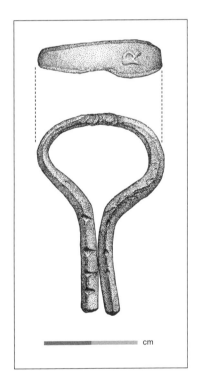

cm

FIGURE 4.30
Above: A round CAMPEN cloth seal, countermarked "4AB" Mitchell site.
(A2005.13BH.99.39).
Rumrill collection, NYSM.
Photo by Ted Beblowski.

FIGURE 4.31
Left: A brass mouth harp stamped with the letter R.
After Bradley 2005:137
Figure 14c.

ARTIFACT
PROFILE 9

The Pipes of Edward Bird

By 1640, pipe making was an established business in Amsterdam with large quantities produced for export as well as local use. One of the most successful members of this community was Edward Bird, a native of Surry who had left England in 1624. As a man who, literally, left his mark in many places, Bird's story is best traced through a combination of documentary and archaeological evidence.

Archival records indicate that Bird married Aeltje Govaerts, an Amsterdam woman, in June 1630. By 1638 he had purchased his burgher right (the right to do business) and by 1644 he had taken on an apprentice. As Bird's business and family grew, he bought property in the Jordaan, a newly created working-class neighborhood. He also appears to have worked cooperatively with neighboring pipe makers such as Willem Hendricks. Bird had contacts with New Netherland as well. In 1646 he loaned 200 guilders to Brian Newton, a military officer in the service of Petrus Stuyvesant on his way to New Netherland. Bird also distributed pipes through New Amsterdam merchants such as Reinier Rycken. When Bird died in May 1665, he left behind a second wife, Anna Marie (Aeltje had died in 1658), and a son, Evert. Anna Marie married again in 1668. Her new husband, Hendrick Gerdes, was listed as a pipe maker when he died in 1684.[68]

Edward Bird was a successful and prolific pipe maker. Some idea of the scale of his production comes from an inventory of his estate in 1665. More than 600,000 finished pipes were found in his shop. These included four distinctly different styles: 66 cases of "glossy pipes," 9 cases of "short fine pipes," 23 cases of "bulbous pipes" and a large number of

FIGURE 4.32

*Pipes of
Edward Bird.*

*a. Three
different pipe
bowl styles.*

*b. Three
varieties of
the EB mark.*

*Drawing by
Ellen Chase and
Gordon DeAngelo.*

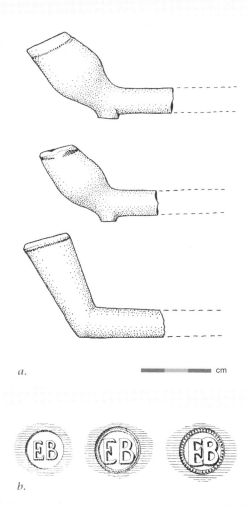

a.

cm

b.

"long pipes."[69] Clearly, one pipe maker could produce a wide range of styles.

This variety is borne out by the archaeological evidence. By 1650, pipes with at least three distinct bowl sizes or shapes as well as at lease three different styles of EB mark were being sent to New Netherland. The question for the archaeologist is what does this variation mean? Is there a chronological pattern to the different bowl shapes and size, to the various EB marks? At present, we don't have enough information to answer those questions.

However, this is not the end of the EB story. Bird was also significant as an innovator who produced a new style of smoking pipe, one made specifically for the New Netherland market. These pipes have a distinctive straight-sided, funnel-like bowl, very different from the typical bulbous shape of other Dutch pipes. These funnel bowl pipes first appear during the late 1640s and become common after 1650.[70] They continue to occur on Dutch as well as Native sites until the final decades of the 17th-century. While EB is the most frequently occurring mark on these funnel bowl pipes, other initials also occur during the 1650s and 1660s. These include WH, possibly Bird's neighbor Willem Hendricks; ID, possibly John Draper, another English pipe maker in Amsterdam; and an abstract version of the Tudor rose (FTO #49) whose maker remains unidentified (*See Figure 4.33*). Eighty-eight funnel bowl pipes with this mark have been recovered from the Monte Christi wreck dated to 1652–1656.[71]

These funnel bowl pipes tell two stories. First they provide an extraordinary view into the small but highly interconnected world of Edward Bird, his pipe-making family and their associates. Second, unlike the other pipes Bird made, these funnel bowl pipes represent a new kind of product, one made specifically for the fur trade. Funnel bowl pipes occur rarely in the Netherlands and are not known on Dutch-related sites outside North America. Conversely, they are most common on Iroquois sites and Dutch sites strongly linked with the fur trade such as Fort Orange and Arent van Curler's house at the Flatts.

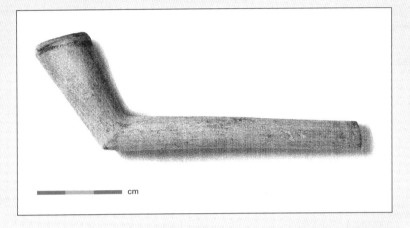

Where did the inspiration for these unique pipes come from? Several researchers have suggested that they are patterned after Native American examples and this seems likely, but what was the connecting link? Who brought this distinctive shape to the attention of Bird and other pipe makers? I think it is no coincidence that EB pipes in general, and funnel bowl pipes in particular, become common in New Netherland after 1648, the year Van Curler returned from the Republic. Like the newly available flintlock muskets and brass mouth harps, these pipes appear to be the material evidence of new kinds of trade goods that Van Curler ordered during his stay.

FIGURE 4.33
A funnel bowl pipe, with an FTO #49 heel mark, found in Amsterdam.
Courtesy of the AHM/BMA.
Photo by Wiard Krook, afdeling Archeologie.

Glass Beads. Beads had been a mainstay of the fur trade from the beginning and, as we have seen, changed frequently in terms of the preferred colors, shapes and sizes. During the period when Van Rensselaer was building up the trade, round turquoise blue beads, either without (IIa40) or with white stripes (IIb56), were the most common style. In terms of the Mohawk, this horizon occurs at the Naylor, Bauder and Oak Hill sites. By the mid 1640s, dark blue tubular beads (IIIa12) have begun to replace these round varieties. Unlike earlier styles of tubular beads, these have sharp, unfinished ends. Basically, these beads are the production tubes from which finished beads were made. However, someone like Van Curler figured out that it would be cheaper to buy and ship these instead of finished beads. And if they broke along the way, that didn't matter. These unfinished, blue tubular beads remain the predominant style well into the next decade and are the most common bead on Mohawk sites such as Yates II, Mitchell, Janie and Lipe.

It is likely that these blue tubular beads were produced at "The Two Roses" glass house located on the Keizersgracht in Amsterdam. Recent research indicates that between 1630 and 1650, a change in color preference took place with a greater emphasis on blue tubular beads.[72] Closer to home, more than ten percent of the beads found at the Flatts and virtually all of the hundreds of beads from Douw's cellar were blue tubular beads.

European Smoking Pipes. By the early 1640s, Dutch pipes were an important item in the trader's inventory. Pipes from a dozen different Amsterdam and Gouda makers have been recovered from Mohawk and Mahican sites of this period. As the instructions sent with a cargo shipped to Rensselaerswijck in March 1644 indicate, they were to be "bartered to the Indians and other inhabitants of the country for tobacco, furs and other produce."[73]

By the mid-1640s it is likely that pipes made by Edward Bird, an English expatriate who worked in Amsterdam, were included. Bird was a successful and prolific pipe maker, a man who literally left his mark around the world. In New Netherland, his pipes are rare until the late 1640s. By the early 1650s, EB pipes dominate the trade and are the most frequently occurring pipe on Mohawk sites such as Mitchell and Lipe. While EB pipes also occur on Dutch sites, they tend to be concentrated on those with strong trade associations. More than 125 examples were recovered from Van Curler's house at the Flatts. EB-marked pipes were also found in Douw's cellar at the KeyCorp site in downtown Albany.

Firearms. During the 1640s, firearms along with gunpowder and lead were the items most requested by Native people. It was a demand that private traders were eager to supply, even though it often meant considerable risk. The archaeological evidence from sites of the early 1640s (Rumrill-Naylor, Bauder and Oak Hill) indicates that the first firearms the Mohawks received were an eclectic mix of old and new weapons. A decade later, the situation was quite different. Although some of the older varieties were still in use, most of the firearms from sites such as Mitchell and Janie are first-class-quality snaphaunce or flintlocks of standard design. An increase in the occurrence of bar lead, bullet molds and shot accompanies this change. The only Dutch sites that have produced evidence of these firearms and their accessories are those known to be involved in trade, the Flatts and Douw's cellar.

In addition to these specialty items for the fur trade, the private traders' assemblage includes a much broader range of consumer goods. The fur trade was an extremely volatile and speculative business. Trade merchandise was usually purchased on credit and paid for after a successful season. Especially as the local Dutch population began to grow, a smart entrepreneur made sure that at least a portion of his (or her) stock could be sold to neighbors as well as Native customers.

The new merchandise that began to appear during the mid-1640s falls into four categories. Better grades of woolen cloth were the first.[74] Lead cloth seals from several textile-producing towns occur on Iroquois sites during this period. Second were utensils for eating and drinking. These include pewter and latten spoons, new styles of roemers and small Westerwald jugs, often embellished with the Amsterdam coat of arms. The third category was a much wider array of tools, especially woodworking tools such as chisels, gouges and drawshaves as well as drill bits and files. Finally, the new merchandise contained more items for recreation and amusement. These included small brass mouth harps, mentioned above, small sheet brass bells and, of course, smoking pipes. Unlike the specialty items made for the fur trade, these new consumer goods are frequently found on Dutch domestic sites as well as Native ones.

Not all trade merchandise was imported. One of the hallmarks of the private traders was a willingness to experiment with producing their own wares. For example, while wampum was made primarily by the coastal tribes of southern New England and Long Island, there are hints of wampum production at Fort Orange. Huey recovered shell blanks, partially drilled beads and drills from both components 83 and 82. However, as the Dutch quickly learned, making wampum was too difficult and tedious to be worth the effort, especially when large quantities could be obtained easily through trade. It would be decades before the Dutch revived wampum production as an activity for the poor.[75]

Assembling firearms was far more profitable. This meant carving the stock, producing the necessary hardware (butt plate, trigger guard and ramrod pipes) and putting a functional weapon together. This resulted in a close

working relationship between gunstock makers and blacksmiths, two of Beverwijck's important trades. It also provided the opportunity to collaborate on making other kinds of small brass items, such as conical pipe liners and tobacco or tinder boxes, as a sideline. While many of the brass and copper objects found on Mohawk sites of this period were Native-made, some show the signs of European craftsmanship and technology.[76]

Perhaps the most unusual of these home-grown enterprises was the making of pewter pipes. As unappealing as the idea may sound to us, pipes made of pewter were a bright, shiny silver color when new and very attractive in terms of Native aesthetics. They became wildly popular among Native people during the 1640s and 1650s. Stem fragments begin to occur on Mohawk sites by the early 1640s, and by the end of the decade pewter pipes were widely used. We know from Radisson's personal experience that the Mohawks were smoking them in 1652.[77]

Like their more common white clay cousins, pewter pipes came in two basic forms, those with a bulbous bowl and those with a funnel shaped bowl. The earliest examples appear to be straightforward copies of white clay pipes. However, by the late 1640s these pipes were often embellished with effigy figures and are more reminiscent of the elaborate stone and wooden pipes made by Native people. The kinds of effigies portrayed also reflect Native tastes. These included long-bodied, long-tailed animals, often described as otters or panthers, as well as hawks or other raptorial birds. Other more quirky motifs, such as a seated monkey playing or smoking a pipe, suggest a European sensibility or sense of humor. Whoever made them, these pewter pipes were clearly designed to work both sides of the rapidly changing cultural frontier.[78]

So, who produced this strange, highly specialized product, and why is it likely that they were a local product instead of an

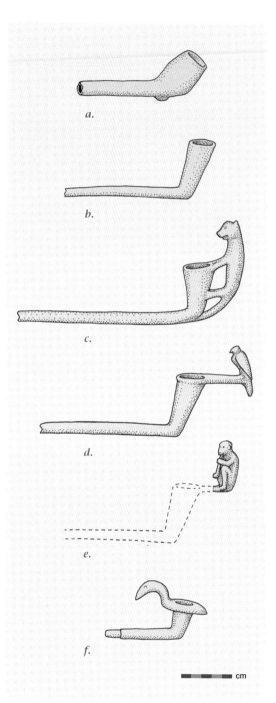

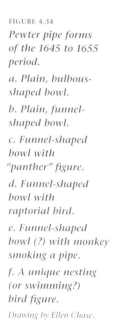

FIGURE 4.34

Pewter pipe forms of the 1645 to 1655 period.

a. Plain, bulbous-shaped bowl.

b. Plain, funnel-shaped bowl.

c. Funnel-shaped bowl with "panther" figure.

d. Funnel-shaped bowl with raptorial bird.

e. Funnel-shaped bowl (?) with monkey smoking a pipe.

f. A unique nesting (or swimming?) bird figure.

Drawing by Ellen Chase.

imported one? Archaeologically, pewter pipes are essentially unknown in Europe. In fact, the only known examples found in Amsterdam were made as advertising models and are not functional pipes. If pewter pipes had been produced in the Republic, there would be more documentary or archaeological evidence of them. More important, these pipes reflect an intimate knowledge of Native taste and even local circumstances. Finally, while these are technically sophisticated castings, they were well within the ability of Dutch settlers. As excavations in Amsterdam have demonstrated, the small-scale casting of pewter and brass items such as buttons, buckles and brooches was not uncommon. Although the documentary record does not list any pewterers working in Beverwijck, there is one intriguing hint that supports the local production of these pipes. In 1666, when a small-time trader and gunstock maker named Cornelis Bogardus passed away, a "pipe mold" was listed in the inventory of his estate. It was purchased by Abraham Staats, another more successful trader.[79]

Although our focus has been on the changing nature of trade within the Dutch community, it is important to remember that this was the period when competition with both English and the French traders was increasingly intense. As early as 1640, Van Rensselaer complained that English traders from the Connecticut Valley were "drawing everything away from us" by dealing with the Mahicans and, through them, the Mohawks.[80] This concern over English interference grew steadily throughout the period. Archaeologically, however, the English presence is elusive and evidenced only by an occasional pipe or cloth seal. French influence, on the other hand, is much clearer. Typical French items – folding knife blades, tanged iron points and iron scrapers – occur on Mohawk sites throughout the period. Given the aggressive expansion of trade under the new Paris-based Company of One Hundred

Associates, and the establishment of Montreal in 1642, this is no surprise.[81] The Jesuits' increasing interest in making friends among the Five Nations is also clearly evident during this period. Finger rings with Roman Catholic religious inscriptions are the most obvious evidence of this effort. These begin to appear on Mohawk sites during the early to mid 1640s and, by the early 1650s, have become fairly common.[82]

Adapting and Adopting

Just as the region's Native cultures helped to shape the ways in which the Dutch settled permanently into a new homeland, European materials, technologies and even ideas exerted an increasingly powerful influence on Native people and their way of life. These changes are especially evident during the 1640s and early 1650s, a period of intense internal and external stress. Nearly continuous warfare and the ongoing adoption of captives continued to redefine what it meant to be Mohawk. New diseases and the availability of alcohol, plus the exposure to Christianity, created factions and put added strain on the traditional bonds of family and community.

By 1650, at least two generations had come of age since Hudson's visit. This meant that European objects, whether re-processed into traditional forms or used as intended, were now an established part of Native life, things that most Native people had grown up with. At the other end of the population, at least two generations had largely passed on, taking their knowledge and preferences with them. These changes are clearly apparent in the archaeological record. Native ceramics are a good example. Although still present, pottery is not used as much as on the earlier Mohawk sites and many of the vessels that occur show the influence of captives, especially Hurons.

Similar changes can be seen in Native-made pipes. However, as we have seen, smoking pipes are complex objects, ones that tell many

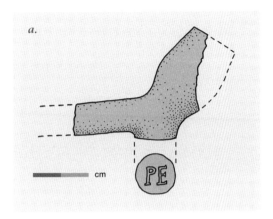

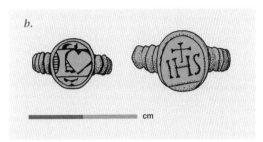

FIGURE 4.35

Evidence of Other Outsiders.

a. English PE pipe
After McCashion 1991: Plates V and VI)

b. Jesuit rings: L with heart and IHS with cross styles.
Drawings by Ellen Chase.

stories. This is particularly the case during the 1640s. On one hand, there is a dramatic increase in the Native use of European white clay pipes. Yet, at the same time, Native clay and stone pipes continue to be a strong presence. Often these were embellished with effigies, such as the examples found at Fort Orange, but a wide range of styles occur, both in traditional shapes and those reflecting the influence of captives. Wooden pipes also were used throughout this period. Often the only evidence of these elegant pipes is the conical brass bowl liner, but occasionally the rare survival indicates how elaborate these wooden pipes could be.

Pipes were important because, like wampum, they had value on both sides of the cultural frontier and were frequently used by Native people and the Dutch for diplomatic purposes and gifts. As a result, some unusual pipes come from the sites this time of dynamic change. Native people made a wide variety of stone pipes during this period, some in traditional

ARTIFACT
PROFILE 10

First-Class Firearms: From Contraband to Commodity

Two Dutch visits to the Mohawks demonstrate when and how quickly firearms became a part of Native culture. When Van den Bogart traveled to their villages in 1634, he was continually asked to fire his weapon. Clearly, firearms were still a novelty. Nine years later during Van Curler's visit to Mohawk country, he and his companions were obliged to wait "fully a quarter of an hour" before each castle while

By 1639, an ordinance forbidding the sale of guns to the Indians, on pain of death, was passed. A second ordinance prohibiting the sale, repair or even lending of a firearm to a Native was signed by Van Curler two years later.[84] By then, however, large quantities of guns had begun to reach the Iroquois, a situation that everyone (the Dutch, English and French) blamed on each other.

FIGURE 4.36
Re-constructed musket with flint lock mechanism and fittings similar to those recovered from Mohawk sites and the Flatts farm.
Drawing by Ellen Chase.

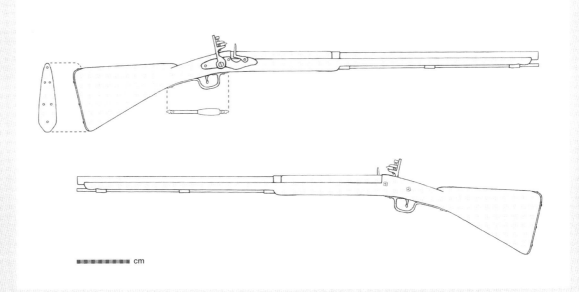

the Mohawks fired their muskets in salute. Isaac Jogues, a Mohawk prisoner at the time, reported that they had nearly three hundred muskets and were skilled in using them.[83]

The Dutch certainly brought firearms to New Netherland both for hunting and protection. From the early 1630s on, muskets, spare parts, bar lead for bullets and gunpowder were part of the supplies sent to the Colonie. The trick was keeping them in the right hands.

The reality is that private Dutch traders probably were responsible for most of the firearms that the Iroquois obtained during the 1640s. As John Winthrop noted in his journal during March 1644, a Dutch ship on the way to Fort Orange had been intercepted and its cargo of "4,000 weight of powder and 700 pieces to trade with the natives" was confiscated by the governor. Other shipments got through successfully, as the archaeological evidence clearly shows. Stuyvesant also tried to enforce the ordinances prohibiting the sale of firearms, prosecuting two prominent traders in 1648. However, by then the economic value of the trade, as well as the political necessity of keeping the Mohawks happy, quickly rendered the rules irrelevant and by 1650 firearms had become an accepted part of the traders' merchandise.[85]

There was another important reason why Dutch traders provided most of the guns – during the early 17th-century, the Dutch Republic was the world's largest producer of armaments. Although the revolt against Spain had stimulated the manufacture of weapons, the arms trade continued to expand, especially in Amsterdam, as the market for weapons grew. By the first quarter of the 17th-century, the Republic not only exported huge quantities of weapons to France and other countries, their firearms also had an outstanding reputation for quality.[86] As the Thirty Years' War came to an end in Europe, it is not surprising that Dutch manufacturers were eager to find new markets for their wares.

Recent research has provided a much clearer view of what kinds of firearms the Mohawks began to receive from Dutch traders during the 1640s. These were not obsolete or inferior products. They were first-class firearms, up to date even by European standards. It appears that barrels and locks, probably produced in Utrecht or Amsterdam, were shipped over in bulk and then assembled in New Netherland. During the 1650s, several Beverwijck businessmen listed themselves as gun stock makers.

The weapons themselves included pistols, muskets and long-barreled fowling pieces with a range of caliber between .50 and .65. While

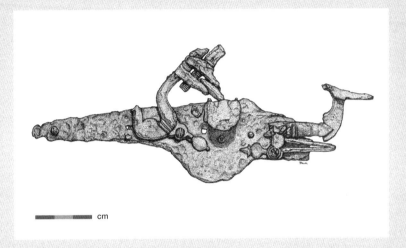

cm

several kinds of firing mechanisms were used, there was a trend toward greater uniformity with first snaphaunce, then flintlock mechanisms of increasingly standard design. Of particular note is Puype's Type II lockplate whose "bellied" shape appears to derive from Dutch wheel locks of the 1620s. This is one of the most common lock forms found on 17th-century Iroquois sites.[87] Two of these lockplates, plus associated parts and evidence of repairs, have also been found at the Flatts. This suggests that Van Curler was the one who had ordered these locks and who supplied them to the Mohawks and others.

FIGURE 4.37
Snaphaunce lock on a Type II lock plate. Power House site (Seneca), RMSC #6242/24. Identical locks were found at the Flatts farm.
Courtesy of the RMSC. Drawings by T. Miller.

ER

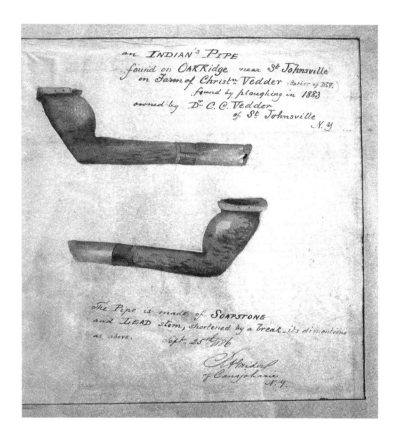

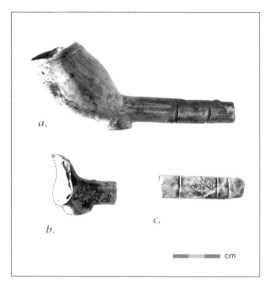

FIGURE 4.38

Above: Drawing of a stone pipe with lead collar, by Rufus Grider. Sketchbook I:47.

Courtesy of the New York State Library Manuscripts and Special Collections.

FIGURE 4.39

Above Right: Very large white clay pipes.

a. A nearly complete but unprovenienced example. (NYSM A-16849).

b. A bowl fragment from the Oak Hill site.

Courtesy of Wayne Lenig.

c. A stem fragment from the Rumrill-Naylor site (A2005.13BM.99.128).

Rumrill collection, NYSM. Photo by Ted Beblowski.

forms, others replicating European shapes. All sorts of combinations occur as well. A good example is a stone pipe found near St. Johnsville. A Native interpretation of a European white clay pipe enhanced with a cast lead or pewter collar, it is truly a transcultural object (*See Figure 4.38*).[88] Extremely large European clay pipes are another group of unusual pipes from this time period. Several pieces of these oversized pipes have been recovered from the Oak Hill and Rumrill-Naylor sites.[89] In a world where the size of a gift was often equated with its importance, these pipes would have made an impressive present. When Van Curler visited the Mohawks in 1643, he reported that they had been received with "great joy."[90] Could these oversized pipes have been part of the reason for his success? Taken together, these unusual pipes provide an insight into the changing nature of Native-Dutch relations. It was no longer just about trade. Now it was a matter of figuring out how to communicate and find ways to live together.

Just as Native pottery was fading away along with the older generations, so too the use of stone, bone and antler for tools was disappearing. A few chert triangular points and

a.

b.

an occasional antler harpoon occur on these sites, but by the end of the period, nearly all the tools are of European material if not manufacture. There are a few exceptions. Native-made gunflints continue to be produced in large numbers demonstrating that lithic reduction skills had been transferred to a new form rather than lost. Still, it is the rapid replacement of traditional forms by European ones that marks this period. Even the evidence for re-use of European objects and their conversion into Native forms decline as the quantity of finished European goods available continued to increase.

However, this hardly meant the end of Native culture. One of the trends that characterized Native-made objects during the first half of the 17th-century was a greater degree of elaboration, an increased use of motifs and forms that were symbolically charged. A good example is the use of effigy figures on pottery, pipes and combs, although why this occurred is the subject of much discussion. Certainly in

times of stress and change, people tend to be more concerned with spiritual matters. For the Native people of the region, good relations with the spirit world had always been essential since that is where the important issues of health, abundance and success in hunting or war were determined. The greater use of figurative forms, whether they represented animals, man-beings or manitous, may have been one of the material ways in which Native people tried to invoke help at a time when things were not going well.

This tendency for Native material objects to be more elaborate extended beyond ceramics. The widespread availability of metal tools was certainly a factor. These gave Native people the means for greater artistic expression in other traditional mediums such as antler, wood and shell. As Van der Donck observed, the older men now spent their time carving wooden bowls and spoons, not just knotting fish nets. It is likely that they were making pipes, combs and clubs as well. Nor was this renaissance in

FIGURE 4.40

a. Wooden pipe with copper bowl and insets, from the Seneca Dann site. (Wray collection #815/28.) Similar to the wooden pipe shown in Figure 3.27.

b. X-ray of same pipe showing copper bowl and insets.

Courtesy of George Hamell and the RMSC. Drawing by Gene Mackay.

cm

effigy figures, crescent and claw-shaped objects as well as massive columella beads from large whelk shells.[92] Like wampum, these shell artifacts were not made by the Mohawks but acquired through trade or as tribute for the coastal tribes of southern New England and Long Island. The sheer quantity of shell that occurs on sites of this period can be astonishing. As many as 12,000 beads have been reported from a single burial; all were probably from a large wampum belt. It is during this period when the use of wampum belts became widespread and these belts may be another indication of the period's intense warfare and diplomacy. However, wampum served many functions. Along with furs, it was the accepted form of currency between Native people and the Dutch. It was also, as Van der Donck noted, "in general use for buying everything one needs." Beyond belts and currency, wampum was used extensively by the Mohawks to adorn their bodies and clothing. Van der Donck describes necklaces and bracelets as well as "beautiful girdles of wampum around the waist" and skirts "wholly embroidered with wampum."[93] Clearly, these small shell beads continued to play many roles within Native culture.

This burst of cultural creativity also extended to new materials. Early in the period, the first attempts to work with lead occur. On sites such as Rumrill-Naylor, these are primarily simple effigies made from sheet metal or flattened musket balls and experimental inlays on stone pipes. On the sites of the later 1640s, such as Mitchell, Lipe and Janie, working with lead and pewter expands in a new direction. Casting becomes an established skill as the numerous small lead effigies of four-legged figures, usually described as turtles, from these sites demonstrate.[94] Casting was not restricted to musket balls and small effigy figures. Collars for stone and possibly wooden pipes were also made and there may even have been some attempts to cast simple pipes as well.[95]

carving limited to wood. Antler combs and ladles, often in styles that combined traditional motifs with European forms, are also typical of this period.[91]

Another indication of cultural elaboration is a dramatic increase in the amount of wampum and other styles of shell ornaments on Mohawk and Mahican sites. These include

One of the greatest changes of this period was the widespread use of firearms. Contemporary descriptions make it clear that the Mohawks were skilled in the use and maintenance of their weapons. On one level, the concepts involved in a flintlock mechanism were not alien. Snares and deadfalls required triggering mechanisms and the use of flint and steel to make a spark was certainly understood. Major repairs, such as welding or tempering, were another matter. These aspects of European technology would take a lot longer for Native people to learn. In the meantime, the tendency was to keep as many spare parts as possible and hope that they could be made to fit.[96]

One other European product began to play an important, if disruptive, role during this period – alcohol. It is hard to gauge how much of a problem drinking was by the early 1650s. According to Van der Donck, "most of them have no taste for liquor at all" and considered drunken men to be fools.[97] There were also strict laws against giving or selling alcohol to Native people, but they were not always enforced. Unlike firearms, liquor leaves little archaeological trace. The best evidence is indirect, the increased presence of European faience and stoneware vessels in Native sites.

Yet even here, in the midst of this flood of European material, Native tastes and preferences continued to operate. Two pieces from the Lipe site provide an example. One is half of a small round pendant made from the body of a large faience (delft) jug, a near-perfect copy of its marine shell predecessor. The second is a small Westerwald jug decorated with the Amsterdam coat of arms.[98] While this may have served as a durable canteen, its ornamentation was also appealing. To Native eyes, the three St. Andrew's crosses on the shield were a familiar device, a pattern of opposed triangles, while the lions on either side were reminiscent of the panthers that embellished Native pipes and combs.

FIGURE 4.42
Top: Lead inlay, an X facing the smoker, on a stone pipe from Rumrill-Naylor site (A2005.13BM.99.13). Rumrill collection, NYSM. Photo by Ted Beblowski.

FIGURE 4.43
Above: Cast lead figures from the Michell and Janie sites (A2005.13AY.99.18). Rumrill collection, NYSM. Photo by Ted Beblowski.

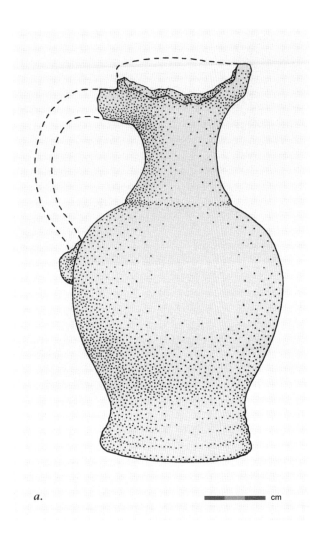

a.

cm

b.

cm

FIGURE 4.44

European ceramics from mid 17th-century Iroquois sites.

a. A white faience jug from the Seneca Dann site (#21571/656).
Courtesy of the NYSM. Drawing by Ellen Chase.

b. A Westerwald stoneware jug with the Amsterdam coat of arms, from Lipe site.
Courtesy of Wayne Lenig and the Mohawk-Caughnawaga Museum.

Summing Up

By 1652 many things had changed. The Dutch were no longer newcomers. In addition to forts and farms, they had begun to establish communities strong enough to withstand the rigors of a new environment as well as political and economic uncertainty. Although the population of these settlements was ethnically diverse, the structure and values on which they were built were firmly Dutch.

Even though the fur trade continued to dominate relations between Native people and the Dutch, other factors had become equally important. Land had to be purchased as settlements grew. This, and the need to have neighboring tribes as allies and not adversaries, resulted in a shift from trade-based to politically-based relationships. This was especially the case with the Mohawks. Arent van Curler appears to have played a central role in this process both through his familiarity with Mohawk people and his close ties with the Van Rensselaer family.

The growing hostilities with England, regionally and around the globe, increased the sense of Dutch nationalism in New Netherland and strengthened emotional ties with the Republic. However, it was during this period that Dutch settlers also began to think of themselves not only as transplanted Europeans, but something else – citizens in a new country, one with its own distinct opportunities and problems.

For Native people, the situation was very different. A permanent Dutch presence changed everything – from how they used the land to their ties with other tribes. In addition, the new material goods brought by Europeans had transformed the way in which tools, utensils and all the things needed to sustain the community were obtained. From a Native point of view, these changes had not occurred only in the material world; the balance seemed to have shifted in the spirit world as well. By 1650 they were confronted by diseases that traditional ritual could not cure and a self-sustaining cycle of warfare and revenge. Faced with additional stresses, such as the availability of alcohol and aggressive Christian missionaries, the challenge for Native people was to find a way to live with these difficult new neighbors before discord and fragmentation overwhelmed them.

The First Anglo-Dutch war (1652–1654) reset the board yet again. If the old Protestant allies had become enemies, other former adversaries quickly became friends as greater threats emerged. The dispute between the Colonie and the Company, so central during the previous decade, faded to insignificance with the Dutch defeat in Europe and aggressive Puritan neighbors in New England.

The war was a hardship for New Netherland, cutting supply lines at the time when the trade was strong and new settlers were finally coming to the province, but it was also fought far away. Locally, things were looking up. With the departure of Van Slichtenhorst in 1652, Kiliaen van Rensselaer's son, Jan Baptist, became director of Rensselaerswijck and took up residence in the Colonie. The new community of Beverwijck began to take shape as Stuyvesant issued lots to residents in 1652 and 1653. In September 1653, the Five Nations signed a peace treaty with the French, after much internal wrangling. Even though the Mohawks were reluctant participants, the agreement was a hopeful sign that the ongoing cycle of intertribal warfare could be broken. However, that was not to be.

Setting the Pattern

The Anglo-Dutch war ended in the spring of 1654 just as Cromwell's fleet was about to seize New Amsterdam. Although New Netherland would not be so lucky the next time, this gave the province ten more years to stabilize and fully develop its Dutch character and communities. The war with England was not the only setback the Dutch suffered in 1654. After an eight-year-long revolt, the Portuguese evicted the WIC from Brazil, whose sugar plantations

were one of the Company's few remaining assets.[1] Ironically, these reverses benefited New Netherland. With the loss of Brazil, the Company finally focused on North America and began to provide some of the support that New Netherland had long needed.

The establishment of Beverwijck transformed the local situation. Within the arc of 600 paces that Stuyvesant drew around Fort Orange, inhabitants were "excused" from their obligations as Rensselaerswijck tenants and given the opportunity to become *burghers,* or citizens, of the new town. Burghership was the basic organizing principle of Dutch communities. It gave an individual the right to practice a trade, guaranteed due process in the court and allowed for participation in town government. In return, it required service in the militia and the payment of taxes.[2] It did not take long for the region's artisans to realize that citizenship in Beverwijck was a much better deal than indentured servitude to the patroon, and the new town grew rapidly. There were still problems. In the spring of 1654, the river flooded again, pushing more people out of Fort Orange and into the town. But as property lines were surveyed, streets laid out and artisan neighborhoods established, Beverwijck looked increasingly like the well-organized, typically Dutch town that it was.

These were good years for the trade and busy ones for men like Arent van Curler. Although his primary interests remained the Flatts farm and the fur trade, he also found a little time for politics. Van Curler had certainly met Jan Baptist and his younger brother Jeremias during his extended stay in the Republic. Ten years older than his cousin, Van Curler was in a position to befriend and advise the Colonie's new director. This cordial relationship expanded to include Jeremias after he came to the Colonie in 1654 and Van Curler became the connecting link between two generations of Van Rensselaer traders.

Others prospered too. Volckert Jansz Douw had become an extremely successful merchant, one who provided goods both to Native customers and the rapidly growing town. He had come a long way from his days of illicit trading. By the mid-1650s he was a magistrate and one of the community's wealthiest and most respected members. Another newcomer, Philip Schuyler, also did well. Arriving from Amsterdam in 1650 and working as a gunstock maker, he married Van Slichtenhorst's daughter, which made him a member of the Van Rensselaer party. By mid-decade he too was a wealthy trader and a high-level speculator in land. However, the prosperity was short-lived and the signs of trouble were evident, if one cared to look for them. Wampum's value as currency dropped steadily throughout the decade.[3] Also, as the town grew, so did the number of people who wanted to be traders. Most important, there was no long-term stability among the region's Native people.

For them, these had not been such good years, especially for the Iroquois. The peace of 1653 did not last and internal problems between the Mohawks and Onondagas had grown dangerous. The establishment of a successful Jesuit mission among the Onondagas in 1654, and a small French settlement there (Ste. Marie among the Iroquois) two years later, had brought the Mohawks to what a Jesuit observer described as "a jealousy almost verging on fury." This time the dispute had gone too far for an easy reconciliation. As one Jesuit observer noted, "The two sides fought with each other until the ground was stained with blood and murder. Some believe that all this was a mere feint to mask the game better;... I greatly doubt whether [even] Iroquois policy can go so far."[4]

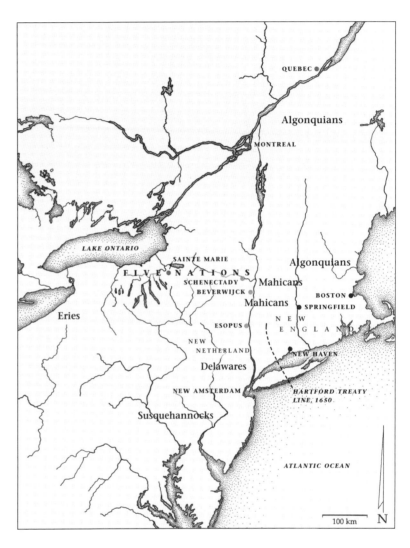

It was indeed a bad time for the Five Nations to be fighting among themselves. After decades of intertribal warfare, they had made enemies on every side of their expanded territory, and paid a huge price for these victories in terms of their own losses. But Mohawk anger over the threat to their position as the eastern "door keepers," and therefore the ones to broker the trade with Europeans, would not be soothed. Mohawk war parties continued to intercept furs headed for Montreal and Quebec as well as raid French settlements along the St. Lawrence River. Meanwhile, Mohawk diplomacy cut away support for the French among the rest of

FIGURE 5.1
Northeast regional map, 1652 to 1664.
Map by Booth Simpson

the Iroquois. By March 1658, when it was clear the new settlement of Ste. Marie was doomed, the French quietly abandoned it. Shortly after, amidst the mutual recriminations, war resumed between the Five Nations and the French along with their Algonquian allies.[5]

The return to hostilities had profound effects. It all but killed the fur trade. With wide spread fighting, no one had time to hunt for furs. Nor was it always safe for traders, Native or European, to be out and about their business. For Beverwijck, collapse of the fur trade brought long-standing problems to a head. Too many traders were competing for too few furs and this produced serious internal feuds within the town. Another result was the very aggressive, even abusive, attitude that developed toward the few Mohawks who did come to trade, a situation that only strained relations further.[6]

All this was aggravated by another problem. During the 1650s, alcohol, usually in the form of brandy, became a significant part of the trade. It was illegal to sell liquor to the Natives but, like firearms a decade before, this did not stop people from doing so. The Mohawks quickly realized how destructive alcohol was and, in September 1659, requested that the Dutch "bung up the casks" and sell no more brandy to them. As if to prove the point, a new war, fuelled in part by alcohol, broke later that month between Dutch settlers in the lower Hudson Valley and the local Esopus Indians.[7] In the face of these external problems, the magistrates of Beverwijck decided it was time to enclose the community within a stockade.

With trouble in the lower Hudson Valley, the Dutch could not afford bad relations with their Mohawk neighbors. The Mohawks certainly had their own list of grievances – Dutch stinginess with gifts, being charged for powder and the repair of weapons, the abusive behavior and lack of hospitality. These may seem small issues to us but to the Mohawks they symbolized the larger problem. "The Dutch

say, we are brothers, and joined together... but that lasts only as long as we have beavers," their representatives complained. To reassure their allies, the Beverwijck court decided to send a delegation to Mohawk country that September. The goal of this diplomatic mission was "to enter into a further alliance" with the Mohawks and "to thank them for their old and continued friendship." Among those who volunteered were Jeremias van Rensselaer (now the director of the Colonie), Arent van Curler, Volckert Jansz Douw and Philip Schuyler.[8] This embassy "for the peace and well-being of this country" was one more step away from the old fur trade partnership and toward a new treaty-based relationship between two nations.

By 1660, Beverwijck had changed, economically and physically. Although the fur trade did revive, it never regained its former vigor and merchants like the Van Rensselaers began to diversify into other commodities such as tobacco, lumber and grain.[9] The town, however, continued to grow. Not only did settlement spread out beyond the stockade, Beverwijck was now large enough to serve as the jumping-off point for groups of settlers intent on establishing new communities. The first new settlement had been built sixty miles to the south along Esopus Creek in 1653. In 1661 it was granted its own court and re-named *Wiltwijck* (now Kingston). That same year, Arent van Curler led another group of settlers west of Beverwijck to begin the village of Schenectady. His goal was to replicate the Flatts model by combining the best agricultural land with the most advantageous location for trade. To some degree, these new settlements relieved the pressure within Beverwijck, now a town of nearly 1,000 people. They provided new opportunities for land and, some hoped, trade. However, these new Dutch communities also served another important purpose – they helped to check English attempts to build their own settlements in the Hudson Valley or even farther west.

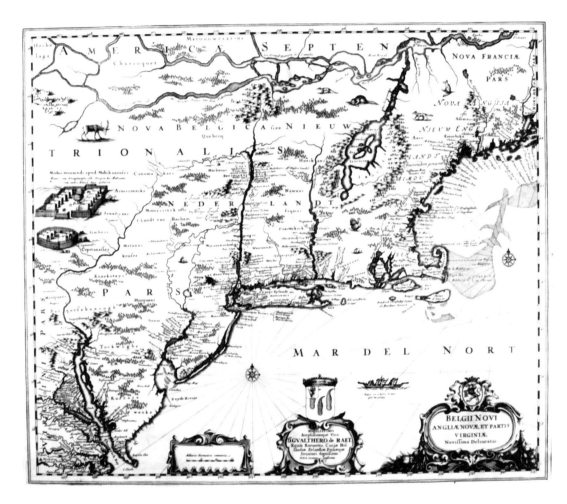

FIGURE 5.2
*Belgii Nova
(New Netherland)
ca. 1651, the Nicolaes
Visscher map.*
*Courtesy of the New York
State Library, Manuscripts
and Special Collections.
Photo by Ted Beblowski.*

While the Dutch began to branch out from Beverwijck and establish new communities, the cycle of Native warfare continued unabated. "The Iroquois of this country [the Mohawks] will never make peace" lamented Jerome Lalemant, the Jesuit Father Superior in 1661. However, by the spring of 1663, peace embassies from the Five Nations, led by the Onondagas, were again on their way to Quebec. Even the Mohawks were present, and the reason why was soon clear. They were "no longer in a condition to make war, being reduced to a very small number by famine, disease and the losses they have suffered in the last 2 or 3 years," Lalemant observed. Yet this attempt at peace was no more successful than

its predecessors, leaving one French observer to comment that "if the Mohawk could be defeated militarily by the French, the other Iroquois Nations would be glad to compromise with us."[10] That prediction would be fulfilled within a few years.

Meanwhile, the warfare continued. Most troublesome for the Dutch was the renewal of hostilities between the Mahicans and the Mohawks. By 1660, the Mahicans were closely tied to the western Abenaki and other New England Algonquians who, as allies of the French, were therefore implacable enemies of the Mohawk. This left the Dutch in the middle and although their towns and farms were safe enough, it was a difficult and uncomfortable

FIGURE 5.3
*"A View of Fort
Orange, 1652."
In the foreground,
the ship Geldersche
Blom (the Flower of
Gelderland) prepares
for departure after
unloading colonists
and supplies.*
Courtesy of L. F. Tantillo.

situation. By 1664, the fighting had resulted in "great losses on both sides" and made travel dangerous.[11] Things were even worse farther south. In June 1663, a large party of Esopus, angry over new Dutch settlements and ill treatment, attacked Wiltwijck, killing several of the inhabitants and carring off many more. While the Dutch quickly regained the military advantage, the troubles left the lower portion of New Netherland frightened and jittery. Even with these problems, Beverwijck continued to grow. By 1664, it was a settled and successful Dutch town, very similar to its sister town, New Amsterdam, at the mouth of the Hudson River. However, in spite of the progress, New Netherland remained just a pawn in a much larger game.

The great game of world domination also continued to evolve during the early 1660s as old players dropped out and new ones emerged. With Cromwell's death in 1658 and restoration of the Stuart monarchy, many in the Republic hoped that good relations with England could be rebuilt. However, passage of

the Navigation Act of 1660 was one of Charles II's first actions, a clear indication that English imperial designs were not waning. Across the Channel, a twenty-three-year-old Louis XIV also exercised his royal prerogative, revoking the charter of the Company of One Hundred Associates and making New France a royal colony. New Netherland as well as the region's Native people suddenly found themselves squeezed between two new and very ambitious powers. The good old days of laissez-faire economics, uncomplicated by political considerations, were over. Events would now be played out on an imperial stage, one that had repercussions around the world. In fact, the Second Anglo-Dutch war (1665–1667) might be more accurately considered one of the first world-wide wars. With background grievances in Indonesia and a practice run along the West African coast, the English takeover of New Netherland in September 1664 served as the dress rehearsal for a war that formally started several months later.[12] The line between local and global events had become fuzzy indeed.

Changes on the Land

Although the 1650s and early 1660s were marked by economic turmoil and nearly continuous warfare, this was the period when the Dutch put their stamp most firmly on the region's landscape. By 1664, they had settled much of the best farmland while scouting out and purchasing still more. They continued to explore the region's waterways, looking for good landings and potential mill sites. They had even begun to build a few roads. The new town of Beverwijck quickly became not just a regional center but the point of departure for settlers heading farther inland. By the time of the English takeover, the region's settlements and institutions (as well as the customs and values on which they were built) were solidly Dutch, even if the population was a much more diverse mix. All this put even greater pressure on the region's Native people, forcing them to consider how best to preserve their own culture and values.

Fort Orange. In 1652, Fort Orange was still the region's most important place. Although the new town of Beverwijck was just getting started, the better houses and nearly all the important institutions were located within the fort. By the end of the decade, the situation had reversed and Fort Orange was little more than a storage area for the merchandise that flowed in and out of the adjacent town.

Archaeology documents this transition in several ways. One is the gradual abandonment of the fort as the preferred place to live. During his fieldwork, Huey located two residences from this period, both of which were built prior to 1652. One was the house of Abraham Staats, a trader, whose wife built the house in 1648 and sold it to Johannes van Twiller in 1655. Van Twiller stayed in the house for only two years, returning to the Republic in 1657, and leaving the property to his cousin Jeremias van Rensselaer. Although Jeremias tried hard to rent or sell the property, no one was interested.

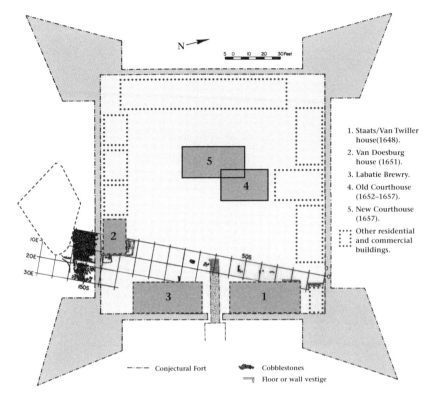

1. Staats/Van Twiller house (1648).
2. Van Doesburg house (1651).
3. Labatie Brewry.
4. Old Courthouse (1652–1657).
5. New Courthouse (1657).
- - - - Other residential and commercial buildings.

- - - Conjectural Fort   Cobblestones
   Floor or wall vestige

By September 1661, Jeremias wrote to his uncle that the house was almost a total loss, more expensive to repair than it was worth. Although Huey uncovered only a small portion of the Staats-Van Twiller house, the site was well preserved. Six stratigraphic components tell the story of this structure from its construction in 1648 until it finally burned down twenty-one years later.[13]

The second house was that of Hendrick van Doesburgh, a gunstock maker, who emigrated from Amsterdam with his wife Marietje Damen in 1651. Although Hendrick Andriessen appears to have been a successful craftsman, the historical documents suggest that Marietje was the real business force in the family. A successful merchant and trader, she also bought and sold real estate. In 1657, the couple bought a house in Beverwijck and probably moved into town. By 1660, the house in the

FIGURE 5.4
Plan view of Fort Orange with structures from the 1652 to 1664 period.
After Huey1988:728.
Map by Booth Simpson.

SITE PROFILE 4   The Van Doesburgh House, 1651–1664

During his excavations at Fort Orange, Huey uncovered the eastern end of the Van Doesburgh house. This was the largest and most complete structure found in Fort Orange and it provides some basis for reconstructing how an early 1650s Dutch house might have looked.

Located against the south wall of the fort near the southeast bastion, the house was 21 feet wide and at least 30 feet in length. Like most mid 17th-century houses, it was probably of timber frame construction, had one and a half stories and a steeply pitched roof. It was set over a wooden lined cellar with an outside shed entrance. The back wall of the house appears to have been an integral part of the fort's exterior curtain wall.

Although archaeological evidence provides some clues, it is unclear exactly what the house looked like above ground. We do know that it was a substantial house with a pan tile roof and a chimney of yellow and red brick. It may have had a brick end wall as well, one secured to the frame with a large iron masonry anchor. Brick would become the fashionable building material within the decade. The primary entrance and windows would have faced the courtyard. The interior, like Van Curler's house at the Flatts, was stylish and decorated with the same delft wall tiles and red earthenware hearth tiles found in prosperous merchant houses back in the Republic.

FIGURE 5.5
Sketch of the Van Doesburgh house, Fort Orange, ca. 1656.
Courtesy of L. F. Tantillo.

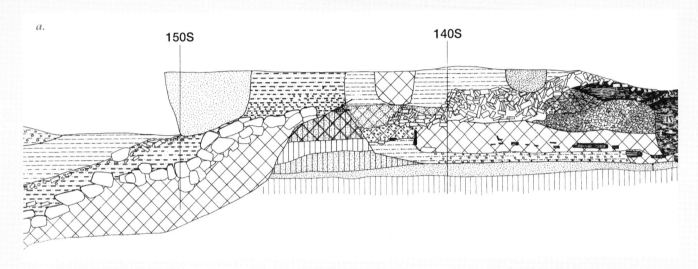

a.

150S

140S

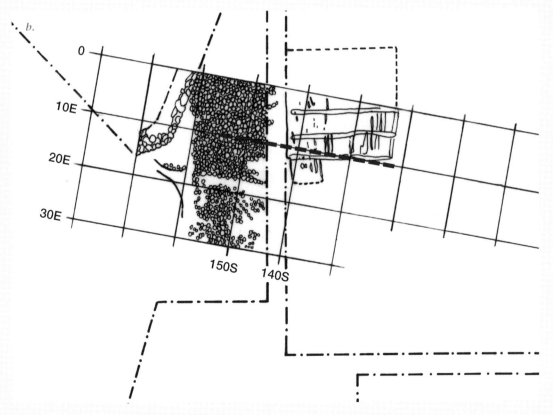

b.

0

10E

20E

30E

150S   140S

FIGURE 5.6

a. **A portion of profile D showing the cobble-lined ditch on the left and the Van Doesburgh house cellar on the right.** *After Huey 1988:750.*

b. **A plan view of Huey's excavation showing the location of profile D.** *After Huey 1988:757.*

a.

b.

cm

One surprising indication of affluence and sophistication was the recovery of several pieces of leaded glass window with enameled decoration. These fragments appear to be from a coat of arms and contain the name "Jacob" and the date "1650." Similar windows with coats of arms in roundels are shown in Dutch paintings of the period. Another example of enameled glass from Beverwijck is a surviving window from the blockhouse church. Made in a slightly different style, this window does not contain roundels and is dated 1656.[14]

FIGURE 5.7

a. Interior with a Woman at a Spinning Wheel, Esaias Boursse, 1661. Note the enameled roundels in the windows.
Courtesy of the Rijksmuseum, Amsterdam.

b. Fragments of comparable enameled window glass dated 1650 from the Van Doesburgh house, Fort Orange.
Courtesy Paul Huey and OPRHP.

fort was falling apart. Damaged further by the flood of 1661, it finally collapsed in 1664.[15]

By 1660, these once stylish houses had been abandoned as residences and were used for storage or worse. As Jeremias van Rensselaer observed in July 1659, "the fort is considered no more than a nest, as no business is to be done there and not many people go there."[16] With the construction of the first Beverwijck stockade later that year, Fort Orange became even more isolated from the community it once had nurtured.

This did not mean the fort had been abandoned. It was still the town's major defensive structure and, though decrepit, several efforts were made to repair the walls and mount additional cannon during the early 1660s. Fort Orange also continued to serve as the landing place for sailing vessels from Manhattan and remained the Company's major distribution point up-river. Most important, the court was still located within the fort, making it the legal center of the Company's operations. By 1657, the "old" court building, a clapboard structure with a shingle roof built in 1652, was so dilapidated that it was torn down in order to build a more permanent structure. The new courthouse was a large, more elaborate brick building and it continued to serve the community until the English takeover.[17] While Huey's excavation did not find either of the court buildings, he may have discovered evidence that they were nearby – their garbage.

The use of the fort for waste disposal was another indication of its declining status. The cellar of the Van Doesburgh house contained a considerable amount of garbage, unusual for a house that was not occupied. Since the kitchen of the new brick courthouse was close by, Huey

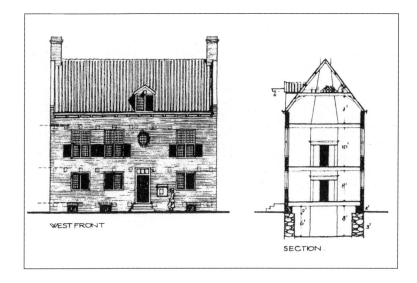

WEST FRONT

SECTION.

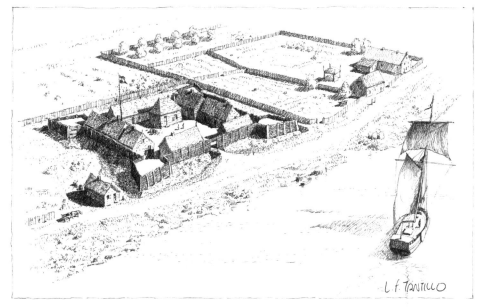

L.F. TANTILLO

FIGURE 5.8
Top: Drawing of the new brick Courthouse, Fort Orange, ca. 1660.
Courtesy of Jaap Schipper.

FIGURE 5.9
Above: A sketch of Fort Orange, ca. 1656, looking northwest.
Courtesy of L.F. Tantillo.

suggests that this may have been the source of the refuse, Nor was this the only example of illegal dumping. Several taverns were located just outside the fort. One of these, owned by Adriaen Jansen Appel, operated just south of the fort between 1654 and 1663. Here Huey found that large amounts of garbage had been dumped into the fort's protective ditch. Composed primarily of food waste, drinking glasses and bottle fragments as well as broken pipes, this deposit clearly came from a nearby tavern, probably Appel's.[18] Even when faced

FIGURE 5.10
Brass weathercock from the 1656 blockhouse church, Beverwijck.
Courtesy of the First Church in Albany (Reformed).

with an English invasion, the fort's ditch was still viewed as a handy place to dump rubbish.

By 1664, Fort Orange was an artifact of an earlier era. Once the center of settlement and trade, it had been reduced to a port facility and dumping ground. The Court of Fort Orange and Beverwijck still met there, but the real center of activity had shifted to the town of Beverwijck a decade before.

Beverwijck, While the Fort dwindled into obscurity, the town prospered and grew. Within a few years, all the institutions that defined a Dutch community – court, church and poorhouse – were present. The war with England made defense a primary concern. While Fort Orange provided protection to the south, additional defenses were built north of town. By 1655, a guardhouse had also been constructed on the hill at the head of what is now State Street. A second blockhouse was proposed in April 1656, this one at the foot of the hill. When the project ran short of money, the appeal for funds was broadened to include a new Dutch Reformed church. The "blockhouse church" as it was known was completed later that year and quickly became a community landmark. Located in the intersection of the town's two major streets (State Street and Broadway), the church's large brass weather vane could be seen from all directions.[19]

Construction of the blockhouse church was a major step in the shifting the community's institutions out of Fort Orange and into the new town. Other social services had already led the way. By 1653, a house for the poor was under construction, charity being a core value in Dutch communities. A separate poor farm was established four years later. Well before 1660, all the important community institutions, except the court, were located in Beverwijck.[20]

The greatest change in the town's character, aside from its rapid growth, was the decision to build a palisade. The attack on Esopus in September 1659 frightened the inhabitants of Beverwijck, who quickly decided that a "much-needed defense" had to be built "as speedily as possible." The result was a "plank fence" that surrounded much of the town. In terms of construction, the palisade was to be "eight boards high" and supported by posts, very similar to the curtain walls of Fort Orange. A series of bastions would protect the walls,

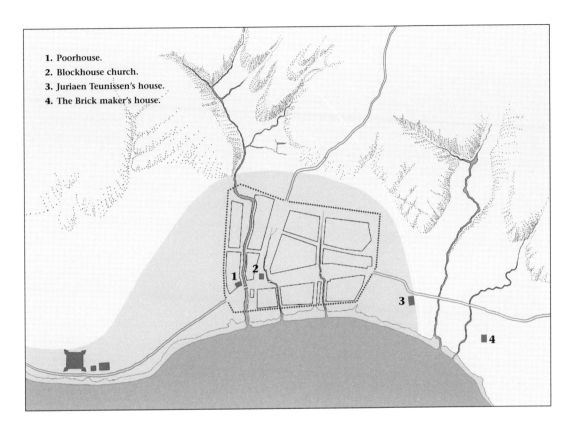

1. Poorhouse.
2. Blockhouse church.
3. Juriaen Teunissen's house.
4. The Brick maker's house.

FIGURE 5.11
Map of Beverwijck, ca. 1664, showing the stockade and street plan.
Map by Ellen Chase and Booth Simpson.

and gates were to be erected where the major roads left the town. What was actually built is not known. Although portions of the palisade may have been encountered during the 19th century, no evidence of these early fortifications has been documented by recent archaeological work.[21]

The palisade represented more than community defense. Enclosing the town gave it a defined character, a boundary, something familiar to Europeans who had grown up in walled cities and towns. Once stockaded, Beverwijck began to take on other, more urban characteristics – streets that ran parallel and crossed at more or less right angles, houses built close together facing the street with fenced-in lots behind them, artisan neighborhoods and a centrally located church.[22]

However, the town had also sprawled out along the river during the 1650s, well beyond the area that would be enclosed

by the palisade. This portion of Beverwijck included houses, workshops and taverns, landings along the river and most of the inhabitants' gardens. A good example is Juriaen Teunissen's house, a fragment of which was uncovered during archaeological excavations at the DEC site. After losing his first house in the 1648 flood, Teunissen appears to have rebuilt on the same parcel but farther back from the river. He received the patent for this property in October 1653 and was listed as a glazier. A year later he was in court because of a fight in his tavern. Like many of his fellow Beverwijck neighbors, Teunissen clearly had more than one thing going. By the late 1650s, however, he had sold the property and moved on. Although only a corner of the structure survived, the archaeologists also found a large deposit of window glass and scrap, more than 100 pounds, strong evidence that they were on Teunissen's lot.[23]

FIGURE 5.12

*An 1807 drawing
of the Jacob de
Hinse house,
Beverwijck,
built ca. 1658.*

*Drawing by Ellen Chase,
after Budka 1965,
figure 66.*

Teunissen's combination of house, tavern and workshop illustrates how complex mid 17th-century sites can be. It also demonstrates the changing nature of the town's identity and how it was defined. Although on a Beverwijck lot and within Stuyvesant's boundary markers, Teunissen's property was well outside the area that would be palisaded. Perhaps Teunissen chose this peripheral location on purpose, a spot where he could do business with less regulation and fewer noisy neighbors. We don't know. What does seem clear is that after 1659, the stockade removed such ambiguity, defining the community physically and sharpening the town's sense of identity as separate from the fort where it had originated.[24]

As Beverwijck grew and changed, so did the houses within the town. Until the mid-1650s, nearly all the buildings built by the Dutch were modest frame structures without brick or stone foundations. The problem was that these wooden houses tended to "wear out in a few years," a fact that archaeological investigation has confirmed. After 1655, this began to change

as the new houses built in Beverwijck were, literally, town houses. Venema estimates that there were roughly 120 houses in Beverwijck by 1657. These were closely spaced, one-and-a-half or two-story houses with their gable end right on the street. Another indication of more permanent construction was the preference for stone or brick-lined cellars instead of wood-lined ones.[25]

Town houses also meant a shift toward brick construction and away from wood. In part this was a safety issue. Wooden houses were a significant fire hazard and as the town grew, local ordinances required tile instead of thatched roofs and brick chimneys rather than wooden ones.[26] The preference for brick was as much a matter of style as of safety and durability. In the Republic, successful townspeople lived in brick houses, and as Beverwijck prospered, local residents made the same choice. Brick, previously an expensive import, also became more affordable as local brickyards began to operate during the 1650s.

Throughout the 1650s, carpenters, masons, glaziers and blacksmiths created the fabric of the new town. These buildings housed not only Beverwijck's residents but their workshops and offices as well as the bakeries, breweries and taverns that served the community. The historical documents tell us a great deal about this side of life in Beverwijck. Archaeology, unfortunately, has yet to contribute very much. Although there have been several opportunities to investigate sites within the area enclosed by the 1659 palisade, little excavation has occurred and few reports have been published. See Site Profile 5.

Beverwijck was not just institutions and houses. Like all towns, it also contained roads, burial grounds and garbage. Here archaeology provides us with a little more information. Roads are an example. Unlike New Amsterdam where some of the streets were paved, there is no record of what Beverwijck's roads were like. However, early in 1973, Paul Huey noticed the

FIGURE 5.13
A section of mid 17th-century corduroy road preserved beneath Broadway.
Courtesy Paul Huey and OPRHP. Photograph by Joe McEvoy.

remains of a corduroy road in a utility trench nearly four feet beneath the surface of Broadway, often referred to as "the street" during the 17th-century. This road surface was composed of small pine branches and logs from 1.5" to 8" in diameter. Mid 17th-century artifacts such as pieces of brick, pipe fragments and a glass bead were found above and among these logs.[27] This style of road building was often used in marshy areas to keep wagons and carts from getting bogged down.

A very different kind of site was discovered in June 1986 when human remains were found off Beaver Street at the location of a proposed parking garage. Documentary research indicated that this was the probable site of the burial ground associated with the nearby "blockhouse church." Initial field testing by Hartgen Archaeological Associates, Inc., showed that a portion of the cemetery remained intact. After considerable political wrangling with the city, additional excavations were done. These revealed the remains of twenty-eight individuals, most of whom had been buried in wedge-shaped wooden coffins with gabled lids. Although the investigators suggested that this cemetery was used between 1677 and 1710, it seems likely that the Beaver Street burial ground did date from the Beverwijck period.[28]

As the town grew, so did the waste it produced. Unlike today, there was no system for trash removal. Each household was responsible

for disposing of its own refuse. Generally, this meant that trash went about as far away as it could be thrown, or was used to fill in nearby low areas or ditches. One such area has been reported at the DASNY site, a mid 17th-century drainage ditch that had been filled with trash, but no details are available.[29]

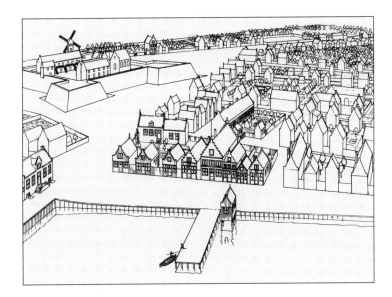

FIGURE 5.14
Below: A view of New Amsterdam in 1664. Schematic drawing by Paul Hendrikse based on the Castillo Plan.
Courtesy of the Municipal Archives, Amsterdam.

By 1664, Beverwijck was a large, prosperous and ethnically diverse Dutch town, very much like New Amsterdam in size and appearance. In fact, the two communities were quite similar. Both were densely settled towns of about 1,200 people. With their orderly streets, rows of townhouses and fortifications, they probably looked very much alike.[30]

147

SITE PROFILE 5   Archaeology in Beverwijck: Lost Opportunities

Over the past twenty years, new construction has substantially changed the look of downtown Albany. As these buildings have gone up, they have also gone deeper down, destroying whatever evidence of older occupations was present. This period of urban growth could have been the ideal time to learn more about Beverwijck through careful archaeological study. Instead, it has largely been a story of opportunities lost. Four projects, all within the bounds of the original Beverwijck stockade, tell the tale.

KeyCorp. In 1985, Hartgen Archaeological Associates, Inc., examined an area off Norton Street where a new bank was planned. Initial testing indicated that little had survived in the lots behind the existing buildings.[31] However, during construction, an interested amateur noticed that at least one 17th-century cellar had survived beneath the 19th-century buildings. While the developer allowed a brief period for Hartgen to salvage a portion of the site, most of the KeyCorp site was lost. The lesson from KeyCorp was clear – important sites do survive in the downtown area, but to find them, testing had to be thorough and deep.

532-554 Broadway. In 1988, Collamer Archaeological Associates, Inc., conducted initial field testing of this parcel. No archaeological investigation had been done previously in this portion of the original Beverwijck settlement. Based on four trenches, Collamer determined that no undisturbed deposits were present. No additional work was recommended.[32]

102-110 State Street. In 1987, Phase 1 testing of this parcel by Hartgen revealed the presence of intact 17th-century levels and features. Additional investigation was recommended. The Phase 2 contract was awarded to Collamer, who reported that no 17th-century deposits were located. In 1997, Hartgen had a second opportunity to test this parcel. Here they found intact deposits dating from the 18th and 19th centuries; however, the areas near Howard Street that had contained the 17th-century deposits had been removed.[33]

DASNY. In 1996, Hartgen tested the large parcel on the south side of Broadway where the new Dormitory Authority headquarters was to be built. Initial trenching across the site by Hartgen indicated that 17th-century levels and features were present in several areas as well as deposits from later periods. Additional testing by Hartgen documented this potential further and recommended additional work. DASNY's reluctance to comply resulted in a lawsuit filed by the New York Archaeological Council (NYAC) against DASNY for noncompliance with the state's environmental laws. A court-ordered settlement did result in additional investigation, which was done by Collamer Archaeological Associates, Inc. Although fieldwork was completed in early 1997, other archaeologists were not allowed to view the excavation or to examine the artifacts recovered. As of June 2006, a report on this project has yet to be submitted to the institution that curates the collection.[34]

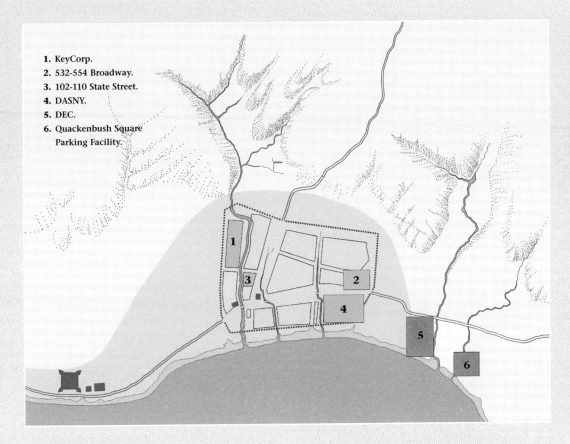

1. KeyCorp.
2. 532-554 Broadway.
3. 102-110 State Street.
4. DASNY.
5. DEC.
6. Quackenbush Square
   Parking Facility.

FIGURE 5.15
Development parcels in relationship to Beverwijck.
Map by Ellen Chase and Booth Simpson.

We are all the losers when important sites like DASNY are destroyed without proper recording. Medium-size cities, like Albany, are in trouble across this country and need every asset they have to maintain a strong economy and a healthy self-image. Albany is particularly fortunate to have such a rich cultural heritage but, as these incidents demonstrate, it is a resource that all too often has been squandered.

Since the DASNY debacle, the situation appears to have improved. Archaeological investigations conducted elsewhere in Albany, notably at the DEC headquarters and the Quackenbush Square Parking Facility, have demonstrated, once again, that important

sites do survive even in densely built areas. Background research has identified the most significant areas within Beverwijck where sites are likely. Recently, the City of Albany has strengthened its preservation ordinances, designating certain areas as "archaeologically sensitive" and adding two archaeologists to the Historic Resources Commission.

However, the real test will come the next time investigation of a potential site conflicts with a developer's plans. Then we will see whether the city's decision makers view the past as an asset or a liability.

Outside the Town – Colonie, Rensselaerswijck and beyond. North of the town's boundary marker was Rensselaerswijck or Colonie as it was increasingly known. Here people were still under the jurisdiction of the patroonship instead of the Company, although that distinction meant less than it had ten years earlier. In addition to a scatter of houses and

FIGURE 5.16
The Pieter Bronck house, Coxsackie, ca. 1663.

taverns, this is where the region's industrial sites – mills, tanneries and brickyards – were increasingly located.

Recent archaeological work near Quackenbush Square has provided a glimpse of how dynamic life was at the edge of Beverwijck during the 1650s. A portion of the excavation focused on a house site with a complex history. Within a fairly short space of time, a typical Dutch frame house was built, lived in, then demolished and the remnants burned. The flood of 1654 appears to have inundated the site shortly afterwards; however, the house was

then rebuilt with a different orientation, and reoccupied. The nearby brickyard is key to understanding this site. While determining who lived here is as complex as the archaeology, it appears that this was the house of Johan de Hulter, a brick maker, and his wife Johanna who arrived in 1653. After her husband's death, Johanna sold the house to Arent van Curler in November 1657 although another brick maker, Pieter Bont Quackenbos, and his family lived there.[35] How long the family stayed in this house is not clear, but their long-term residence in this location is reflected in the area's present-day name – Quackenbush Square.

Elsewhere in the Colonie, individual farms still dominated the landscape, although mills and small settlements had begun to spread along the Hudson by 1664. These ranged from the Wynantskill to Claverack (present-day Hudson) on the east side, and from Half Moon (present-day Waterford) to Catskill Creek on the west side. Although many farmers continued to dabble in trading and other enterprises, farming itself was a profitable business during this period. There was a strong export market and two rapidly growing towns, Beverwijck and New Amsterdam, to feed.

Here too, there was a discernable shift toward more permanent construction. Even more striking was the development of new architectural styles and material preferences, ones quite different from those in the Republic. A good example is the Pieter Bronck house in Coxsackie, probably the oldest standing house in the Capital region. Built around 1663, this small, two-and-a-half-story structure was typically Dutch in terms of its plan and details – one room per floor, a steeply pitched roof and small casement windows with arched lintels. What makes the Bronck house so unusual is its fieldstone walls. Stone construction was virtually unknown on farms in the Republic where building stone had to be imported and only the very wealthy could afford it. In the mid–Hudson Valley, the situation was completely different. Good quality stone was readily available and easy to build with. In a harsh and uncertain environment, stone construction also made good sense, even if there was no precedent for it back home.[36]

The Flatts farm continued to flourish during the 1650s. While it was still the Patroon's farm, and probably "the best" one in Rensselaerswijck, it looked and functioned more like a small village. In addition to the *hallehuis* and the house built for farm hands in 1642, there were probably several other buildings. These would have included a horse barn, a forge and a bake house as well as the other facilities needed to support Van Curler's family and the twenty to thirty laborers and servants who worked there.

This was also the period when Van Curler was most successful in the fur trade, at least until 1658. While the archaeological work done at the Flatts does not tell us much about how the overall farm changed during these years, it does reveal more about the farmhouse (*hallehuis*) and the people who lived there. Cellar #2 in particular contained a great deal of refuse as well as a level of demolition debris. While the former tells us about daily life at the Flatts farm, the latter gives us an indication of what the building may have looked like.

As discussed in Chapter 4, Van Curler and his wife made substantial changes in the farmhouse after returning from the Republic in 1648. Building-related artifacts from the two cellars provide evidence for the kinds of improvements that were made. The presence of brick, some with plaster and even white-wash, suggests the addition of an interior firewall and chimney. Pantile fragments indicate that, on a portion of the roof probably around the chimney, tiles had replaced thatch. On the interior, the recovery of many tin-glazed wall tiles,[37] as well as plaster fragments and a piece of cast iron fireback, suggests a typical Dutch open hearth.[38] Lead-glazed tiles may have formed the hearth or covered a portion of the floor. Other improvements

probably included casement windows with leaded glass panes, shutters and interior partitions. All in all, the Flatts farmhouse was a comfortable and well-appointed residence during the years Van Curler lived there.

While the Flatts farm prospered, Van Curler's interests moved on. By 1657 he was wealthy enough to buy property of his own and began to purchase houses in Beverwijck. By 1659 it appears that Van Curler had left the Flatts behind in order to pursue his plans for a new settlement on the Great Flats (*Groote Vlackte*) west of Beverwijck on the Mohawk River.

Farms also began to play another role during this period – providing a country home for wealthy merchants who did not want the clutter and inconvenience of town life. Volckert Jansz Douw was just such a man. In 1653, Douw and two associates leased one of the Papscanee farms several miles southeast of Beverwijck. Five years later, they purchased the farm along with additional land bought from the Mahicans. At some point during this period, perhaps as early as 1653, Douw may have made Papscanee his primary residence.[39] At present, not enough is known about the Van Buren site to determine who lived there. However, there are some intriguing hints that suggest it may have been Douw. The location was perfect for someone involved in the wampum trade, and many of the artifacts recovered from the site indicate that trade was an important activity. Of all the Rensselaerswijck farms, only the Flatts has more evidence of trade than Van Buren.[40]

Branching Out. Besides farmsteads, another kind of growth took place – the establishment of new communities. The first movement out of Beverwijck occurred in June 1653 when a small group of families set up farms along Esopus Creek. Several of these were Rensselaerswijck people anxious to have land of their own. Other families were recent immigrants from Europe also attracted by the area's excellent soil.

FIGURE 5.17

Above: A typical mid 17th-century Dutch hearth with tin glazed wall tiles and a cast iron Hollandia fireback.

Courtesy of Jan Baart.

FIGURE 5.18

Tin glazed wall tiles from cellar #2, the Flatts farm.

a. A vase of flowers (bloemvaas) with oxhead corners.

b. A goat with Wan-Li corners.

c. A small dog(?) with oxhead corners.

Courtesy of Bobby Brustle. Photo by Joe McEvoy.

cm

Unlike the situation in Beverwijck, there were problems from the beginning between the settlers and the local Esopus, a Delaware-Munsee people related to the Mahicans. Not all the Esopus agreed about selling their land and many resented the high-handed treatment they often received from the newcomers. A brisk trade in liquor quickly aggravated these grievances. Like the Mohawks, the Esopus sachems begged the Dutch "not to sell any more brandy" since it caused internal problems they could not control.[41] However, the Dutch could not control the situation either and, even though serious troublemakers like Hans Vos were prosecuted and fined, the trade in liquor continued and the tensions grew.[42]

As the situation deteriorated, Stuyvesant became increasingly concerned about the settlers' safety. In May 1658, he decided that the farms were too scattered and pressured the settlers to relocate into a centralized community that could be protected by a palisade. This stockade, completed in June, may have been very similar to the one built around Beverwijck later that year. Archaeological investigations along Clinton Street in 1970 exposed a portion of this palisade. Built along the edge of a steep embankment, it was composed of a double row of posts ranging from 8" to 12" in diameter. It was built none too soon. That September, a group of Dutch soldiers assaulted some drunken Indians outside the town, killing several of them. The outraged Esopus attacked the next day, besieging the community for several weeks. As the fall and winter wore on, an uneasy truce prevailed and by the following summer a peace treaty was signed. However, none of the underlying issues had been resolved.[43]

The Dutch quickly turned their attention to rebuilding. In the spring of 1661, Stuyvesant visited Esopus again, distributing more parcels of land and directing the expansion of the stockade. A section of this new palisade was uncovered in 2001 during excavations by Joe

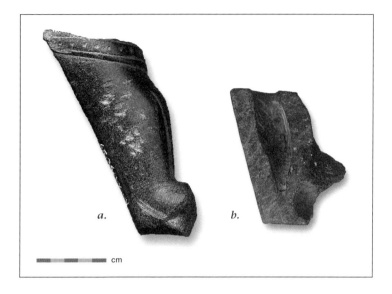

a.

b.

cm

Diamond beneath the Matthew Persen house.[44] Stuyvesant also sought to strengthen the community in another way. As director-general, he had the authority to create new towns, as he had done with Beverwijck. In May 1661, he exercised that authority again, establishing a local government "in conformity with the customs of the city of Amsterdam in Holland." The new village, which Stuyesant re-named *Wiltwijck* (or the Indian District), had its own magistrates, sheriff (*schout*) and court.[45] The hope was that this new village, the first one to be established between Beverwijck and New Amsterdam, would help stabilize the region.

The transformation of Esopus into Wiltwijck may have made the Dutch feel better, but it did little to ease Native concerns. Neither did the building of another settlement, New Village (*Nieuw Dorp*), farther up Esopus Creek the following year. More settlers meant more problems and as Wiltwijck's new sheriff confided to Stuyvesant in September 1662, "if no precautions are taken, we are in great danger of drawing upon us a new war." His prediction was all too accurate. On June 7, 1663, a large group of Esopus attacked New Dorp burning the settlement to the ground. They then proceeded to Wiltwijck where many of the town's

FIGURE 5.19

Two mid-17th-century stone pipes from Dutch domestic sites.

a. A "Narragansett-style" pipe bowl, the Van Buren site.

b. A pipe broken during the process of drilling, the Flatts farm.

Courtesy of Paul Huey and OPRHP. Photo by Joe McEvoy.

FIGURE 5.20

A portion of the 1658 Esopus stockade, looking northwest, Kingston, NY. Note – The oyster shells were stacked on the postmolds in order to increase their visibility; this is not the way postmolds normally look.

Courtesy of Paul Huey and OPRHP.

Photo by Paul Huey.

inhabitants were killed or taken as prisoners.[46]

The events of June 7 were also evident in Diamond's excavations – a clearly defined level of charcoal created by the burning of the town. However, unlike New Dorp, Wiltwijck was damaged but not destroyed. While hostilities were gradually replaced by negotiations, the rebuilding of the town commenced yet again. Among the new settlers was Gysbert van Imbroch, previously the surgeon at Fort Orange. The small dwelling he built between 1663 and 1664 appears to have been the first phase of what now survives as the Persen house.[47]

As the Esopus settlement became Wiltwijck in 1661, another new Dutch community also came into existence. After years of preparation, Arent van Curler was finally ready to launch his new community on the *Groote Vlachte* (the Great Flats) of the Mohawk River less

than twenty miles west of Beverwijck. His first steps were successful. He received permission from Stuyvesant to establish the settlement in June. A month later, three Mohawk sachems signed a deed transferring the piece of (previously Mahican) land known as "Schonowe" to Van Curler. By fall, a road had been built and preparations were underway to clear the land and erect buildings. However, things did not go quite as Van Curler planned, and the problem was not with the Mohawks or Mahicans, but with Stuyvesant.

Dividing the land into individual lots was an essential step and, in April 1662, Van Curler requested that Stuyvesant send the provincial surveyor so that the land could be "surveyed and allotted." When the director-general's reply came a year later, it was not the one Van Curler had expected. Stuyvesant would send the surveyor, but only after the residents promised, in writing, not to engage in the fur trade. Taken aback by this response, Van Curler immediately wrote to Stuyvesant on behalf of all the proprietors pointing out that "the land was bought out of our own purse" and settled at great expense. If the settlers were not given a fair chance to make a living, then "all their work would be in vain and they would be totally ruined." Stuyvesant was unmoved, either by Van Curler's requests or subsequent petitions from the proprietors. The prohibition against trading stayed in effect and instead of becoming a major commercial town (as Van Curler had hoped), Schenectady remained a small, unpalisaded farm community for several more decades.[48] To date, no archaeological evidence from this early period of Schenectady's history has been reported, although the potential is certainly there.

By 1664, the Dutch had developed two distinctly different ways of dealing with their Native neighbors. One differed little from the approach used by the neighboring English colonies. Basically, Native people and their wishes were ignored or bullied out of the way while the Europeans took what they wanted. This was the approach Willem Kieft had used in the lower Hudson Valley, with disastrous effect, and the one that brought such misery to the Esopus valley fifteen years later. There was a second, very different strategy, the one that reflected the procedural and pragmatic side of Dutch culture, and that served as the foundation for Dutch settlements in Rensselaerswijck. This was the approach that Van Curler perfected, one that focused on finding some level of mutual self-interest, of common ground. The results weren't always neat or painless but, over time, problems got solved legally and diplomatically, instead of by force. By 1660, a new kind of political arrangement had come into existence between the Dutch and the Mohawks – a covenant designed to maintain "the peace and well-being of this country." This successful model for political alliance

based on mutual self-interest and reciprocal obligations would long outlive the people who created it.

Mahican Sites. As Beverwijck grew and smaller Dutch settlements began to fill in the landscape, the Mahicans found themselves increasingly squeezed out of the center of their territory. This process had started decades earlier when the land for Rensselaerswijck was sold to the patroon's agents. But since the newcomers had been slow to occupy their new domain, the impact of these sales was not immediately apparent. By the 1650s, however, Dutch settlement had spread broadly throughout the Colonie making it more difficult for Mahican people to continue to use the lands they had sold. In addition, there were many potential settlers and speculators anxious to buy land outside the boundaries of Rensselaerswijck. This pressure (or opportunity) resulted in a series of new sales of Mahican land, especially south of Beverwijck and the Colonie, throughout the 1650s and 1660s.[49]

A significant result of these sales was the splitting of Mahican people into two distinct groups. One was centered south of the Dutch settlements in what is now Greene and Columbia counties. This traditional Mahican core area extended from Little Nutten Hook to "Klaver rack" (Hudson) on the east side of the Hudson River, and from Coxsackie to "Katskil" on the west. By the late 1650s, a distinction was being drawn between Mahican and Katskil people, at least by the Mohawks. After 1660, this usage appears to become widespread. The refocusing of Mahican settlement did not mean a withdrawal from regional events. To the contrary, the Mahicans remained deeply involved in affairs unfolding around them. For example, under the leadership of Aepjen, the Katskils often tried to mediate the troubles between the Dutch and the Esopus. The Katskils also appear to have been on better terms with the neighboring Mohawks, and even allied with them on occasion. In August

1663, Arent van Curler and Jeremias van Rensselaer meet with representatives of the Mohawks and Katskils to ensure that the latter "remain in our league… as brothers."[50]

In contrast, the second group, usually referred to as Mahicans or the Loups (Wolves), was strongly allied in a different direction – with the western Abenaki and other New England Algonquian tribes who were closely linked with the French. This group was located north of the Dutch settlements in the traditional Mahican core area that extended along the Hudson River from Lansingburgh north to Schaghticoke on the east side and from Cohoes to Fish Creek (present day Schuylerville) on the west (*See Figure 5.21*). This location not only kept many of the best fishing areas along the Hudson under Mahican control, it also allowed them to challenge the Mohawks when they traveled north to the St. Lawrence via Lake George and Lake Champlain. Unlike the Katskils, the old anti-Mohawk antagonisms still burned bright among the Loups. Not only were previous humiliations remembered, but the ongoing sale of "conquered" Mahican land by Mohawk entrepreneurs (such as the Schenectady and Half Moon tracts) kept the fires of vengeance fully fueled.[51]

Though less visible than the Mohawks in the historical documents of the period, the picture of the Mahicans that emerges during the 1660s is not one of a cowed or defeated people. To the contrary, it was often the Mahicans who took the initiative and when hostilities did break out, the Mahicans usually gave as good as they got, or better. By the spring of 1664, Lalement reported that "the Mahicans render the roads very dangerous" and occasionally even attacked the Mohawks within sight of their own villages. But these could hardly be considered victories since "there were great losses on both sides."[52] By the time the English took control of New Netherland, Mahican – Mohawk hostilities remained stuck in a deadly stalemate.

Mahican sites, always small and elusive, are especially difficult to see during this turbulent period. However, several are known and they confirm the patterns indicated by the documentary record. Five sites have been reported from Greene and Columbia counties. Most are small, multi-component sites – fishing camps or rock shelters – that have produced artifacts diagnostic of this period. The site in Leeds may represent a larger village, and fragments of other large sites may still lie buried beneath Catskill and Hudson.[53] To the north, two large sites are known with components from this period, one in Lansingburgh, the other at Winney's Rift. Here too it is likely that there are more Mahican sites to be found.

By 1664, two distinct groups of Mahican people existed, each with its own allies and political strategy. The Katskils chose to stay with the Dutch, and therefore the Mohawks, while the Loups remained with their Algonquian kin and the French. For each, this also meant some degree of withdrawal from traditional lands. But whether they moved south, north or even farther east, another piece of the emerging regional pattern was set. Although many families and individuals would stay in the Hudson Valley for years to come, the Mahicans as a people would ultimately choose to survive by leaving their valley behind.

Mohawk Sites. For the Mohawks, the choices were very different. After decades of warfare with their Native neighbors, there was no other place for them to go. They had Native enemies to the north, east and south, and their Confederacy brethren on the lands directly west. There just was no room to move. So, even though much of their traditional territory had been "hunted bare"[54] they chose to hunker down in their own beloved valley and find a way to make things work.

Meanwhile, things were falling apart. At one time or another during this period, the Mohawks were at war with virtually everyone – the French and their Native allies, the Mahicans, the Susquehannocks, even (briefly) their Onondaga brothers. And this was in addition to the ongoing wars that took Mohawk warriors into the Great Lakes region, the Ohio Valley and beyond. It was an unsustainable situation. By 1660, the Mohawks had lost and replaced such a large percentage of their population that they were, literally, a different people. As Lalement observed in the Relation of 1660, they were "for the most part, only aggregations of the different tribes they have conquered." Foreigners were now "the largest and best part" of the Mohawks.[55]

The internal results of such change were devastating. As strangers made up more of the population, it became increasingly difficult to maintain traditional ways or even remember what the traditions were. Since their villages were the closest to Dutch settlements, the Mohawks also suffered more from the exposure to alcohol, new diseases and other, less pleasant aspects of cross-cultural contact. Christianity, which the Mohawks fiercely resisted because it came with the French, also made significant inroads during this period, in large part because many Christian Huron (previously converted by the Jesuits) were now adopted Mohawks. It is not surprising that under the pressure of all these forces, Mohawk culture began to fragment and splinter into factions.

By the early 1660s, the Mohawks were in serious trouble. Early in the decade, Jesuit analysts estimated that the Mohawks could still field five hundred warriors. A year later, that number had dropped by more than half to "two hundred men, all told, in the country." As Lalement observed, "one would never believe how few they are." While it is more difficult to estimate changes in the overall size of the Mohawk population, it clearly dropped precipitously during this period as well. By the spring of 1664, the Mohawks were "no longer in a condition to make war" and were "within two finger-breadths of total destruction."[56]

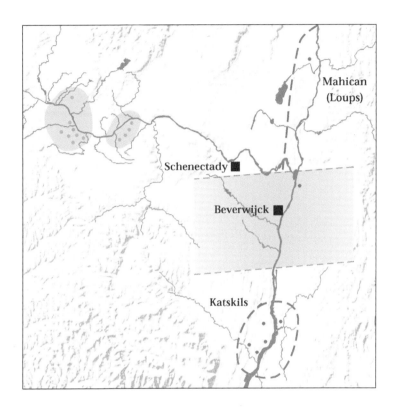

As a result of these changes, the once mighty Mohawks found themselves not only on the defensive but in the new and uncomfortable position of supplicant. In June 1657, three sachems from the three Mohawk castles requested to speak to the Court of Fort Orange and asked the Dutch help them repair their stockades, give them each a cannon and protect their women and children if attacked. Two years later, the same request was made again. The Mohawks certainly needed the help. Their "castles" were in terrible condition. As Lalement noted, their villages "have no palisades, except here and there some stakes as large as a man's leg, through which one could easily pass."[57] This was not a good state of affairs when surrounded by enemies and it is unclear from the documents to what degree the Dutch responded.

FIGURE 5.21
Mahican and Mohawk sites, 1652 to 1664.

SITE PROFILE 6

The Jackson–Everson Site

FIGURE 5.22

*a. A Huron-style
ceramic vessel
from the Jackson-
Everson site.*
Courtesy of Wayne Lenig.
Drawing by Ellen Chase.

*b. A reconstructed
wooden pipe with
pewter inlays.
While a similar
pewter mouthpiece
was found at
Jackson-Everson
by Don Rumrill,
this reconstruction
is based on a
complete example
from the Seneca
Rochester Junction
site.*
Courtesy of George
Hamell. Drawing by
Gene MacKay.

By the 1660s, Mohawk sites looked very different than they had at the beginning of the 17th-century. The Jackson-Everson site is a good example. This small, unpalisaded village is located on an upper terrace along the north side of the Mohawk River. Information on this site, which dates between ca. 1660 and the mid-1670s, comes from excavations done by Don Lenig during the 1930s and the SUNY Albany field school conducted by Dean Snow and Robert Kuhn in 1983.[58]

In terms of European influence, Jackson-Everson is much like Freeman and the other large Mohawk sites of the period. Not only are European ceramics and utensils common on the site; the presence of pig and cow bones indicate the profound level of change occurring within Mohawk culture. The presence of elaborate lead castings, religious rings and other French-related trade materials also place this site securely within the 1660 to 1670s period.

Still, this site has some unusual traits. In addition to the European artifacts, it contains a surprisingly high proportion of Native-made artifacts such as stone and antler tools as well as ceramic pottery. In this regard, Jackson-Everson looks more like a Mohawk site of thirty years earlier. However, the reason for all these old-fashioned artifacts is that this was a village of captives. The vast majority of pottery is Huron, not Mohawk. Eighty percent of the pottery from Jackson-Everson has classic Huron traits

a.

⬛⬛⬛⬜⬜⬛⬛⬛ cm

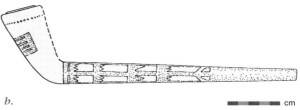

b.

⬛⬛⬛⬜⬜⬛⬛⬛ cm

including low collars with typical Huron motifs, turret castellations and carinated shoulders (*See Figure 5.22a*). Not surprisingly, few firearms have been found on this site.

The Jackson-Everson site provides archaeological confirmation for statements made by French Jesuits that, by 1660, adoptees were the majority in some Mohawk villages, outnumbering their captors.

Archaeological evidence helps to fill in the picture. Several Mohawk sites are known that date from the 1652 to 1664 period. Based on diagnostic artifacts such as glass beads and smoking pipes, these fall into two groups – sites that were occupied between ca. 1652 and 1658, and those that date between ca. 1658 and 1666.[59] Here again, since few large-scale excavations have been done, only limited information is available. Like the sites of the 1640s, most of the Mohawk sites of this period are on the south side of the Mohawk River. Some, like Printup, Fiske and Freeman, are fairly large, two to three acres in extent, and set in the traditional Mohawk locations – high, defensible hilltops or plateaus set back from the river. Some of the other sites are small, an acre or less, and located in more diverse settings. Most are simply not well-enough known to estimate their size. While some of these sites were palisaded, excavations at the Freeman site suggest that the Dutch did respond to Mohawk requests for help in strengthening their defenses. Here members of the Van Epps-Hartley Chapter found evidence of a more European-influenced fortification with straighter palisade walls and a corner bastion.[60]

By 1664 the Mohawks had decided how they would deal with their not-so-new and now permanently established neighbors. Unlike the Esopus, who chose resistance, or the Mahicans, who either elected to leave or learned to become invisible, the Mohawks chose to tough it out. This made good sense since they had a treaty-based relationship with the Dutch, one that had been in operation for more than fifteen years. This meant that they could demand equal treatment and complain when the Dutch called them "dogs and rascals." In Mohawk eyes, the treaty also empowered them to speak on behalf of all the region's Native people to ensure that the Dutch "do not harm to any of the Mohawk, Mahican or Katskil, but live with them as brothers."[61] For the Mohawks, it was a good arrangement, and one they were quick to renew with the English in 1664.

Comfort and Style

New Netherland was far from a failed colony when the English took over in 1664. It was prosperous, stable and stylish. With a highly profitable fur trade throughout most of the 1650s and rapidly growing population, Dutch settlement in and around Beverwijck grew in wealth as well as in size. Just as its buildings and town plan reflected an increasing sense of order and affluence, so did the possessions of its inhabitants. For some, this was a period of great wealth. This was especially true for the most successful traders and land speculators, men such as Philip Schuyler, Arent van Curler and Volckert Jansz Douw.[62] While not everyone was that rich, times were good enough that most people could afford the material goods that made life comfortable and even fashionable.

Wealth aside, the other factor that differentiated households was location, specifically whether they were in town or out in the country. As Beverwijck grew, its households took on a more urban, European character while those on the outlying farms were more likely to show a mixture of European traditions and adaptations to the local environment. Food preferences demonstrate this difference. On Beverwijck archaeological sites, such as the brick maker's house, cattle and pigs are the most common large animal food refuse while deer remains have dropped to a minority. Among birds, chickens occur more frequently than wild fowl for the first time. In addition, these bones indicate that much of this meat had been purchased as select cuts from a butcher instead of killed and dressed by the consumer. By contrast, at farm sites like the Flatts, the pattern is quite different. Here there is considerable evidence for butchering and processing. While cattle, pig, sheep and chickens are well represented, there is a much larger component of wild game, especially deer, but also bear and smaller mammals. Ducks and other wild birds as well as sturgeon are also

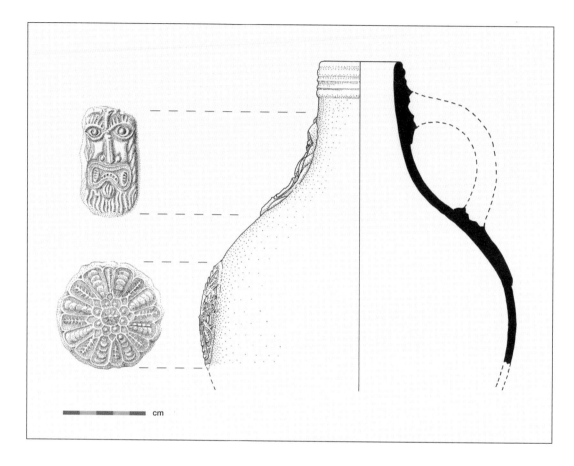

FIGURE 5.23
A German stoneware Bartmann jug, from cellar #2 at the Flatts farm.
Courtesy of Bobby Brustle. Drawing by Ellen Chase.

plentiful. Either country people had more diverse taste than their neighbors in town, or they were less picky eaters. The one exception was oysters. Whether rich or poor, in town or on the farm, it seems that everyone ate oysters.[63]

Dutch Domestic Assemblages after Midcentury. The increased emphasis on comfort and style is clearly visible in the artifacts from this period. In previous chapters, we looked at the ceramic vessels used for storing, preparing and serving food to see how they reflected the circumstances of their times. Here the ceramic evidence indicates both greater availability and affluence.

In terms of food storage, nearly every household now used German stoneware for storing liquids. Especially popular were the large, bulbous jugs, often decorated with bearded faces and medallions, known as bartmanns. After 1650, many households also began to use large, unglazed storage jars from the Iberian Peninsula, an indication of changing economic realities. Traditional Dutch lead-glazed red earthenware pots, bowls and colanders remained the standard for cooking in every household.

It is in the choice of serving and eating vessels that the evidence of wealth and taste are most apparent. Prior to 1650, most of the eating plates used by the wealthy were imported from Italy or Portugal, while Dutch-made vessels were used primarily for serving or for display. People of more moderate means used pewter or wooden plates. By 1650, however, Dutch potters were producing tin-glazed wares in quantity as well as new styles.

By 1660, most eating plates in the Republic were of Dutch faience, or delft as it was increasingly known. With greater availability and the money to purchase them, it was not long before these new delftware plates appeared on tables of prosperous merchants in New Netherland as well. Several examples of these stylish plates were recovered from the Van Doesburgh house.[64]

Stylish tableware included more than plates. In fact, many of the dishes that appeared on tables during this period were as much for show as for use. These included large "fruit bowls" with their blue-on-white floral motifs as well as all-white vessels such as jugs for serving wine, porringers and elaborate lobed dishes. These vessels occur not only in wealthy households such as Van Curler's, but in those of successful merchants and tradesmen like Van Doesburgh.[65]

Fashionable as these tin-glazed wares were, it was the porcelain they mimicked that conferred the highest degree of status. Ever since the first captured Portuguese cargoes had been auctioned in Amsterdam early in the century, porcelain was the ultimate expression of style and prosperity. By the 1650s, there was sufficient wealth in and around Beverwijck to import and display this prized commodity. Wan-Li-style plate and tea cup fragments have been found at the Flatts while pieces of a porcelain mustard pot were recovered from the Van Doesburgh cellar.[66]

The emphasis on comfort and style is also reflected in personal possessions – the clothing, furnishings and valuables of the period. Perhaps the clearest evidence comes from estate inventories, such as the one prepared after the death of Jonas Bronck. Among the items listed were numerous books and manuscripts, elegant clothes including "a black satin suit," pewter plates, silver spoons, a gold signet ring, two mirrors, "one with an ivory frame, the other gilt" and "various pieces of porcelain."[67] Since Bronck's widow, Antonia Slachboom,

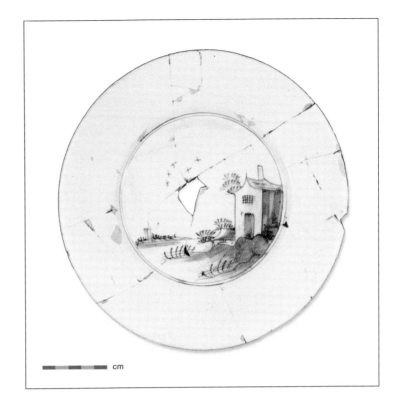

later married Arent van Curler, some of these objects may have ended up at the Flatts.

While archaeological evidence for all these fine things is rare, it confirms the basic pattern. Most sites of the period produce brass and pewter buttons as well as clothing and, occasionally, shoe buckles. Wealthier households such as the Flatts also yield fancier materials like fragments of gilt braid and the lead seals from superior quality cloth such as Haarlem linen. Some sense of period furnishings also survives on sites, usually in the form of furniture hardware, book clasps and hinges and the occasional fragment of mirror glass.

One indicator of style actually has survived better in the ground than in documents from the period. Many of the fine majolica and faience plates were designed not only for table use. Made with a small hole in the foot ring, these plates could also be hung on the wall. Sometimes, when a plate was damaged, the edges were carefully trimmed away so that

FIGURE 5.24
Delftware plate from the Van Doesburgh house, Fort Orange.
Courtesy of Paul Huey and OPRHP.
Photo by Joe McEvoy.

161

Cultural Re-mixing and Global Style

By the 1650s, the global nature of Dutch commerce was reflected in a series of new styles that combined shapes and motifs from cultures around the world. Edward Bird's funnel bowl pipes, an adaptation of a Native American form, is one example. Dutch wall tiles with their mix of Renaissance, Iberian, Chinese and typically Dutch motifs are another. However, nowhere is the complexity and interactive nature of this mixing better illustrated than in ceramics.

With the collapse of the Chinese porcelain trade in the 1640s, Dutch potters quickly adjusted their output to meet the demand. The result was not only greater production. A new style emerged as potters in Delft and Haarlem experimented with the four elements that created a vessel – its shape, glaze, border motif and central motif.

Fragments of two large majolica bowls recovered from cellar #2 at the Flatts are a good example. Known as "fruit bowls," these vessels were made for show more than for use. While the shape was Italian, the borders were decorated in a new, more open style known as "flower work." With its repeating pattern of a single flower and leaves, this design was a de-constructed version of traditional Chinese porcelain motifs. At the center, these bowls had a vase of flowers, a common Dutch motif. The Flatts examples were probably made by Willem Jansz Verstraeten, a Haarlem potter who worked between 1625 and 1650. Fragments of his majolica plates as well as faience examples made by his son Gerrit were also found in cellar #2. Identical plates were included in the cargo of the Monte Cristi wreck, located on the north side of the Dominican Republic and recently excavated by Jerome Hall. This unidentified vessel, which sank between 1652 and 1656, also contained bulbous bowl pipes marked EB, and funnel bowl pipes with the abstract Tudor rose motif shown in Figure 4.34. The vessel was apparently headed for New Netherland.[68]

However, this is not the end of the story. By the late 1650s, faience plates with "flower work" motifs had been sent to Japan, where they were copied in porcelain at the shops of Arita. These porcelain versions of Dutch plates inspired by the Chinese have been found on several sites in Amsterdam. A decade or so later, when the Chinese porcelain industry was re-organized under the Manchu emperor K'ang-hsi, potters began to incorporate Dutch motifs such as tulips on the plates made for shipment back to the Republic.[69]

Although sites in New Netherland, such as the Flatts, may have been at the periphery of the Dutch commercial empire, they were still participants in what had become a global economic system.

cm

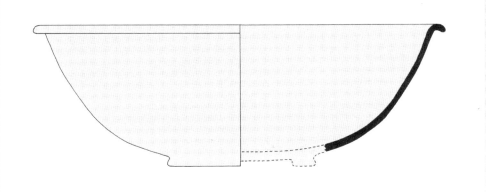

FIGURE 5.25
Plan and profile
views of a majolica
'fruit bowl' with a
flower work motif
around the rim,
from cellar #2 at
the Flatts farm.
Courtesy of Bobby Brustle.
Drawings by Ellen Chase.

cm

cm

FIGURE 5.26

Top: A complete Wan-Li style porcelain plate from Amsterdam.

Courtesy of the AHM/BMA. Photo by Wiard Krook, afdeling Archeologie.

FIGURE 5.27

Above: Fragments of a Wan-Li style porcelain plate, from cellar #1 at the Flatts.

Courtesy of Paul Huey and OPRHP. Photo by Joe McEvoy.

the central motif could still be used as a wall decoration. While not considered important enough to list in an inventory, these plate bases are often found on sites in the Republic. Huey recovered one such example at Fort Orange[70] (*See Figure 5.28*).

Archaeology is better at documenting the mundane, the commonplace objects of everyday life, than the exotic. And here too, it is easy to see the evidence of more consumer goods. In terms of recreation, smoking remained popular along with eating and drinking, as both domestic and tavern refuse clearly attest. This evidence also indicates that most Dutch smokers had a clear preference for bulbous bowl pipes. Funnel bowl pipes are found only on sites where there was a significant involvement in the fur trade.[71] Other traditional Dutch forms of entertainment continue throughout the period. Nearly every site produced brass or iron mouth harps, pipe stem whistles and clay marbles. There is also evidence of other games, such as bone dice, from the KeyCorp site.

The broader range of personal items that occur on period sites is another indication of the changing nature of Dutch communities. Articles such as eyeglasses and ointment jars indicate more elderly people in the population. Also, by the mid-1650s, Beverwijck was no longer a community primarily of men. More women and families were present and they too are evident in the material record. Most household assemblages now include domestic implements – pins, thimbles and embroidery scissors – as well as unusual items such as a pewter nursing nipple from the Flatts. Bodkins (ornamental hair pins), fancy combs and other similar items also indicate the presence of women.[72]

Many of these personal items also reflect the ongoing Dutch passion for curiosities, both local and from around the world. For example, among the objects mentioned in Bronck's inventory were "six little alabaster saucers"

164

cm

FIGURE 5.28
A majolica plate base reworked for use as a wall plaque from Fort Orange (A.FOR.1971.1) and a complete plate of the same style (AIAH 1983.5.3).
Courtesy of Paul Huey and OPRHP.
Photo by Joe McEvoy.

and "a Japanese cutlas," undoubtedly a samurai sword. While most of the combs from this period are of bone or walrus ivory, one example from the Flatts is made from elephant ivory. The comb from the Van Doesburgh house is of tortoise shell, probably from Jamaica.[73] While many of these exotic objects came through established trade networks, local items were still of considerable interest. Quartz crystals (Herkimer diamonds) continue to be found on Dutch domestic sites as do Native-made artifacts. For example, several pipe stems and a fragment of finely made bear effigy pipe were recovered from the brick maker's house.[74]

Some curiosities reached the Beverwijck area as a result of its own traders' activities. As the Flatts farm developed a reputation for fine horses, Van Curler traveled extensively, buying and selling stock. He made at least

two voyages to the West Indies, one to Barbados in 1650 and another to Antigua two years later. Among the objects recovered from cellar #2 at the Flatts were several pieces of coral and two sea shells of West Indies origin[75] (*See Figure 5.30*). Given the Dutch fascination with exotic shells, it would have been surprising if Van Curler had not collected a few specimens to take home during these trips.

Return of the Van Rensselaers

While the economy of Beverwijck and the surrounding region began to diversify during this period, it was still driven primarily by the fur trade, at least up through 1658. True, the war with England disrupted the shipment of merchandise, and the increased competition from nearby French and English colonies cut into profits. Even so, these were lucrative years.

Finding Individuals in the Archaeological Record

As people acquired more personal property, there was a greater tendency to mark their possessions. This gives us the unusual opportunity to see individuals in the archaeological record, people who otherwise would be invisible. These marked artifacts also help us identify specific archaeological sites by linking them with the historical records. Here are three examples.

In early 1657, Jeremias van Rensselaer received a case of "duffels from Campen" along with a letter from his mother updating him on family matters. The case in which they were shipped was marked JVR. During excavations in the Staats-Van Twiller house cellar, Huey uncovered two lead seals very close together. One was a large CAMPEN cloth seal, the other a small personal seal marked JvR[76] (See Figure 5.29a and b). These seals provide good evidence that Jeremias used the house to store trade merchandise after his uncle returned to the Republic.

Glass case bottles and the pewter screw caps used to seal them are common artifacts on mid 17th-century Dutch sites. More than a dozen pewter caps were found in the two cellars at the Flatts. Several of these had marks scratched on them. Often referred to as "house marks," these informal tallies served to record use or indicate ownership. On one of these, the letters AVC had been quickly incised, confirming that this was the household of Arent van Curler (See Figure 5.29c and d.).

a. ▬▬▬▬▬▬▬ cm

b. ▬▬▬▬▬▬ cm

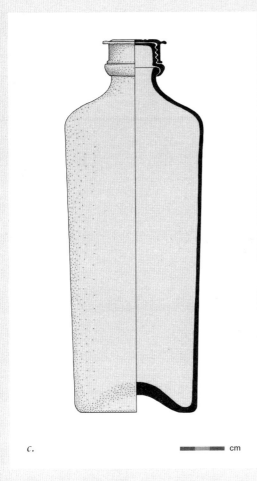

e.

During the 1960s, excavators found an unusual object in the middens of the Oneida Quarry site – a silver alloy bodkin marked with the name "Zarra * Rulofsen." Sara Roelofs was one of three daughters born to Roelof and Anneke Jansz and she lived in Rensselaerswijck as a child. A skilled translator, she lived most of her adult life in Manhattan, although she maintained close ties with family and friends in Beverwijck.[77] How such a personal item ended up on a mid 17th-century Oneida site is a mystery (*See Figure 5.29e*).

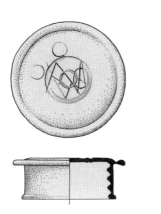

c.   ▬▬▬▬ cm

FIGURE 5.29

A CAMPEN cloth seal (a.) and a personal seal marked 'JvR' (b.) found together in the cellar of the Staats-Van Twiller house, Fort Orange.
Courtesy of Paul Huey and OPRHP.
Photo by Joe McEvoy.

A profile view of a glass case bottle with a pewter screw top (c.) and a plan view of the top (d.) from from cellar #2, the Flatts farm. Note the monogram 'AVC' scratched on the top.
Courtesy of Bobby Brustle.
Drawings by Ellen Chase.

A silver bodkin engraved with the name 'Zarra Rulofsen' (e.) from the Oneida Quarry site.
Courtesy of A. Gregory Sorweide.

d.   ▬▬▬▬ cm

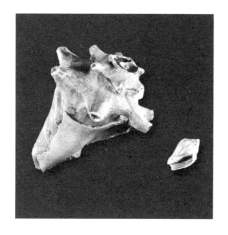

FIGURE 5.30

Above: Two West Indies seashells from celler #2, the Flatts farm.

a. A Fighting Stromb (Strombus pugilis).

b. A small Music Volute (Voluta musica).

Courtesy of Bobby Brustle. Photo by Joe McEvoy.

FIGURE 5.31

Above right: Still Life with flagon, Pieter Claesz, 1640, William Ray Adams Memorial collection 47.2.

Courtesy of the Indianapolis Museum of Art.

The 1650s also saw the return of the Van Rensselaers. After Kiliaen's death, the patroonship had gone to Johannes, the eldest son and half brother of Jan Baptiste and Jeremias. Since the new patroon cared little about New Netherland, it was up to the younger brothers to salvage what was left of the family's inheritance.[78] In this, the brothers received significant help from their uncle, Arent van Curler. No one knew the trade better and Van Curler had his own personal reasons to assist the family that had supported him for many years. With Van Curler's knowledge of the market plus the family's resources and connections in the Republic, the Van Rensselaers again became a major economic and social force within the Colonie.

But even in good years, the trade was a risky business. A trader had to have stock, and that meant borrowing against anticipated profits. For example, in August 1652, Van Curler signed a promissory note for more than 2,000 guilders "for merchandise received to my satis-

faction" to be repaid with the next year's beaver. As a result, the trade tended to run in boom-or-bust cycles – one either made great profits or went into an equivalent degree of debt.[79] The possibility that cargoes could be lost through shipwreck or capture only made the risks greater.

Smart traders cushioned themselves against such losses in two ways. They invested their money in land, ships or other tangible assets, and they diversified. The Van Rensselaers did both. While they continued to import goods for the "Indian trade," cargoes also contained a large component of clothing, supplies and luxury items intended for Dutch residents. In 1658 when Jan Baptiste returned to Amsterdam, leaving his brother Jeremias as director of the Colonie, he continued to channel the family's fortune into the shipping and provisioning end of the trade. Between 1659 and 1664, he chartered and outfitted no less than six ships for the voyage to New Netherland.[80]

Defining Trade Assemblages between 1652 and 1664. Although the trade in general became more diverse during the 1650s, the merchandise intended for Native people did not. By 1652, the era of experimentation was over and a well-defined set of trade goods and suppliers had been established. Many of these were the commodities that Kiliaen van Rensselaer had pioneered and Arent van Curler perfected – woolens from Campen and Leiden, smoking pipes and glass beads from Amsterdam, firearms and other ironwork from Utrecht.[81]

Yet the Indian trade was hardly static. The volume of material goods available to Native people during the 1650s was vastly greater than it had been ten years earlier. Some changes in trade stock continued to occur but these reflected a fine-tuning rather than a rethinking of the inventory. Axes are an example. During the 1650s, smaller, lighter axes begin to occur on Mohawk sites along with the large ones for domestic use. It is likely that these "belt axes"

glass bead assemblages now contain a roughly even mixture of long red-and-blue tubular beads with unfinished ends as the most frequently occurring varieties. This shift in color preference is best explained by consumer demand since these beads, like the blue tubular beads of the 1640s, were basically production stock and sent over in bulk. Like the earlier varities, these beads were probably made in the Two Roses glasshouse on the Keizergracht by Claes Claesz Jaquet.[82]

Other key components of the trade assemblage during the 1650s include CAMPEN cloth seals and EB marked pipes. While both bulbous and funnel bowl varieties occur, the latter are now common for the first time. Gun parts are common on sites of this period as are a series of other consumer items. These range from domestic objects such as scissors and thimbles to pewter spoons and European ceramic vessels as well as tools and specialty items including brass mouth harps, small brass bells and pewter pipes. Indeed, it is the abundance of material

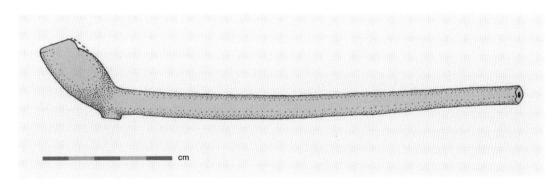

FIGURE 5.32
A complete but unused pipe from cellar #2 at the Flatts. Unmarked, unburnished and off center, this pipe was a definite 'second.'
Drawing by Ellen Chase

were intended as weapons, no surprise given the ongoing hostilities. A similar change occurs with kettles as smaller, more portable styles occur along with the standard large sizes.

Glass beads also reflect the evolving nature of the trade. Not only are they far more common on Native sites; several changes in style help us to distinguish sites of this period from those of earlier and later periods. On Mohawk sites of the 1650s, such as Printup and Fiske,

wealth that sets Native sites of this period apart from those that follow.

On sites of the 1658 to 1664 period, several changes are evident. On the Dutch side, fewer excavated sites show evidence of trade assemblages. By this time, Van Curler had left the Flatts to pursue his plans for Schenectady while Van Doesburgh and most others had moved out of Fort Orange and into Beverwijck. Equally dramatic is the decline in quantity

SELECTED SITES	DATE RANGE	HEEL MARKS			
		EB	WH	ID	*
Dutch sites					
Fort Orange:					
Component 83	c. 1640 to 1647	1			
Component 82	c. 1648 to 1657				
Component 96	c. 1651 to 1657	6			
Component 66	c. 1664	8			1
Component 71	c. 1664	3			
Brick maker's house					
Occupation I	c. 1648 to 1654	1	2		
Occupation II	c. 1654 to 1658+			1	
The Flatts farm	c. 1643 to 1660	13	8	12	1
Van Buren farm	c. 1640 to 1666	9	1	3	1
Monte Christi wreck	c. 1652 to 1656				88
Native sites					
Mohawk:					
Janie	c. 1645 to 1652	2			
Printup	c. 1652 to 1659	2	4	1	
Freeman	c. 1659 to 1666	3			
Jackson-Everson	c. 1660 to 1674	3			
Onondaga:					
Lot 18	c. 1650 to 1655	2			
Indian Castle	c. 1655 to 1663	5	2		
TOTAL		**58**	**17**	**17**	**91**

TABLE 5.1 Occurrence of marked funnel bowl pipes on Dutch and Native sites between ca. 1645 and 1665

of trade material on Mohawk sites such as Freeman and Jackson-Everson. Nearly all the same artifact classes are represented, just in smaller amounts. Another clear change occurs in glass beads. Sometime around 1658, short tubular beads with finished ends replace the long tubular beads. These new beads are predominantly red, although several striped varieties occur as well. The same size and shape as wampum, these glass beads could be strung into belts as well as onto clothing and regalia.[83] Funnel bowl pipes are now at their greatest popularity. Most are marked EB, although some WH and unmarked examples occur as well.

Lead and pewter pipes also continue to occur on Native sites throughout this period. Whoever made them, the popularity of these pipes had not diminished. In fact, a whole series of new effigy forms characterize these pipes. Here again, there is a combination of traditional Native motifs – such as herons, raptorial birds and man-bird beings – as well as whimsical styles that seem to reflect a European sensibility or sense of humor. These include a seated dog, a different style of monkey with a pipe and a generic human figure with a blanket roll.[84] Although both the Mohawks and the Mahicans were starting to cast more sophisticated objects by this time, this mixture of Native and European-inspired motifs suggests that these effigy pipes continued to be a specialty trade item made in Beverwijck.

Just as the decline in Dutch trade is evident by the reduced quantity of trade goods on Mohawk sites after 1658, so too the steady increase in French influence is clearly reflected in the artifactual record. Religious rings are common on sites of this period as are other indications of French trade – tanged iron points, iron scrapers, stepped awls and folding knife blades. Surprisingly, given the concerns of Stuyvesant and others, there is

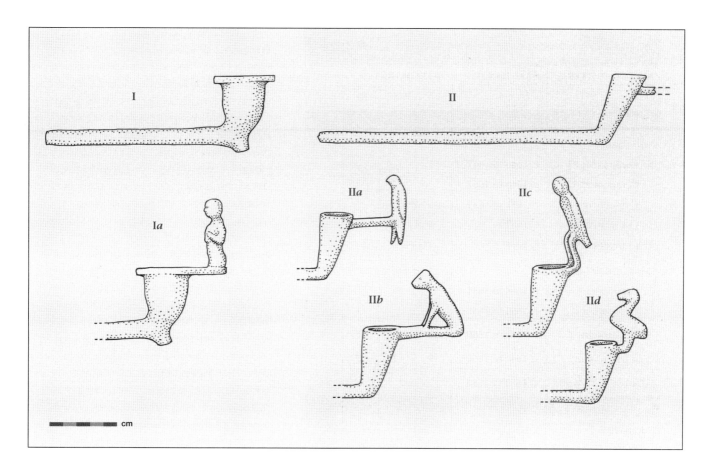

very little archaeological evidence of the English. Those changes would not come until decades later.

Trauma and Choice

Just as the archaeological record indicates increased comfort and affluence in Dutch communities, it also demonstrates the cultural disruption that Native people faced after 1650. The traumatic effects of warfare and disease continued to deplete Mahican and Mohawk populations while the pressures of assimilating captives and adapting to Europeans diluted traditional ways. After mid-century, both the Mahican and the Mohawk people were confronted by hard choices in terms of what their culture was and how to protect it from further loss.

FIGURE 5.33

Pewter and lead pipe forms of the 1655 to 1670 period.

I. A flanged bulbous bowl with a distinct heel.

Ia. A flanged bulbous bowl with a distinct heel and "person with blanket roll-style" figure.

II. A plain, funnel-shaped bowl.

IIa. A funnel-shaped bowl with "bird-man-style" figure.

IIb. A funnel-shaped bowl with "sitting dog-style" figure.

IIc. A funnel-shaped bowl with a "man-bird-style" figure.

IId. A modified funnel-shaped bowl with an "erect bird-style" figure.

Drawings by Gene MacKay and Ellen Chase.

171

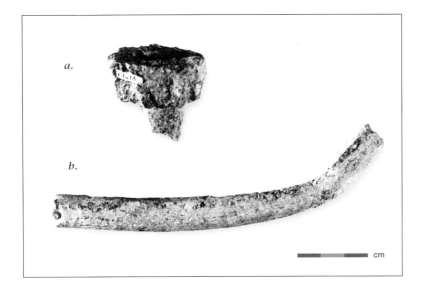

FIGURE 5.34

Above: Examples of possible Native casting.

a. A pewter pipe bowl from Printup site, (2005.13BJ.99.22).

b. A lead pipe stem from the Rumrill-Naylor site, (2005.13BM.90.30).

Rumrill collection, NYSM

Photo by Ted Beblowski.

FIGURE 5.35

Right: A lead owl with round blue beads for eyes, from the Seneca Dann site, (NYSM A-21078).

Courtesy of the Rock Foundation.

Drawing by Gene MacKay.

Native Material Culture after Midcentury.

After more than fifty years of contact with Europeans, the changes in Native material culture are obvious and overwhelming. By 1660, most of the traditional Native technologies and materials are gone from the archaeological record. Native ceramics, with the exception of captive pottery from sites like Jackson-Everson, has all but disappeared. The same is true with stone, bone and antler tools. In their place is a nearly complete inventory of European tools and utensils, all the objects that Native people had absorbed into their culture during the previous decades. Of course, much of this assimilation occurred in creative ways, such as cutting up iron axes into celts and recycling brass kettles into a wide range of implements and ornaments. However, by 1660, even the tendency to adapt and re-use European materials began to decrease. Axes, knives and kettles were so readily available that it was no longer worth the effort to re-process them. After midcentury, most broken or worn-out items were simply discarded. In fact, as European ceramics and bottle glass begin to appear in Native refuse along with white clay pipe stems, nails, broken gun parts and the bones of domestic animals, Native archaeological sites do not look that different from the sites of the more rural Dutch farms.

But this is only half the story. If the utilitarian side of Native culture was submerged by the sheer quantity and availability of European material goods, the spiritual and aesthetic side of Native culture, and its expression in smoking pipes, combs and other artifact forms, remained dynamically alive. Native smoking pipes of pottery, stone and wood continue to be made throughout the period. These reflect both long-established Mohawk styles and the cultural traditions of adopted and captured people. The same is true with antler combs, wooden bowls and other objects that rarely survive in the archaeological record. Shell ornaments continue to play an important

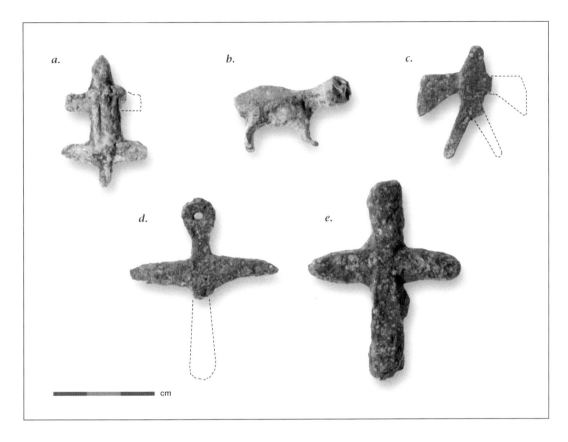

FIGURE 5.36

Additional examples of Native casting.

a. A 'turtle.'

b. A bear/man being or piasa.

c. A thunderbird.

d. and e. Two Christian crosses.

All are from the Printup site, (A2005.13BJ.99.19) for a.-d. (A2005.13BJ.18) for e.

Rumrill collection, NYSM. Photo by Ted Beblowski.

part of Native material culture. Wampum remains common on sites of this period as well as marine shell discs (also known as runtees), crescents and a variety of effigy forms. A new material, catlinite, begins to occur more frequently on these sites. Catlinite, a fine-grained red stone quarried in Minnesota and used for pipes and ornaments by Native people of the northern Plains, serves as another indicator of how far west Mohawk interactions extended.

The vitality of Native culture was not limited to traditional materials. In fact, Native-made lead and pewter objects provide some of the most compelling evidence from this period. As we saw in the previous chapter, both the Mahicans and the Mohawks had learned to cast musket balls and simple effigies during the 1640s. By the 1650s, these skills had become sufficiently refined to produce

a wide repertoire of forms. These included elaborate collars for wooden and stone pipes as well as complete pipes and other forms.[85] As casting became more widespread, it also became a means for expressing the shifting political and cultural balance between those Mohawks who were Christian and those who sought to maintain time-honored ways. Among the cast objects from the Printup site are both simple Christian-style crosses and the traditional forms used to evoke spiritual help – turtles, thunderbirds and other manitous.[86] Even as their culture underwent cataclysmic change, Native people continued to find ways to express their traditions and beliefs in both new and old mediums.

Summing Up

Between 1652 and 1664, cultural and economic patterns were set that would persist long after the English takeover of New Netherland. By 1660 the Dutch were firmly settled on the landscape. Beverwijck was sufficiently large and prosperous to establish new communities at Esopus and Schenectady. Although the population of these settlements continued to be ethically diverse, the institutions and values on which they were built remained solidly Dutch. However, forty years at the edge of the frontier had also left their mark. In addition to the established Dutch values of entrepreneurialism, community and tolerance, a strong sense of self-reliance and a distrust of authority characterized the region's population.

For the Dutch, two important lessons had been learned. The first was that business across cultural boundaries worked best when Native people were treated as partners instead of property. As Van Curler demonstrated, the effort made to provide Native people with the goods they wanted and to treat them fairly was repaid not just in profits but with loyalty. The second lesson was closely related. By 1660, the "Indian trade" was less about wampum and furs, both of which had lost substantial value, and more about alliances. The real issue was which imperial power would control the access points into the continent's vast interior. Even though the Dutch did not have the opportunity to apply this lesson, their English successors would.

The lessons, and resulting choices, for Native people were far grimmer. It was not just difficult to live with these new people and their strange ways; it began to look impossible. No matter how well intentioned the newcomers were, the differences in how they thought and lived presented a monumental challenge to the region's Native people and the stability of their communities. Faced with this reality, the Native people of the upper Hudson and Mohawk valleys made different choices. The Esopus chose resistance and quickly found out how futile that option was. The Mahicans, split in two by Dutch settlement, made two decisions. Although the Loups would continue to resist for another decade, they would choose to leave their valley and re-settle elsewhere. The Katskils, on the other hand, chose to become invisible, to live as quietly and unobtrusively as possible and hope that this would allow them to survive within their own territory. The Mohawks chose to throw their lot in with the newcomers, to succeed by becoming partners and allies. With treaties to guarantee their rights and privileges, the Mohawk decision was to ride out the storm.

EPILOGUE: Fortuna's Wheel, 1664–1689

In the spring of 1660, as Father Jerome Lalemant composed his report on the previous year's events, he chose a common metaphor to describe the situation among the Mohawks – Fortuna's wheel. From the medieval period through the Renaissance, one's fortunes, whether good or bad, were frequently viewed as part of an ongoing, endless cycle of change. Whoever was up would soon be down. Yesterday's failure might well be followed by today's success. This cycle was often personified by the image of a woman whose wheel drove the unpredictable events that made life both exhilarating and terrifying. Even today, our concept of revolution is based on a turn of Fortuna's wheel.

Lalemant had been in New France since 1638. He traveled to Huron country that year and supervised construction of a new Jesuit mission, Ste. Marie aux Hurons. It had been during his first term as Father Superior that the Mohawks had killed Isaac Jogues, then gone on to destroy Ste. Marie and virtually annihilate the Hurons. Since then, Lalemant had witnessed many events, some hopeful, others horrific. Lalemant was a deeply thoughtful man and as he wrote the section on *The Condition of the Country of the Iroquois and of their Cruelties,* he chose his words with care. While Fortune's "most customary game is to break scepters, abase crowned heads and, in rolling her wheel, raise some to the throne by the same movement whereby she casts others down, ... this blind and fickle dame does not refrain from taking her diversion in Savages' cabins and amidst the forests as well... She can play her game everywhere." The Mohawks were a case in point, Lalemant continued. They have been "so many times at both the top and the bottom of the wheel, within less than sixty years, that we find in history few examples of similar revolutions."[1]

Fortuna's wheel had certainly revolved a few times for the Dutch and English as well. From allies against the Spanish at the beginning of the 17th-century, they had become economic rivals, then bitter enemies by midcentury. The capture of New Netherland by the Duke of York's forces in early September 1664 precipitated a second round of warfare between these two Protestant powers that finally ended in 1667. However, Fortuna's wheel still had some surprising turns to make, ones that nobody in 1664 could have foreseen.

Becoming Albany

The first of those turns occurred nearly ten years later. In 1673, the Dutch recaptured New York from the English during yet another war, only to return it as part of the peace settlement a year later. What changed during those first ten years under the English? In most ways,

very little. In spite of the shift to English sovereignty, things had remained much as they were. Yet, significant changes were underway even if their full implications were not yet visible.

The "conquest" itself was a minimal event. There was no fighting, no loss of life. The most obvious changes were on maps and in what places were called. After naming the city of New Amsterdam and province of New Netherland after himself, James Duke of York also decided to re-name Beverwijck as well. Since New York was already taken, he used his title as Duke of Scotland (or Alba in Gaelic), calling the town Albany.

Name changes aside, not much happened at first. The man James chose to pacify his new domain was Colonel Richard Nicolls, a trusted staff officer who had served with him in France while in exile during the English Civil War. Nicolls was a seasoned military professional and no fool when it came to operating in hostile territory. One of his first acts was to appoint four new magistrates for Albany – Arent van Curler, Abraham Staats, Philip Schuyler and Richard van Rensselaer, the youngest of the Van Rensselaer brothers.[2] Nicolls planned to keep the region's leading Dutch citizens both visible and accountable. But Nicolls was also careful not to antagonize. British soldiers were quartered in Fort Orange, re-named Fort Albany, instead of with civilians in the town. As governor, Nicolls also re-confirmed most Dutch land holdings and left the existing political structure in place. The Dutch too were careful to cooperate. So were the Mohawks, who quickly signed an agreement with the English in late 1664 that kept their alliance and source of supplies intact. In all these negotiations, the Mahicans were not mentioned.[3]

In spite of the political change, everyday events proceeded much as they had before the takeover. In the spring of 1666, another major flood swept down the Hudson River, washing

FIGURE 6.1
Overleaf: Fortuna and her wheel. After Lydgate's Falle of Princis, 1494, in Patch 1927, Plate 10.
Redrawn by Booth Simpson

away more of Fort Orange and causing extensive damage. Forty houses and barns were carried off including the patroon's house, Jeremias van Rensselaer's farm, and the house of Volckert Jansz Douw at Papscanee. A different kind of disaster struck the Mohawks that fall when the French made good their threat "to teach them a lesson." In September, a thousand French troops under Prouville de Tracy marched into Mohawk country, burning their villages and destroying the harvest. The Mohawks, devastated by the loss, reluctantly agreed to sign a peace treaty the following June. The key intermediary in these delicate negotiations was Arent van Curler. However, in July 1667, on the way to Quebec to finalize arrangements, Van Curler drowned in Lake Champlain when his canoe overturned under questionable circumstances. The man known to the Mohawks as *Corlear* was gone, but his utility as a symbol was just beginning to become apparent.[4]

With the end of the Anglo-Dutch war in 1667 and peace with the French, hopes were high that the fur trade could be revived. Although the terms of surrender permitted the Dutch to continue trading, it was unclear exactly what this meant. In October, ex-governor Stuyvesant wrote to the Duke of York asking that the inhabitants of New York continue to "have liberty to trade with their own correspondents in Holland." The beaver trade had always depended on goods such as "Campen duffels, hatchets and other ironwork made at Utrecht," he explained and "if those commodities should fail… the very trade itself would fall" to the French.[5] Stuyvesant's appeal resulted in a temporary relaxation of the Navigation Acts, but there was little patience with foreign competition in the British imperial system and the exception was revoked a year later.

Historians have made much of the commercial side of the conquest. One has argued that patterns of trade were so radically altered that Dutch commercial activities in North America

were "destroyed." Another concluded that "in less than one generation" the ethnic Dutch merchant establishment was supplanted and anglicized at a surprisingly rapid pace.[6] Certainly changes did occur, but the archaeological evidence indicates a very different picture. We will return to this below.

Meanwhile, life went on in its more mundane aspects. In 1668, Jeremias van Rensselaer wrote to his brother Jan Baptist that the farmhouse at the Flatts had collapsed and had to be completely repaired. Jeremias did rebuild the house for his younger brother Richard. However, when Richard decided to return to the Republic, the farm was sold to Philip Schuyler. From 1672 on, the area would be known as the Schuyler Flatts.[7]

Even at peace with the French, the Mohawks remained depleted and deeply divided. One of the settlement terms was an agreement to accept Jesuit missionaries into their villages. By 1668 a chapel had been built in one of the main towns and there were several priests in residence. This aggressive Christian presence split the fabric of Mohawk culture further, often dividing families and speeding the breakdown of traditional clan and village structure. Fragmented by religious tension and alcohol internally, and beset by the Mahicans outside their palisades, many Christian Mohawks took a previously unthinkable step – they left. During the late 1660s, several new Indian settlements were established along the St. Lawrence near Montreal. Some of these even bore the same name as Mohawk towns back in the Valley. For Christian Mohawks, these new communities were a refuge and a place where they felt welcome. For traditional Mohawks, these defections were a loss worse than death and only enflamed their hatred of the French further. But the exodus continued nonetheless, and it was not only women and children who left. By 1673, the Jesuits could claim that more Mohawk warriors now lived near Montreal than in the Mohawk Valley.[8]

Across the Hudson River, the Mahicans continued to leave as well. Although often successful in their ongoing battles with the Mohawks, the Mahicans were increasingly involved in the affairs of their Algonquin relations and allies in northern New England. Split by the growing Dutch settlements, many Mahicans felt it was better to sell what land they could and move on.

FIGURE 6.2
*Map of
the Northeast,
ca. 1676.*

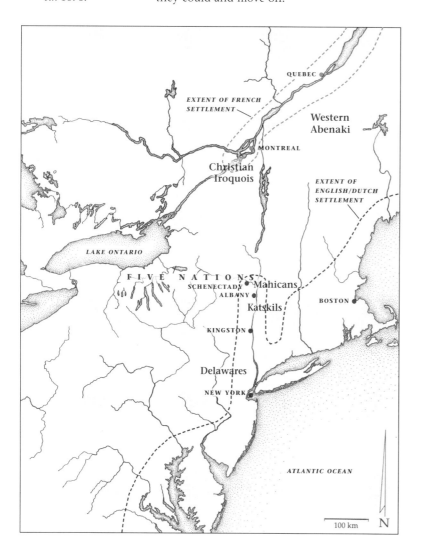

Ten years after becoming Albany, it was not clear how much had changed. In many ways, it was a Dutch town with an English name. Albany remained the center of the Indian trade and the place where conferences were held and treaties signed. Documents were kept in Dutch. The Dutch Reformed Church was still the predominant social institution and continued to be governed under the Classis of Amsterdam. While a few houses may have been influenced by the new "English" style, most buildings in town and outside it remained resolutely Dutch in character. In fact, many of the residents continued to describe themselves as living in Beverwijck or even the Fuyck.[9]

The real conflict embedded in the English takeover was not military or even economic. It was the clash of two very different sets of values. Even though the Dutch and English had much in common – both were Protestant and shared considerable cultural heritage – they were profoundly different in important ways. English society was still a feudal system, based on the authority of the sovereign. Especially under the Stuarts, English kings tended to see themselves as divinely appointed to their task. That task was to rule through a class of nobles, parceling out land to loyal retainers who, in turn, used their tenants to protect the land and make it profitable. This was a hierarchical system based on everyone knowing his or her place and staying there. It was also an authoritarian system, quick to reward and quick to punish, one in which wealth and status conveyed a clear message of royal approval and favor.

By contrast, the Dutch operated under a republican system that grew up during the Renaissance, one in which independent cities and towns voluntarily joined together for mutual defense and economic advantage. This was the basis of the Dutch Republic. Under this system, political authority resided in the elected officials of each city or town. Land ownership, like all business arrangements,

E P O L O G U E

was a private matter, one based on negotiation and contract, not the whim of a sovereign. Disputes were resolved by presenting one's case to other members of the community, not appealing to a higher authority. This was a system that valued enterprise and innovation, understood the need for tolerance and tended to downplay differences in wealth and status.

In Albany, these broad cultural differences were augmented by another factor. By 1674, the Dutch had had fifty years of very independent living along the Hudson River, whether the settlement was called Fort Orange, Beverwijck or Albany. This community, although firmly rooted in Dutch institutions and values, had also absorbed the lessons learned from a new environment and its Native people as well as the extreme diversity of its own population. With its own strong set of values that emphasized entrepreneurialism, community and tolerance, Albany was not a good candidate to become an imperial command center.

For the Dutch, the period from 1664 to 1674 was another ten years of the life to which they had become accustomed. For the agents of English imperial policy, the lesson was quite different. De Tracy's invasion pointed out both the potential and the vulnerability of Albany's location as a strategic outpost. If the king's dominions in North America were to be protected and expanded, then it was time to get this unruly colony and its wayward people in order.

This task fell to a new governor, Major Edmund Andros, who arrived in October 1674, at the end of the Third Anglo-Dutch War. His task was straight forward – to "civilize" the locals, Native and European alike, and to make Albany into "an English place." This was a military occupation and to underscore that point, Andros had the remnants of Fort Orange pulled down in 1676 and a new defensive position built on the hill above the town. Called Fort Albany, this new stronghold

served as much as the garrison for an occupying force as it did to protect the local population from outside invasion.[10]

Recognizing their strategic importance, Andros quickly turned his attention to the Iroquois. Andros was an imperial agent and assumed from the beginning that the Iroquois and their land were a part of his charge. Here his goal was simple – to make them into subjects and instruments of imperial policy. In August 1675, Andros took the unprecedented step of visiting the Mohawks in their own towns to impress them with his potential as a friend and protector.[11] The Mohawks were impressed. Not since Van Curler's death had anyone in power approached them on their own ground. Andros had picked the moment well. The Mohawks were in the midst of traumatic changes. Desperate for assistance and passionately anti-French, they were ideal partners for Andros' plan.

The Mohawk response was predictable. Andros was given the title of *Corlaer* in memory of their late friend and in expectation that the English governor would provide for them accordingly. This agreement would serve as the basis for what came to be known as the Covenant Chain, a series of treaties and agreements, recorded both on paper and in wampum belts, that specified the relationship between the English and the Iroquois.[12]

Andros had good reason to be pleased with this result. With the outbreak of King Philip's War in New England and another round of ugly hostilities between the Mohawks and Mahicans, the governor needed to know on whom he could count. As it turned out, many Mohawks were willing to serve as mercenaries against the New England tribes, even though it was afterward claimed that they had fought only "as servants and souldjers" of the English. Andros also made a gesture toward the Mahicans and other displaced New England tribes, encouraging the latter to settle at Schaghticoke, but it was mostly show.

With the Mohawks, Andros had the allies he needed. The Mahicans, on the other hand, no longer commanded an important place on the imperial game board. But the Mohawks would pay a high price for their privileged position. For them, and the rest of the Five Nations, the Covenant Chain would become chains indeed, ones that bound them to an imperial system that would reduce them to the status of military auxiliaries and economic dependents over the next fifty years.[13]

Andros was also quick to begin the second part of his charge – civilizing the Dutch population of Albany. Here the first step was control of the land. Since all land was under royal authority, more precise boundaries and public record keeping were required. Instead of the traditional Dutch orientation to the water, it was now proximity to "the king's highways" that determined where one lived. Within a few years, additional changes would require that deeds be recorded with civil officials instead of the traditional notaries and that records be kept in English. Disturbing as these changes were, it was a shift in tax structure that caused the greatest concern. The traditional Dutch method of raising public money was through an excise tax, one based on goods and services. Under the English, taxes would now be based on property.[14]

Political reform was next on Andros' agenda. In 1675 he re-structured the town's court to include the garrison commander as well as local burghers. He also appointed a newcomer, Robert Livingston, as court secretary. Subsequent changes would shift court proceedings away from Dutch precedents toward those of English common law. As part of his strategy to weaken the community's major Dutch institutions, Andros may also have encouraged the Lutheran minority to obtain land and build a church of their own.[15]

While Andros had no particular interest in disrupting Dutch commerce, trade under the English was also "a Prerogative Royall" and therefore to be brought into line with imperial policy. By 1679 many of the traditional Dutch trading practices were discouraged or banned. Native people were no longer permitted within the town but restricted to "Indian Houses" built outside the palisade. Andros also denied trading rights in Albany to several merchants from Manhattan. When local merchants explained that connections with suppliers in New York and overseas were a traditional privilege and essential for the trade, Andros bluntly informed them that they could either trade for furs or trade overseas, but not both.[16]

For many of the Dutch residents, these enforced changes ran against the grain of established business and political practices; they were deeply offensive to the community's social values as well. Property holdings were a private matter. Public displays of status and social ambition were distasteful. English treatment of Native people made no sense either from a business or a neighborly point of view. Of course, not everyone opposed these changes, and deep divisions ran through the town.

Andros was recalled to England in 1681 and it was two years before his successor, Colonel Thomas Dongan, arrived. Nearly twenty years after the English takeover, Albany was still not significantly different from Beverwijck. It remained a frontier market town where the Indian trade, and to a lesser degree agricultural products, dominated. Most householders continued to engage in more than one occupation, as had long been the case.[17] A town of burghers, Albany was exactly the kind of independent-minded community that men of a royalist temperament, like Nicolls and Andros, disliked and distrusted. By then, however, the last of the old Dutch leadership was gone; both Volckert Jansz Douw and Philip Pieterse Schuyler died in 1683. The question was – where would the new generation of merchants and political leaders, men like Peter Schuyler who had grown up in a divided society, stand in this conflict of values?

If the Albany Dutch thought that any one would be better than Andros, they were quickly disappointed. Dongan not only continued his predecessor's work; he substantially picked up the pace. Shortly after his arrival in 1683, the new governor enacted a "Charter of Liberties and Privileges," the goal of which was to construct an English political structure within a colony. One immediate consequence was the creation of counties throughout New York. With the creation of Albany County, the next step was to prepare the town to serve as its county seat. The following year Albany was divided into four wycks, or wards. This not only facilitated the taxing of property, it was a step toward residency as a requirement for holding office.[18] The final step in Dongan's plan occurred in 1686 when the governor signed a new municipal charter creating the city of Albany.

It remains unclear whether this action was taken at the request of a group of Albany merchants or initiated by Dongan. However it came about, the charter changed Albany in fundamental ways. It defined the city's boundaries, specified the rights of its citizens and laid out how the city would be governed. To many people, it seemed like a good deal. Albany was now guaranteed "the sole and only management" of the Indian trade in "his Majesties Dominion." To participate in the trade, one now had to be a "freeman" and "actual Inhabitant" of the city. As the fur trade expanded into the western Great Lakes and beyond, this monopoly virtually guaranteed Albany's economic health for some time to come. There was a price, of course. Albany would now be governed by English legal principles and practices. Initially, the governor would name all municipal officials. While elections could be phased in for aldermen and other minor officials, the mayor and sheriff would remain appointed.[19] Dongan planned to keep his charges on a very short leash. Among the new officials, Peter Schuyler was

named mayor, as well as clerk of the market and coroner, while Robert Livingston became town clerk.

How the public received the news of the charter is as ambiguous as who instigated its creation. Schuyler and Livingston brought the document back to Albany in July 1686 where it "was published with all the joy and acclamations imaginable." However, as one later scholar has noted, these words were added in the margin of the original court records. It is not clear that everyone was so enthused.[20]

For Dongan, the Albany Charter was another successful step in the imperial plan. It extended and protected royal control while giving worthy local clients an opportunity to profit. For some Albany residents, this was a logical and necessary step, a re-assertion of Albany's rights over those of neighboring communities like Schenectady. In this, it differed

FIGURE 6.3
The first page of the Albany Charter of 1686.
Courtesy of the Albany County Hall of Records.

FIGURE 6.4
Settlement plan at the Vedder site (Caughnawaga).
Courtesy of Wayne Lenig and the Mohawk-Caughnawaga Museum.

little from Stuyvesant's creation of Beverwijck thirty years earlier. However, for others in the Dutch community, this was a deal with the devil, one that traded economic advantage for the yoke of English boundaries, English laws and English government. Like the Covenant Chain for the Mohawks, the Charter was the means by which the Dutch inhabitants of Albany would finally be made into good imperial subjects.

These successes were only the beginning of James' ambitions. With the death of his brother Charles II, James became king in 1685 and New York a royal colony. As James II, the new king undertook a vast plan to re-organize all the northern colonies, enfolding New York along with Massachusetts Bay, Plymouth and the others into a new creation called the Dominion of New England. However, these plans crumbled as Fortuna intruded with

yet another, unexpected turn of her wheel.

In June 1688, a son was born to James and his queen. Since James was a practicing Catholic and a great admirer of Louis XIV, his divine-right neighbor across the Channel, a royal son meant the continuation of a Catholic, absolutist monarchy. This was too much for the increasingly powerful Protestant-dominated Parliament, which quickly encouraged Willem of Orange, stadholder of the Dutch Republic and husband of James' daughter Mary, to intervene and assume the throne. William and his army landed in England that November and James fled to France. Crowned William III the following year, the new king would reign into the next century. William and Mary's rule did bring stability and prosperity to England, but the irony was not lost. After three bitter wars between 1652 and 1674, England had a Dutch king. Old enemies had become allies again, this time against the French.[21]

Reading Rubbish

Since this is a story about archaeology, not just history, what do the sites and artifacts tell us about these complex events? While a thorough answer to that question would require another book, or even several, a brief review will help us complete this story.

A basic premise of this book is that people's actions, as reflected in the things they leave behind, can be a more accurate indication of what they thought and did than what they may have said. This does not mean that trash always tells the truth, but it seldom lies. If we, as archaeologists, work within the rules that govern interpretation – sample, context and scale – we have a good chance of reading more of the message that past people have left about themselves buried in their rubbish.

Although the documentary record indicates that Mahican people were still present, very few Mahican sites that post-date 1664 are known from the region. These sites are small and ephemeral, probably short-term camps used by family groups. Even at large sites like Winney's Rift and Lansingburgh, where the evidence indicates a continuous Mahican presence from the beginning of the 17th-century, it appears that, by the 1670s, the Mahicans were gone.

The Mohawks, on the other hand, remain clearly present throughout the period. Among the known sites are several, such as Freeman and Allen, that were burned by de Tracy in 1666. However, the Jackson-Everson site appears to have been spared, a fact that is not mentioned in the historical record. This may have been because the majority of its inhabitants were of Huron descent, Christian and pro-French. After de Tracy's attack, the Mohawks returned to the north side of the Mohawk River to rebuild their villages. These include the sites from late 1660s into the 1680s, such as Fox Farm, Schenck #2 and White Orchard, as well as the subsequent sites, such as Veeder, that date from the late 1680s. Some of these late 17th-century sites, with their straight walls and more orderly layout, show the influence of European ideas in their settlement plan (*See Figure 6.4*). Sites such as Veeder are where many of the Mohawks lived until 1693 when they were, once again, destroyed by the French. Although the Mohawks continued to sell off parcels of land throughout this period, all of it was land that had previously belonged to the Mahicans. The Mohawks sold no land of their own until after 1700.[22]

The artifact assemblages from these sites testify to the changing nature of Mohawk culture. Most striking is the pervasiveness of European materials. Only a few remnants of Native ceramics, lithics and bone tools continue to occur in the archaeological record, reflecting a nearly total dependence on European utilitarian objects. This does not mean that Native culture had disappeared. Much of what was most distinctive – carved wooden ladles, bowls and clubs as well as woven bags and sashes, quill work and beaded

FIGURE 6.5
Antler comb from the Fox Farm site, Swart collection, NYSM.
Photo by Ted Beblowski.

clothing – simply has not survived. Other traditions also remained strong, especially the production and use of elaborate pipes, antler combs, and a wide variety of marine shell, catlinite and metal ornaments. However, many of these reflect the cultural traditions of adopted people and serve as an indication of how ethnically diverse the Mohawks had become. The artifacts document other changes as well. For example, many Jesuit-related religious objects, especially rings and small medals, have been found on sites from the 1660s and 1670s, while virtually none occur on later sites like Veeder. By that time, the Jesuits and most Christian Mohawks had left for Canada.

Throughout this book, we have looked at certain classes of European objects – particularly glass beads, cloth seals and smoking pipes – and how these help us understand larger social and economic changes. During the years 1664 to 1689, these small artifacts continue to illuminate much greater events.

TABLE 6.1   Glass Bead Horizons on eastern Five Nations sites: 1665 to 1750

Glass Bead Horizon	Mohawk Sites, Eastern	Mohawk Sites, Central	Mohawk Sites, Western	Oneida Sites	Onondaga Sites
Round Red Beads green core (IVa5) ca. 1665 to 1675 no core (IIa1) ca. 1675 to 1690	Fox Farm	Schenck #2	Jackson-Everson' White Orchard	Sullivan	Indian Hill
Round Black Beads (IIa6) ca. 1690 to 1700	Veeder, Milton Smith	Horatio Nellis	?	Upper Hogan	Weston Jamesville/Pen
Polychrome Revival Beads (IIbb13, IIb'7, IIj1-2) ca. 1700 to 1715	Milton Smith Auriesville	Allen	Galligan #2 Ganada #2	?	Jamesville/Pen
Wire Wound Beads (WIb2, WIIc12) ca. 1715 to 1750	Auriesville Fort Hunter		Prospect Hill Sand Hill Indian Castle	Primes' Hill Lanz	Sevier Coye, Onondaga

Drawings by Ellen Chase

Glass beads, in particular, continue to change although it is not always clear why. The short, tubular red beads, so common during the late 1650s and early 1660s, were replaced by round red beads during the mid-1660s. These predominate through the 1680s. By the late 1680s, round red beads were, in turn, superceded by round black ones. One is tempted to call these "English" beads, since their appearance seems to correlate, first, with the 1664 takeover, and then with Dongan's arrival. However, the evidence indicates that these beads were almost certainly produced in the Dutch Republic. The first round red beads have the same characteristic green core as their short tubular predecessors and were probably made in the Two Roses glasshouse on the Rozengracht in Amsterdam. This glasshouse produced beads until at least 1671. In 1676, the entire operation was sold, and then moved to the neighboring city of Haarlem where it continued to operate until at least 1697.[23] It is likely that the plain round red and black beads of the late 1670s to 1690s period were made there. By 1697 several glasshouses were again operating in Amsterdam and Dutch bead production may have continued well into the 18th-century.[24]

Cloth seals also suggest that the transition from Dutch to English goods was not as rapid or straightforward as historians have suggested. On eastern Iroquois sites of the "round red bead" period, cloth seals from Campen continue to occur. Clearly, traditional Dutch suppliers remained involved in the fur trade through the 1670s and possibly later. By the 1680s, however, the majority of cloth seals found on Native sites suggest an English origin and may indicate a shift from duffels to strouds.[25] These may also reflect the changes in trade policy undertaken by Andros and Dongan. But such English commercial successes were the exception and Dutch products continued to dominate both Iroquois and "Dutch" domestic sites in upstate New York until the end of the 17th-century.

Nothing demonstrates this more clearly than clay smoking pipes. Pipe smoking remained popular throughout the century, and both the English and Dutch made them for their own use as well as for trade. As a result, pipe fragments provide an excellent means for tracking the origins of trade merchandise. Pipe fragments are also important because, like today's cigarette butts or coffee cups, no one thought much about discarding them. This means that it is usually possible to get a larger, more representative sample of pipes from a site than is possible with other kinds of artifacts.

In earlier chapters, we tracked the development of pipe making in Amsterdam, especially Edward Bird and his role in developing pipes specifically for the New Netherland market. When Bird died in 1665, the story of EB pipes did not end; it became more complex. Bird's son, Evert, inherited both the rights to his father's EB mark and his extensive property holdings. Evert also continued the family business of making pipes. When Bird's widow remarried three years later, her new husband, Hendrick Gerdes, became a pipe maker too. However, it is unclear whether he marked his pipes HG or EB.

What is certain is that Bird's ongoing success soon resulted in others copying both the EB mark and his father's funnel bowl design. In 1672, an Amsterdam merchant, Adrian van der Cruis, registered the EB mark in the city of Gouda and hired a local pipe maker, Jacobus de Vriend, to produce pipes for him. De Vriend already made bulbous bowl pipes for export under his own mark, the hand. It appears that Van der Cruis also contracted with pipe makers in other towns to produce pipes marked EB.[26] By 1676 several Gouda pipe makers were producing pipes in the funnel bowl style and stamping them with their own marks.[27]

All of this was part of a larger economic shift. Just as bead making moved from Amsterdam to Haarlem during the 1670s, the focus of pipe making shifted away from Amsterdam to Gouda. By 1678, Evert Bird may have begun to feel the financial pressure, selling the family property on the Egelantiergracht. Five years later, the end came. Bird sold the remaining house on the Rozengracht at a loss and declared bankruptcy.[28] But while pipe making may have been over in Amsterdam, it continued to flourish in Gouda. In fact, pipes with Gouda marks, such as the orb, HG and crowned HG, are the most commonly occurring pipes on Native sites during the last quarter of the 17th-century.[29] It is not until after 1700 that English-made pipes, especially those of Robert Tippett and other Bristol makers, begin to appear on Mohawk sites in more than trace amounts (*See Table 6.2*).

Two other trends in pipes are significant during the last quarter of the 17th-century. One is the rapid decline in quality as the quantity of pipes increased. These pipes are less-carefully made, often poorly fired and frequently unmarked – all signs of cheaper or second-class products. The other trend is notable by its absence – a nearly complete lack of English-made pipes. As we saw in Chapter Three, pipe making actually began in England

FIGURE 6.6
Gouda pipe marks from the 1670 to 1695 period – goblet, hand, orb, HG and crowned HG.
After Bradley and DeAngelo 1981.

TABLE 6.2   Pipe Horizons on Eastern Five Nations sites between 1666 and 1700+

Pipe Marks	Mohawk Sites	Oneida Sites	Onondaga Sites
EB (funnel and bulbous bowls). ca. 1666 to 1674	Jackson-Everson	Sullivan	Indian Hill
EB (bulbous bowls) and Gouda morks such as the orb, hand, and bell. ca. 1674 to 1683	Fox Farm White Orchard	Upper Hogan	Indian Hill Weston
HG and crowned HG (funnel and bulbous bowls), other crowned marks. ca. 1683 to 1695	Veeder	?	Weston Jamesville
English pipes – RT, TO as well as Gouda marks, after ca. 1695	Milton Smith	Primes Hill	Jamesville

during the 1590s and was brought to the Republic by Protestant expatriates during the early decades of the 17th-century. By the mid-century, English pipe making had shifted away from London to the western city of Bristol, which organized its own pipe guild in 1652. As with Gouda, it did not take long for Bristol makers to recognize the success of Edward Bird's funnel bowl design and, by the 1660s, they began to experiment with their own version of a heel-less pipe for the Indian trade.[30]

What is surprising is that these pipes do not occur on Iroquois sites of the 1660s and 1670s.[31] In fact, the only site within the region where these pipes have been found is Fort Orange, British headquarters in Albany until 1676. During his excavation, Huey uncovered a large number of pipes from component 66, a brick pile located above the remains of the Van Doesburgh house and dating between 1664 and 1676. This sample of pipes was interesting as it contained both classic Dutch funnel bowl pipes stamped EB as well as several similar pipes. These unmarked pipes have a softer, chalky finish and a slight curve to the bowl. By contrast, the Dutch pipes have a rouletted rim on the bowl, a burnished finish and are straight-sided (*See Figure 6.7*). Described by Joe McEvoy as "good, utility grade soldiers' pipes," these unmarked pipes appear to be what Bristol makers were producing during the late 1660s and early 1670s.[32]

Although the English pipes from Fort Orange are unmarked, they may have been produced by the Evans family in Bristol. By the 1660s, several members of that family were pipe makers and at least two of them, William and Llewellyn, marked their work.

These funnel bowl pipes were stamped either WE or LE on the back of the bowl facing the smoker, and are similar in shape to those from component 66 at Fort Orange. Evans pipes of this style are also common on English colonial sites of the last quarter of the 17th-century from Maine to Maryland, except in New York. North of Kingston, these English pipes simply do not occur.[33]

So, who were the merchants that continued to import Dutch merchandise in violation of the Navigation Acts and the explicit orders of men like Andros and Dongan? Before answering that question, let's look briefly at the archaeological evidence from Dutch sites in New York.

Since few Dutch domestic sites from this period have been excavated, our sample size is small.[34] However, the domestic material culture of 17th-century Albany appears to have been much the same as that of Beverwijck. Red earthenware vessels and Rhenish stoneware jugs were still used for food preparation and storage. Meals were served and eaten from tin-glazed (delftware) dishes. English ceramics, such as the buff earthenwares from Staffordshire, do not appear until the 1690s. (See Figure 6.8) The same Amsterdam and Gouda pipes seen on Native sites characterize Dutch domestic assemblages as well. Another distinctive Dutch trait, pipe stem whistles, has also been documented on several of these sites.[35] In general, domestic assemblages from the 1670s and 1680s do not differ much from those of two decades earlier. The sense that emerges from these artifacts is one of cultural conservatism and a reluctance to change.

Dutch sites related to the "Indian trade" during the period 1664 to 1690 are even scarcer than the domestic ones. Aside from Fort Orange, which continued to be used as a staging area until 1676, the only sites known to be involved with trade are Schuyler Flatts and Van Buren. Although Albany was the

official center of trade, no trade-related sites from this period have been found within the city limits. Even so, a comparison of trade goods between Mohawk sites and important trading centers like Schuyler Flatts is instructive. Once again, smoking pipes provide the best evidence. Basically, all the Gouda pipes that occur on Mohawk sites of the 1670s to

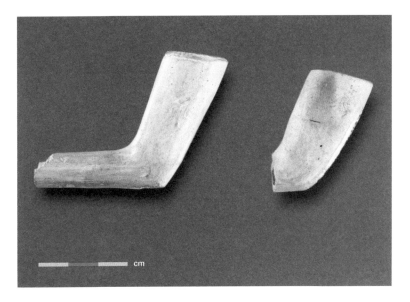

1690s are also represented at the Flatts. These include the orb, HG and crowned HG as well as CDP.[36] The other similarity is that, just as on Mohawk sites, virtually no English pipes of the 1670 to 1690 period have been recovered from the Flatts.

While archaeological investigations at Schuyler Flatts are far from complete, reading the rubbish provides us with an unmistakable message. Even if the sources of supply were different, the inventory of successful trade goods remained basically the same as that pioneered by Kiliaen van Rensselaer and perfected by Arent van Curler – one that contained smoking pipes, blankets and good quality flintlocks in addition to the usual kettles, knives, axes, awls and glass beads. From the 1670s through the 1690s, the majority of these goods were imported from

FIGURE 6.7
A comparison of a Dutch funnel bowl pipe and an English copy from components 65 and 66, Fort Orange.
Courtesy of Paul Huey and OPRHP.
Photo by Joe McEvoy.

FIGURE 6.8

Artifacts from the Mortar Hill site, Scotia, NY.

Ceramics include three pieces of Dutch lead glazed red earthenware (a., b. and d.) and two pieces from a German stoneware Bartmann jug (c. and g.)

Pipes include a Gouda-style example with a plain heel (e.) and several unmarked funnel bowls (f.).

Courtesy of Gary Bernhardt. Photo by Joe McEvoy.

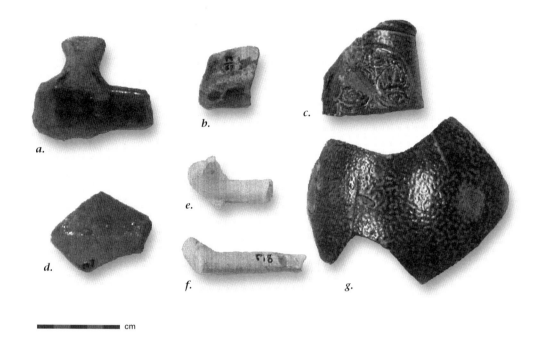

the Dutch Republic.[37] Whoever was in charge was still deeply connected to Dutch suppliers, regardless of what the rules were or what the historical documents indicate. The man in charge, of course, was Peter Schuyler.

Peter Schuyler: A Man in Two Worlds

If one of our goals is to understand behavior, especially when people are caught in difficult conflicts, there are few better candidates than Peter Schuyler – a man who straddled two worlds. Peter Schuyler is usually portrayed as a good servant of the new order and, superficially, this certainly appears to be the case. During his nearly fifty years in public life, Schuyler held many important and powerful posts. He served as Albany's first mayor, from 1686 to 1694, and was later a member of the Royal Governor's Council. He was also the Superintendent for Indian Affairs. A respected military commander, Schuyler was ceaseless

in his efforts to protect the New York frontier from the French. He was also a successful diplomat. In 1710, he traveled to London with four Mohawk and Mahican tribal leaders, introducing them to Queen Anne and creating a social sensation.

Schulyer was amply rewarded for his services. He was one of the largest landowners in the region and the most successful of its merchants. It is not surprising that scholars have often placed the Schuylers with several of the other wealthy, landed families – the Livingstons, Van Cortlandts, Phillipses and others – describing them as the new Anglo-Dutch elite whose wealth and influence would persist up to the American Revolution.[38]

However, Schuyler can also be seen from a very different point of view. Born in Beverwijck in 1657, he grew up immersed in the Dutch cultural values that defined the community. Given his father's position, he would have known the Van Rensselaers and other important community leaders such as Arent van Curler, who died when Schuyler was ten. In 1672, when Peter was fifteen, his father bought the Flatts farm and made it into the family's principal country house. This is where Peter Schuyler spent much of his adolescence and early adult life.

Schuyler's career parallels that of Van Curler in other ways. Both were highly successful entrepreneurs. Each was also a dedicated public servant, one who continued to serve his community through very difficult times. Like Van Curler, Schuyler had strong personal ties with the Mohawks. And they, in turn, liked and trusted him. It was to Schuyler Flatts that many of them came to live after the French burned their villages in 1693. While Schuyler probably deserved the title *Corlaer* more than any English governor, the Mohawks honored him with a special name of his own, *Quidor.* As a contemporary observer noted, "he hath been the main (if not only) Instrument of preserving the five Nations... from a totall Defection to the french." Although they lived in different times, Van Curler and Schuyler faced similar problems. More important, each served as a model for how to succeed individu- ally as well as on behalf of his community.[39]

It has often been assumed that, because Schuyler was one of the rich and powerful, he was British inside and out. But this is where the material evidence shows us a more complex person. Like many of the Albany Dutch, Schuyler was able to balance his public appearance with the needs of his personal life. One could be a good servant of the empire, yet true to the values of one's upbringing and community.

This view of Schuyler is entirely consistent with the archaeological evidence from the Flatts. As Christian Koot has demonstrated in the West Indies, Dutch merchants continued to operate, even dominate, the trade in English colonies for much of the 17th-century. This could happen in many ways, from exploiting

FIGURE 6.9
Portrait of Peter Schuyler. Attributed to Nehemiah Partridge, ca. 1710.
Courtesy of the City of Albany, Office of the Mayor.

legal loopholes in the law, to the use of agents as intermediaries to smuggling.[40] It was not a black-and-white world, in spite of what imperial policy might dictate. And while Schuyler may be an unusual example, given his high standing in the imperial order, he was not unique in terms of living with divided loyalties.

The ability to live successfully in two different worlds is also reflected in Schuyler's surviving personal possessions. These include stylish furniture such as a William and Mary tea table believed to have been Schuyler's, and side chairs imported from Boston. However, also present is a cast iron fireback from the Flatts farm. This Hollandia-style fireback is virtually identical to the example recovered from Van Curler's cellar (*Figure 4.25*), except that it is dated 1665, the year after the English "conquest."[41]

By 1689, Peter Schuyler and the community he represented were something different. Neither was English, nor were they really Dutch any longer. They were something else, a combination of all the diverse factors that had shaped the Albany area over the past century; something new that we can begin to recognize as "American."

cm

FIGURE 6.10
A cast iron Hollandia fireback, dated 1665, from the Flatts Farm.
AIHA, gift of Mrs. Richard P. Schulyer 1910.2.

190

One Last Turn

Peter Schuyler and Albany in 1689 are a good place to end this story, although it is a tale that continues and becomes increasingly familiar. A Dutchman on the English throne was still a king and royal policies toward the North American colonies did not change significantly. Neither did the conflict in values between those who supported the demands of empire and those who opposed them. The resulting divisions would not be resolved until the events that led to the American Revolution forced people to choose sides. When that decision came, it was no surprise that the Dutch population of Albany sided with the rebels from New England and Virginia, and that another Philip Schuyler, Peter's great-nephew, was among their leaders.

By 1689, events in the Albany area were less about specific tribes or ethnic groups and more about the definition of emerging communities. It was no longer a matter of Mahican or Mohawk history, Dutch as opposed to English. Each of these strands was important, but the reality was that they had become so intertwined that it was no longer possible to separate them. Yet it was exactly this collision of cultures that brought about the "colonial" history we now take for granted. Through all these convoluted rivalries and alliances, conflicts of values and struggles to maintain tradition, choices were made and new solutions found. These in turn became the raw material from which not just Albany and other new communities from Schenectady to Schaghticoke were built, but the culture of a new country.

From our perspective, the events of the 17th-century seem not only distant but incredibly confusing. So why look back? Because it is our history and looking back helps to explain who we are as Americans today. Regardless of our personal identities and histories, we live in a country based on shared values, and many of

those values grew out of the interactions between Native people and Europeans in the upper Hudson River Valley. We still value hard work and making money. Community remains fundamentally important to us, even if the definition of it continues to change. Tolerance – the need to get along, to live together even when we don't like each other – is still one of our core values. While Arent van Curler and Peter Schuyler might not recognize much of their world in ours, these values would be familiar. And in a country as large and diverse as the United States, these values are not just historical oddities or quaint survivals; they are the glue that holds us together.

A Final Thought. What will future archaeologists think of us as they sift through our rubbish? What messages are we leaving behind? Perhaps that is worthy of some reflection, even in our stressed and busy lives.

ABBREVIATIONS

AIHA	The Albany Institute of History and Art
AHM/BMA	Amsterdam Historisch Museum/Bureau Monumenten and Archeologie.
NYSL, MSC	The New York State Library, Manuscripts and Special Collections
NYSM	The New York State Museum
OPRHP	The New York State Office of Parks, Recreation and Historic Preservation
RMSC	The Rochester Museum and Science Center

GLOSSARY

A horizon. The upper, most biologically active layer of soil

Alluvium. Soil deposited by river flood waters.

Anneal. The process of softening a metal, particularly copper or brass, by heating it so that it can be worked further.

Apostle spoon. A popular style for metal spoons during the early 17th-century which had a small figure of one of the Apostles at the end of the stem.

Archaeology. The science of understanding human behavior by looking at its material remains.

Artifact. A material object left, intentionally or not, by past people.

Assemblage. An archaeological term for a set of artifacts used by a particular group of people at a specific time and place.

Bodkin. A blunt needle with a large eye used for lacing. Often highly ornamented, these were also used by 17th-century women as hair pins.

Boslooper. A Dutch term for a skilled woodsman, similar to the French term courier de bois.

Brass. An alloy of copper and zinc. Other metals including nickel, tin, lead, bismuth, even gold and silver often occur in trace amounts.

Case bottle. A style of square bottle used for storing liquor. Six or eight of these bottles were set in a wooden case designed for transportation and storage.

Catlinite. A fine-grained red sedimentary rock found in Minnesota and quarried by Native groups in the Great Lakes and northern Plains. It was used for making pipes and ornaments.

Celt. An ungrooved stone axe. This was a traditional axe form in Native culture prior to European contact.

Chert. A flint-like stone used by Native peoples to make tools. Deposits of good quality chert occur at several locations in the upper Hudson and Mohawk Valleys.

Cog. A broad beamed, shallow draft sailing vessel used by the Dutch during the 15th and 16th centuries for carrying bulk cargoes in the North Sea.

Commis. The Dutch term for business agent.

Columella. The central portion of a whelk shell.

Duffel. A type of coarse woolen cloth.

Earth fast. A type of building construction where structural timbers are set directly into the ground without stone or brick foundations.

facon de Venise. Glass made in the Venetian fashion.

Faience. A tin glazed earthenware of the early and mid 17th-century, popularized in Italy and copied by the Dutch. Unlike majolica, the tin glaze was applied on both the front and back of the vessel. When made in the Republic, the Dutch referred to this as 'Dutch porcelain'. We call this delftware.

Feature. Any sub-surface disturbance of the soil observed during excavation. Features may be the result of natural activities (such as animal burrows or tree falls) or cultural activities (storage pits, postmolds or burials).

Flute. A larger, deeper draft sailing vessel used by the Dutch for long distance exploration and trade voyages during the late 16th and early 17th centuries.

Glass Bead Horizons. A set of twelve glass bead assemblages that reflect the changes in preferred styles on Mohawk and Mahican sites between ~1600 and 1750.

Glass Bead Periods (GBP). A series of five time periods between 1580 and 1640 during which a specific set of glass beads occurs on Native sites (see Kenyon and Kenyon 1983, Fitzgerald et al 1995). Since these were defined on Canadian sites, these periods do not correspond exactly with the occurrence of similar beads on Mohawk and Mahican sites.

Historic period. The period after 1609 when Mahican and Mohawk people had direct contact with Europeans and European materials.

Horizon. An archaeological term used to describe a trait or series of related traits that occur at the same time but across cultural boundaries.

Jambette. A French term for a small, folding pocket knife.

Latten. An alloy of copper similar to brass and commonly used for making spoons.

Lithic. Made from stone.

Locus. An archaeological terms for a concentration of features and/or artifacts on a site.

Majolica. A tin glazed earthenware of the early 17th-century, popularized in Italy and copied by the Dutch. Unlike faience (delftware), the tin glaze was applied only to the front side of the vessel.

Manitous. Powerful spirit beings who controlled the forces of the natural world.

Material culture. The set of physical objects, from small objects to buildings, that defines a particular group of people.

Pakhuis. The Dutch word for a storehouse.

Palisade. A wall of vertically placed logs and brush used to surround, define and protect an Iroquois village.

Patroon. A Dutch word meaning 'patron'. The title given to the owner of a private colony in New Netherland.

Patroonship. A private colony in New Netherland set up under the authority of the West India Company.

Plan. An archaeological term that describes how a site is laid out when viewed from above.

Polychrome. Multi-colored.

Polychrome Bead Horizon. Sites where a specific set of high quality polychrome glass beads are most common. These beads probably represent the trading activities of the New Netherland Company, 1614–1618.

Postmold. The discolored stain left in the ground by a post after it has rotted away or been removed.

Pre-Contact period. The period before 1525, or prior to any known contact with Europeans.

Profile. An archaeological term that describes the vertical sequence of cultural and natural soils encountered during an excavation.

Protohistoric period. The period between ~1525 and 1609 when Mahican and Mohawk people may have had indirect contact with Europeans or European materials.

Roemer. A German style of drinking glass used primarily for beer.

Runtee. A disc of marine shell usually decorated with incised lines and dots. These popular ornaments are found on Native sites in the Northeast during the second half of the 17th-century.

Seriation. An archaeological term for describing the occurrence of a particular trait and how it changes over time.

Sewan. The Dutch term for wampum.

Sherd. A fragment of a pottery vessel.

Site. A location where past people lived or worked. Also used to describe where a particular archaeological investigation has occurred.

Sith. A sharp-edged tool used by Dutch farmers for harvesting wheat, oats and other grains.

Sloep. A small, un-decked Dutch sailing vessel of the early 17th-century.

Snaphaunce. A type of ignition system used on firearms before development of the flintlock.

Stadtholder. A Dutch term for the titular head of the Republic. During the late 16th and most of the 17th-century the head of the House of Orange held this title.

Strouds. An inexpensive woolen cloth produced by mills in the Stroud River valley, England and exported to the American colonies during the late 17th and early 18th century.

VOC The Dutch East India Company or Vereenigde Oost-Indische Compagnie in Dutch.

Weir. A fish trap constructed from rocks and wooden stakes.

Wetu. An Algonquian term for a small dome-shaped house.

Wheel lock. An early type of firearm that used a spring-driven wheel to strike a spark.

WIC The Dutch West India Company or Geoctroyeerde Westindische Compagnie or (GWC) in Dutch.

Whelk. Any of several species of large marine gastropods.

CHAPTER NOTES

CHAPTER 1

1. For a review of regional archaeology see Funk 1976 and Ritchie 1965.

2. A "friendly and polite" people, a "very loving people," Jameson 1909:7, 20-3. General sources on the Mahicans include Brasser 1978, Dunn 1994a and 2000. Also see the papers from the *Mohican Seminar* series, Dunn ed. 2004 and 2005, published by the New York State Museum. I have chosen to use the name *Mahican* in this book for two reasons, even though other scholars such as Shirley Dunn and the federally-recognized descendants, the Stockbridge-Munsee Band of Mohican Indians in Bowler, Wisconsin, strongly prefer *Mohican*. I find that this name, popularized by James Fenimore Cooper in the early 19th-century, is easily confused with Mohegan, a distinct and different Native group who lived in Connecticut. Also, *Mahican* is the spelling used consistently during the 17th-century.

3. Recent archaeological work provides some support for the idea of an ancient homeland for Algonquian speakers in the eastern Great Lakes, Curtin 2004.

4. An initial list of Mahican sites dating from the late pre-Contact and Protohistoric periods include the following. For the Lower Mohawk/Saratoga cluster: Triangle Flats, Pottery Beach, Quinn, Seman, Corp and Winney's Rift. For the Upper Hudson cluster: Peebles Island, Van Schaick Island, Schuyler Flatts, Menands Bridge, Fort Orange, Welling, Goes/Van Derzee, Clarkville, Lansingburgh*, "Troy," Riverside, Sterling, Goldkrest*, Van Buren, Van Vechten, Staats House, and "Castleton." For the Mid-Hudson cluster: Black Duck, Rip Van Winkle, Hamburg*, Leeds, Van Orden, Nachte

Jan's, Little Nutten Hook, Rogers Island and Ford. These sites all produce Garoga horizon ceramics. European material has been recovered from those with an asterisk (*).

5. Lavin et al. 1996; Lavin 2004.

6. Brasser 1978; Dunn 1994:50-62

7. A good general source on the Mohawk is Fenton and Tooker 1978. For more recent studies, see Snow 1995a, Funk and Kuhn 2003, and Lenig 1998. For a general introduction to the Iroquois and their world, see Engelbrecht 2003.

8. "Came out of the earth," Wonderly 2005:229. Migration from farther west, Beauchamp 1905:132-34. Archaeological evidence from movement into the Mohawk Valley around one thousand years ago is summarized by Snow 1995c. For a recent re-assessment of the in situ vs. migration argument, see Hart and Brumbach 2005.

9. The sites listed in Table 1.1 are based on Snow 1995a as revised by Wayne Lenig 1998:37 and personal communication. Recent analysis of the Swart family collection in the NYSM has more than doubled the number of Mohawk sites reported by Snow, Lenig 2003. All the sites in Table 1.1 have produced Garoga horizon ceramics. European material has been recovered from those with an asterisk (*). This list does not include floodplain components or sites in the Schoharie Valley such as Vanderwerken*, Cassedy et al. 1996.

10. For the most current discussion of this site, see Funk and Kuhn 2003. Between 1,400 and 3,000 people lived at this site, ibid., p. 151. Occupied between A.D. 1525 and 1545, Kuhn 2004:150.

11. Kuhn and Funk 2000.

12. For a discussion of population estimates, see Engelbrecht 2003:125.

13. Ancient adversaries, Dunn 1994a:91. The idea that Mahican and Mohawk people were friends and neighbors has also been suggested by Curtin 2004:10-11.

14. One exception to this pattern of similarity appears to be a Mahican preference for chert points with a broader, more equilateral shape (Levanna-like) as opposed to the longer, thinner, more isosceles shape (Madison) favored by the Mohawks. See Ritchie 1961:31-34 for definitions.

15. Kuhn 2004; Funk and Kuhn 2003:157

16. "former friends and neighbors'" Van Laer 1908:306.

17. Funk and Kuhn 2003:157

18. See Brumbach and Bender 2002 for a recent review of Woodland period patterns in the upper Hudson River Valley. For a discussion of cord-impressed pottery in the Northeast, see Lavin 2002:160-62. Although the term "Owasco" has been used to describe this cultural phase, its utility has been questioned by Hart and Brumbach 2003. Fagan 2000 provides an excellent overview of the Little Ice Age and its effects.

19. Brumbach 1975, 1995.

20. Diamond 1999:133; Funk and Kuhn 2003:132

21. This discussion is drawn from the work of George Hamell 1987, 1992 and *Maps and Dreams: Native Americans and European Discovery,* an exhibition at the Robert S. Peabody Museum of Archaeology, Andover, MA in 1992-93. See Bradley 1996.

22. Turgeon 1998; Fitzgerald 1990:21-36; Bradley 2005:99-103.

23. For summaries on Basque whaling sites, see Turgeon 1998, Tuck and Grenier 1981, 1989.

24. For more on banded copper kettles, see Fitzgerald et al. 1993. Rim fragments of these distinctive kettles have been recovered from several Mohawk sites including: Mother Creek (Swart collection NYSM A2002.47ED.1.1), Schenk #1 (Wayne Lenig, personal communication), and Martin, Snow 1995a:244 figure 6.4. Artifacts made from this high purity copper have been found at the Mahican Lansingburgh site (Anselmi 2004:212-13) and the Mohawk (?) Vanderwerken site, Cassidy et al 1996:29-31.

25. Beads are described according to the system developed by Kidd and Kidd 1970. Kenyon and Kenyon first defined a series of "Glass Bead Periods," bead assemblages that occur on sites of a specific period of time, in 1983. These have been refined further by Kenyon and Fitzgerald 1986 and Fitzgerald et al. 1995. A small number of GBP 1 style beads have been found on the Mohawk Chapin and Barker sites, Rumrill 1991:7-8. One frit core bead has also been reported from the Barker site, Wayne Lenig, personal communication.

26. Fitzgerald et al. 1995. Trudel 1973.

27. These styles define Glass Bead Period 2 (1600-1625/30) in Canada, Fitzgerald et al. 1995:122. Small samples of these beads have also been found on early 17th-century Mohawk sites such as England's Woods and Cromwell, Rumrill 1991:8; Wayne Lenig, personal communication. Although Turgeon 2001 has argued that these beads were made in Paris, it is more likely they were produced in Amsterdam. See Chapter 2, note 21.

28. For more on Native copper working, see Martin 1999. For a detailed study on how Native peoples in the Northeast adapted these traditional metal-working techniques to European metals, see Anselmi 2004.

29. Craddock 1995:100-102; also see Martin 1999:125-26. Small sandstone abraiders are common artifacts on Protohistoric Mohawk sites, Wayne Lenig, personal communication.

Examples have been reported from the Cromwell (Kuhn 1994:36) and Martin sites (NYSM Swart collection A2002.10AZ.99.23). While these abraiders could be whetstones, they fit the description of Cushing's grinding stones very well.

30. Large, Basque-style axes have been recovered from Dewandelaer and possibly Chapin, Snow 1995a: 218 Figure 5.13, 201. For more in-depth discussion of what has been found on Protohistoric Mohawk sites, see Funk and Kuhn 2003; Snow 1995a.

31. Bradley and Childs 1991. Though not common, several of these distinctive artifacts have been recovered from the Mohawk England's Woods – one spiral and at least six fragments of spirals or hoops, Snow 1995a:213-15, Figures 5.10 and 5.11; Wayne Lenig, personal communication. Examples have also been reported from Smith-Pagerie (spiral), Wormuth (spiral) and Wagner's Hollow (hoop), Wayne Lenig, personal communication. Three spirals were found at the Mahican Lansingburgh site (NYSM Thompson collection 1914.52/30902a-c).

CHAPTER 2

1. Northern European cargoes and expansion into the Mediterranean, Scammell 1981:373-80; Rietbergen 2004:88. With the closing of the port of Lisbon in 1580, Dutch merchants lost access to the traditional source for porcelain, spices and other exotics goods from the Far East. Direct voyages to the East by Dutch vessels were the result, ibid., p.89; Sheaf and Kilburn 1988:81-82.

2. Amsterdam as the Republic's major trading port, Mak 2000:89.

3. The desire to improve their lives, ibid., pp. 55, 99-108.

4. The Republic's moral geography, Schama 1987:43.

5. "took spoil of them, as they would have done of us." Purchas 1906:348.

6. The river was "at an end for shipping." ibid., p. 369. For the text of Juet's journal, see Purchas 1906 and Jameson 1909. For additional comments on Hudson's voyage, see Milton 1999:162-189 and Shorto 2004:13-36.

7. Demand for beaver fur, Turgeon 1998:599. Within a few years several ships sailed intentionally for Hudson's river, Hart 1959:7-15.

8. Partnership with two Norman merchants from Rouen, Hart 1959:15-16. It is important to note that the distinction we make between "French" and "Dutch" did not exist in the early 17th-century. The people who lived in the broad lowlands between the Somme River and the Schelde thought of themselves as Flemish. Joint ventures among Norman, Flemish and Dutch partners were common as were mixed crews on the vessels that sailed to Terra Nova, Morison 1971:252-61.

9. A three-year monopoly over the trade, Hart 1959:33; Rink 1986:32-46.

10. Jan Rodrigues, Hart 1959:23,26. Jacob [Jaques] Eelkins was another Dutch trader with strong Rouen connections, ibid., pp. 54-55. His claim to have "lived four years with" the Indians (Richter 1992:323, note 18) takes on greater significance when compared with the oral tradition recited by later 17th-century Iroquois speakers, stories about the first European, a man "called Jacques" who "came with a ship… and received them as Brethren." See ibid., pp. 87-89 and Lenig 1999:50-51 for more discussion.

11. Probably remained in use from several more years, Rink 1986:48-49; Huey 1988:12-13.

12. Hendrick Christiaensen was killed during a surprise attack, Hart 1959:52. Even Jacques Eelkins was unable to trade successfully, ibid., p.55. Hontom castrated and killed his hostage anyway, Huey 1988:13-16; also see Richter 1992:90. As Charles Gehring has observed, many of the early participants in the fur trade were war veterans and "a pretty tough bunch."

13. North America was the least of its priorities, Rink 1986:50.

14. List of Mahican sites with artifacts from the Independent Traders period. These sites are: Winney's Rift, Mechanicville Road (Waterford), Menands, Lansingburgh, Pottery Beach, Bethlehem and Goldkrest. All these sites produce polychrome beads. To date, no clear evidence has been found from the Columbia and Greene Counties area although the Hamburg site (CTL 29) and Hudson Fire House site may date from this period.

15. These include in the eastern series: Cromwell and Martin; in the central series: Schenck #1, Rice's Woods and Coleman-Van Duesen; and in the western series: Nelliston, Wagner's Hollow and possibly Kilts (although it is not clear whether this is a habitation site). Polychrome beads have been recovered from all these sites. This list is based on Snow 1995a:239-42 and conversations with Wayne Lenig.

16. Snow 1995a:242. There is no evidence for massive population loss among either the Mohawks or the Mahicans due to the introduction of European diseases during this period.

17. Baart et al. 1977, 1986. Particular thanks go to Jan Baart, director emeritus of the Archaeology Department who has supported this project since its inception, and to Jerzy Garwonski, current director, for his continued support.

18. De Roever 1995:77.

19. "beads, knives and hatchets," Jameson 1909:22. Little that would considered as "trade goods," Braat et al. 1998.

20. Kidd and Kidd 1970. Also see Karklins 1985b for an update and clarification of the Kidd system. For more on Native perceptions of glass beads and color, see Hamell 1983, 1992.

21. For more on bead making in Amsterdam, see Karklins 1974, 1985a and Baart 1988. Comments on the recent excavation of the Carel-Soop glasshouse (KLO9) are based on conversations with Wiard Krook and Michael Hulst, Archaeology Department, Amsterdam, and the author's examination of the excavated assemblage. The excavation revealed the base of a large, circular glass oven, one of three known to have existed in the glasshouse, as well as a small rectangular annealing oven. Materials recovered included large crucible fragments (up to 60cm in diameter), chunks of waste glass in many colors, many production tubes (several of which show the marks from pontil attachment) and many examples of drinking glass and bead production waste.

22. For broadcloth, see De Roever 1995:78-82. For ivory and bone combs, see Baart 1995.

23. See Van Dongan 1995a for a more in-depth discussion.

24. Lambert van Tweenhuysen was a prosperous merchant from Zwolle who, in the tradition of Hanseatic traders, dealt in "everything which could make money." His interests ranged from the Baltic to the Iberian Peninsula to Istanbul. In 1604, he helped establish a company based in Rouen for trade in Terra Nova. Van Tweenhuysen also served as a director of the New Netherland Company, Hart 1959:39-41.

25. This includes the first occurrence of chevron or "star" beads (Kidd #IVk3-4). Based on the presence of production tubes and finished examples at KLO9, it is likely that these chevron beads, as well as most of the glass beads of this period, were produced in the Carel-Soop glasshouse.

26. Kenyon and Fitzgerald 1986. Also Rumrill 1991:11; Fitzgerald et al. 1995:122; Lenig 1999:52. Other bead styles that define this horizon include Kidd #IVb29-36, IIbb1 and IVa19.

27. Among the artifacts recovered during the NYSM excavation at Rice's Woods were one complete pewter spoon from Bu. 2 (A-49460.003) and fragments of others from Bu. 6 (A-49464.004) and Bu. 11 (A-49469.001). Both black and white glass buttons were also recovered from Bu. 6 (A-49464.008). The complete spoon is nearly identical to those recovered from Barentz' camp on Nova Zembla, Braat et al. 1998:238. An ivory comb from Rice's Woods is reported in the William Naylon collection, Wayne Lenig, personal communication. Four additional examples were recovered from the contemporary Seneca site, Dutch Hollow, Sempowski and Saunders 2001 (1):225-26.

28. Several of the exotic objects from Martin, including the matchlock serpentine and two coins – a French copper coin with a 1615 date and a late 16th-century German (Nuremburg?) counter or jetton, are reported in Rumrill 1985:5.

29. Werra and Weser wares are slip-decorated earthenwares made in northern Germany during the late 16th and early 17th centuries, and shipped in vast quantities to the Dutch Republic. Werra ware has a red-brown body while Weser ware is off-white to buff. Both are decorated with bands and dots of yellow and green slip and occur in a variety of vessel forms including dishes, bowls and pipkins, Hurst et al. 1986:242-57. As many as eight pieces of Werra and Weser ware, representing at least four different vessels, have been recovered from the Martin site. Wayne Lenig reports two different rim fragments in the Van Epps-Hartley Chapter collection (4135 VE-H and 39-4135 VE-H), a pipkin handle in the Naylon collection (425-G) and another fragment in the Hartley collection; there are also at least four pieces in the Swart collection (NYSM A2002.10AZ.99.50-52). There is one piece of Weser ware from Rice's Woods is in the Swart collection, (NYSM A2002.10BG.99.15). Among the most interesting European items recovered at Rice's Woods by the NYSM is the male portion of a pewter screw top from a glass case bottle (A-49465.001). Although badly corroded, this piece is very similar to the one found at Nova Zembla, Braat et al. 1998:231, #7724.

30. Aside from Eelkins' claim of living with the local Natives for four years (see note 10 above), Christiaensen was reputed to have made ten voyages to the Hudson River before his death in 1619, Hart 1959:52.

31. This assemblage also appears to be present to some degree at Wagner's Hollow, suggesting that this site continued to be occupied into the 1620s, and at Brigg's Run, suggesting that the Mohawks began to live in this location by the mid-1620s.

32. Little has been published on this site aside from Rumrill 1985:6 and 1991:15-18. Among the objects he recovered were a piece of scissors, half of a lead cloth seal and two iron mouth harps, often referred to as "Jew's harps" in the literature. Rumrill also recovered several musket balls and pieces of casting waste from Coleman–Van Duesen, a distinct change from previous sites. Wayne Lenig reports one piece of Werra or Weser ware from this site. Rumrill also notes the presence of a distinctive new bead style – a "shiny coated" red, barrel-shaped bead with an apple green core and pressed ends that result in "a lip-like ridge around either end," Rumrill 1991 Plate IB, upper left, illustrates an example of this style. These beads (Kidd IVa5/7) are the most frequently occurring style on the site. Examples of this distinctive style also occur at Wagner's Hollow (Wayne Lenig, personal communication) and on the Briggs Run site (Rumrill 1991:9) but not at Rice's Woods or Martin. Nearly identical beads were recovered during the excavation of the Carel–Soop glasshouse in Amsterdam. These red beads with an exterior layer of clear glass have the same barrel-shape with flattened ends as the examples from Mohawk sites. The only difference is that they have a black instead of apple green core (Kidd IVa1).

33. Hart 1959:40.

34. "hanging to their breasts as ornaments," Heckewelter 1971[1876]:74.

35. The two re-worked knife blades as well as a sword blade scraper are from Rice's Woods, the Stillman collection, as drawn by Gilbert Hagerty. They are reproduced courtesy of A. Gregory Sohrweide. The flat tanged knife converted into a harpoon illustrated in figure 2.18a is very similar to another example from the Martin site in the Rumrill collection (NYSM A2005.13BE.99.20). The modified knife blade shown in figure 2.18b may have been indented for use as a crooked knife. See note 41 below.

36. No clear evidence of re-used European ceramics have been reported from Mohawk sites to date. However, two examples are known from other Iroquois sites of the Polychrome Bead Horizon. One, from the Onondaga Pompey Center site, is a fragment of polychrome majolica ointment jar (*zalfpot*) made into a disc-shaped pendant, Bradley 2005:156, plate 11a. At the Oneida Cameron site, seven pieces of a Weser ware dish were found in a sealed refuse pit within a longhouse. Two of these had been ground into gaming discs, Bradley and Bennett 1984.

37. For a pre-Contact example, see the double bird effigy comb from Frontenac Island, Ritchie 1965:116-17. Quotes are from Baart 1995:180 which provides a more detailed discussion of European comb production and use.

38. Perhaps the earliest example of a Native copy comes from the Seneca Cameron site #475/41, Wray et al 1991:217. Wayne Lenig reports one European ivory comb from Rice's Woods in the Naylon collection. In addition to a Native-made copy from Martin in the Swart collection (NYSM A2002.10AZ.02.04), Snow illustrates two other examples from Wagner's Hollow, Snow 1995a:268, figures 6.27 and 6.28. For additional Native style combs, see Snow for examples from Rice's Woods (1995a:224-5), Martin (1995a:248) and Wagner's Hollow (1995a:267). Beauchamp was the first to notice these Native-made brass saws and described two examples from Wagner's Hollow, Beauchamp 1902:76 and figures 18 and 135.

39. The example illustrated in figure 2.21 was recovered from the Wagner's Hollow site by Don Lenig and is reproduced courtesy of Wayne Lenig. Made from a piece of kettle brass, this piece shows embrittlement cracks that resulted from insufficient annealing. Wayne Lenig reports another copper spoon from England's Woods in the Klinkhart collection. Also see Beauchamp 1902:55 and Plate 31 for additional examples.

40. Prisch 1982:3; Sempowski and Saunders 2001 (2):567.

41. The inspiration for the crooked knife may have been a beaver incisor hafted in antler, a traditional wood carving tool. See Bradley 2005:149, 151 figure 17 for two examples of knives converted into crooked knives from the Onondaga Pompey Center site.

CHAPTER 3

1. The image of Fortuna occurs frequently in the Republic during this period. Usually portrayed as a neoclassical goddess, standing on a globe and directing the winds of fate and prosperity, Fortuna was emblematic of the commercial and maritime success we associate with "the Golden Age." This image was frequently depicted on gable stones (*gevelstenen*), carved stone plaques that were set into the front wall of homes and institutional buildings to celebrate or invoke Fortune's blessing. For more on Fortuna, see Patch 1927:101-7. The Company's only real hope for rapid wealth lay in war and privateering, Rink 1986:61. For the text of the original charter see Van Laer 1908:86-115

2. Rink 1986:79-80; Huey 1988:25-27.

3. Rink provides an excellent sketch of Van Rensselaer's background 1986:191-99.

4. Shorto 2004:45; Milton 1999:271-342.

5. "Indians were as quiet as lambs," Van Laer 1924:xix; Huey 1988:26-27.

6. Literally nothing left, Jameson 1909:78; Van Laer 1924:219-20.

7. Keep all these Native tribes "devoted to us," ibid., p. 203.

8. The Natives must be "well treated," Van Laer 1924:200. Also see Shorto 2004:46-47.

9. This "reckless adventure," Jameson 1909:85; Van Laer 1924:214. For more discussion of the Mahican – Mohawk War, see Starna and Brandão 2004; Dunn 1994a:96-100.

10. Ibid., p. 99; Van Laer 1908:307.

11. Trade goods were often in short supply or of poor quality, Van Laer 1924:223, 228, 231-32.

12. Rink 1986:102-3.

13. Van Rensselaer's plan was approved, Rink 1986:94-116.

14. Van Laer 1908:157; Dunn 1994a: 100-2, 279.

15. Zandvliet 2002:166. An original copy of the Rensselaerswijck map, probably drawn by Gillis van Scheyndel in 1631 or 1632, is housed in the New York State Library, Manuscripts and Special Collections. This remarkable map, which is 58cm wide and 179cm long, is accessible through the Library's online catalog.

16. A few "fine farms," Van Laer 1908:308-9.

17. Gehring and Starna 1988:1,13,15.

18. Belonged to England by right of prior discovery, Shorto 2004:69-72.

19. A new settlement called Hartford near the site of an earlier WIC trading house, Jennings 1975:188.

20. Europeans could not be trusted, ibid., pp. 226-27.

21. The trade would now be open to all Dutch citizens, Rink 1986:136-73.

22. A series of new farms along the east side of the Hudson, Huey and Luscier 2004; Dunn 1994b, 2003.

23. The size, color and weave of the cloth, Van Laer 1908:427,468-71, 543, 545-46.

24. "The fur trade begins gradually to get into our hands," ibid., p. 520.

25. Ibid., pp. 433-34, 460. For a biographical review of Van Curler, see Bradley 2005b.

26. Huey 1988:26; personal communication 1/11/05.

27. For the 1630s improvements to Fort Orange, see Huey 1988:37. For building outside the fort, see Van Laer 1908:309. "a wretched little fort," Jogues in Snow et al. 1996:31.

28. Huey 1988: 271-72 for component 96c; pp. 237-38 for the guard house foundation, personal communication 11/16/04.

29. Van Rensselaer's account is reproduced in Van Laer 1908:306-12. Shirley Dunn has also written several important articles describing these early Rensselaerswijck settlements: Dunn 1994b, 1997, 2002b, 2003.

30. There is one possible exception. Level Three at the Sterling site appears to be one of the 1637 period farms, possibly that of Van Buren or Simon Walichsen. For more information, see Huey and Luscier 2004.

31. From north to south, these sites are Winney's Rift, Lansingburgh, Menands Bridge, and Riverside. Dating is based primarily on the presence of a WIC trade assemblage.

32. A few fortified sites, Dunn 1994a:103.

33. Mahican people started to leave the central portion of their traditional territory, ibid., pp. 126-29.

34. For example, Snow places Briggs Run in the preceding Independent Traders period, 1995a:250. Rumrill suggests that both Briggs Run and Swart-Farley predate the 1609 to 1624 period, 1991:9-10.

35. The sites dating from the 1624 to 1635 period include Briggs Run, Yates I, Ford, Swart-Farley, Crouse and Sand Hill. Wayne Lenig has identified additional sites that appear to date from this period as well. Sites dating from the 1635 to 1645 period include Bauder, Rumrill-Naylor, Failing and

Oak Hill. It is likely that the occupation at Oak Hill continued later than that of the other sites.

36. For the complete text, see Gehring and Starna 1988:3-4.

37. For examples see Snow 1995a:280-81; Rumrill 1985; Hagerty 1985.

38. Snow 1995b. For a discussion of estimating population, see Brandão 1997:153-61.

39. For details see Huey 1988:241-43, 266-78; 772. Ceramics are also discussed by Wilcoxen 1987:82-88.

40. Beneath the level of the April 1640 flood, Huey 1988:241.

41. Only nobility could afford to eat game, ibid. For glassware, see ibid., pp. 284-85. It is likely that these beakers, known as *façon de Venise* (made in the Venetian style) were produced in the Carel-Soop glasshouse. For ceramics, see ibid., pp. 285-90. The examples shown in figure 3.15 include: c. Dutch majolica dish decorated in the Italian (Montelupo) style (courtesy of the AIHA, 1983.5.8); the three fragments from Fort Orange shown are catalog numbers A.FOR.1971.207, 271 and 202); d. Dutch majolica dish decorated in the Chinese (Wan-Li) style (courtesy of the AIHA, 1983.5.3); the three fragments from Fort Orange are catalog numbers A.FOR.1971.1, 735 and 702.

42. Expatriate English pipe makers who lived in Amsterdam, Huey 1988: 259-61. The five marks shown in Figure 3.16 are Huey's FTO #1-5, ibid., pp. 277-78.

43. See Huey 1988:278-80 for discussion of WIC armaments. The complete wheel lock (FC.1974.273) and excavated bridle (A.FOR.1971.485) are illustrated courtesy of Paul Huey and OPRHP. The bronze cannon (NYSM H-1937.4.1) is an extraordinary object. It was cast by Assuerus Koster, Amsterdam's official gun founder, as part of a 1630 order for cannon from the West India Company. Among its elaborate Baroque embellishments

are dolphin handles, the relief of a ship under sail and the Company's monogram along the barrel, and the maker's name [AUSSUERUS ∗ KOSTER ∗ MEFECIT ∗ AMSTERDAM 1630] in a band around the breech end. Although donated to the museum by a Van Rensselaer family member, Van Laer concluded that this cannon originally had been at Fort Orange, A. J. F. Van Laer, letter dated December 22, 1930, NYSM.

44. "the smell of the Dutch Republic was the smell of tobacco," Schama 1987:189.

45. For English pipemakers in Amsterdam, see Huey 1988:260, 297-98, 608-9. For an interpretation of the rose heelmark as Tudor-related, see De Roever 1987:51 and Dallal 2004:212. Opinions that these marks were generic are personal communications from Don Duco, 5/10/04 and Jan Baart, 5/22/04.

46. Three IP marked pipes have been recovered from Rumrill-Naylor, Rumrill 1985:14 and Wayne Lenig, personal communication 2/15/05. See Huey 1988:296-97 for information on John Plummer. For the Blowers pipe, see McCashion 1979b:88-91; for a comparable example from Amsterdam, see de Haan and Krook 1988:32 #101.

47. "I know how to get wampum," Van Laer 1924:223-27.

48. For Van den Bogart's word list, see Gehring and Starna 1988:51-65.

49. Predominant varieties include Kidd # IVa11/13, IIa7 and IVa19. For Fort Orange beads, see Huey 1988:782. For Mohawk beads, see Lenig 1999:62-63.

50. For wampum at Fort Orange, see Huey 1988:251-52, 273. For wampum on Mohawk sites, see Snow 1995a:279-80. For Briggs Run, see ibid., p. 255. Information on wampum from Yates I is from Wayne Lenig, personal communication 1/4/05. For Oneida Blowers site, see Bennett 1979:20.

51. A fragmentary Leiden (?) seal was recovered from the Yates I site, Wayne Lenig, personal communication 1/4/05. A partial Haarlem seal is reported from the Oneida Wilson site, Wonderly 2001:21.

52. The apostle spoon from Briggs Run is from the Jackowski collection. Photograph by Gilbert Hagerty, reproduced courtesy of A. Gregory Sohrweide.

53. "the money with which they will buy their food, wood, bark house, and other necessaries," Thwaites 1896-1901 (12):119-21; (7):223.

54. The story of wampum and its changing uses is a long and complex one. Good summaries occur in Hamell 1996, Ceci 1989 and Bradley 2005a:178-80.

55. Eelkins' role in the wampum trade is discussed in more detail by Salisbury 1982:147-50. Also see Jameson 1909:86 for Wassenaer's [1624] account of this event. See Peña 2003 for a discussion of Dutch wampum making.

56. "Strange it was to see the great alteration it made in a few years among the Indians themselves," Bradford 1952:203-4. For archaeological evidence of Narragansett wampum making, see Simmons 1970:74-75, 138, 151.

57. "These [great pipes] commonly come from the *Mauquauwogs,* or Man Eaters, three or four hundred miles from us," Williams 1973 [1643]:127. For examples of these pipes from southern New England, see Turnbaugh 1976; Gibson 1980:42-43.

58. Several of these large stone pipes were recorded in the notebooks of 19th-century historians Rufus Grider and A. G. Richmond. A good example is the complete pipe found near Rice's Woods and drawn by Grider in 1895, Richmond collection, Book 2 p. 217 (NYSL, MSC). There are also many examples on the archaeological side. Snow illustrates a fragment of soapstone pipe stem from Briggs

Run, Snow 1995a:256, figure 8.18. Others have been reported from Rumrill-Naylor, Oak Hill and later sites; these are discussed further in Chapter 4. Most interesting is the heavily curated fragment of a soapstone effigy pipe from the Fiske site illustrated in figure 3.22a (Fea collection, NYSM A-38381). This piece is identical to the large effigy pipe found at the Wampanoag Burr's Hill site in Rhode Island, Gibson 1980:43, figure 18. While large wooden pipes rarely survive in the archaeological record, a few examples collected during the 17th-century exist in European museums. For archaeological evidence of wooden pipes, see note 69 below.

59. For folding knives, see Hagerty 1963; Bradley 2005a:141; Fitzgerald 1990: 106-7, 201 figure 62. For iron scrapers, see Bradley 2005a:145, 227 note 29; Fitzgerald 1990:107-8, 203 figure 58. For iron points, see ibid., p. 109, 204 figure 60. At the Rumrill-Naylor site, numerous iron scrapers in three sizes and nine long tanged iron points were recovered, Rumrill 1985:15. Bauder has produced several scrapers and at least one folding knife blade, Naylon collection, Wayne Lenig, personal communication 1/11/05. Snow reports at least one iron scraper from Oak Hill, Snow 1995a:338. At least two folding knife blades and an offset awl from Oak Hill are also present in the Hagerty collection.

60. For a pewter pilgrim badge from the Rumrill-Naylor site, see Snow 1995a:318 figure 8.17. Rumrill also reports a small religious medal from Oak Hill, Rumrill 1985:17. The more controversial religious items reported from Oak Hill are discussed by Snow 1995a:335-37. Other examples of French religious objects from this period include three religious rings from the Oneida Thurston site, Neill 1991:16-7, Appendix C, and a religious medal from the Onondaga Shurtleff site, Bradley 2005a:136, 138 figure 15a.

61. Dutch pipes from these sites are also more frequently marked. In addition to those described in note 46 above, marked examples from Rumrill-Naylor include: the heel mark IR (1), maker unknown, courtesy of Wayne Lenig; the heel marks VO with a horseman (1), a 1640s Gouda mark, Duco 2003 #160, and EB (2), the mark of Edward Bird, the most prominent of the Amsterdam pipe makers, courtesy of Gary Bernhardt; and a stem marked with PG with fleur de lis on a stem, Rumrill 1985:13. Heel marks from Bauder include: the small tulip or thistle (1), a Gouda mark from the mid 1640s, Duco 2003 #60, and two unidentified, but probably Amsterdam, marks – RH (Robert Henrickse?)(1) and HF (1), Rumrill 1985:12; and two additional Amsterdam marks – WT (1), probably Willem Thomas or Willem Tamkins, Amsterdam pipe makers of the 1640s, Duco 1975:11, and EB (1) in the Hagerty collection . An even larger assemblage of marked pipes has been recovered from Oak Hill. See McCashion 1979a:74-85 and Snow 1995a:356-58 for a discussion of these marks.

62. Rumrill 1991:16. The varieties that define this Blue Bead Horizon are Kidd # IIa40 and IIb56. Nonetheless, the several of the earlier "seed" bead varieties continue to occur (IIa7, IVa11/13) and there is a perceptible increase in tubular beads as well, Lenig 1999:63.

63. Rumrill recovered one tubular CAMPEN seal from Bauder and three examples, two tubular and one round from Rumrill-Naylor, Rumrill 1985:12, 14. Hagerty recovered one "lead bale seal" from Oak Hill (T187). For a recent summary on cloth seals, see Baart 2005.

64. Snow reports several gun parts from Bauder, Snow 1995a:305. A careful examination of these pieces from the Hagerty collection indicates an eclectic mixture of wheel lock and

snaphaunce parts. Rumrill's large assemblage from the Rumrill-Naylor site provides a clearer indication of the diverse nature of these weapons, Rumrill 1985:15-6. They include components from Spanish miquelet locks, wheel locks, English-style "doglocks" (both musket and pistol size) and snaphaunce locks, Puype 1985:85-86. The firearm assemblage from Oak Hill shows a similar mix of styles including two Type I lockplates in the Hagerty collection. One of these is illustrated (upside down) in Snow 1995a:339, figure 8.45. Clearly, these firearms were not standardized for trade and the Mohawks were happy to use whatever they could get.

65. Dutch settlers often used these goods to obtain food, guide services or other necessities, Van Laer 1924:232.

66. Lenig 1999:60. For more on Shantok pottery, see Lavin 2002; Goodby 2002.

67. The frequency of Huron-related pottery is greater than on previous sites, Kuhn 2004:152-53. Additional examples of Mohawk pottery with Huron effigy and castellation forms from the Oak Hill site are in the Lenig collection.

68. A deliberate strategy of capturing other people, Brandão 1997:43.

69. Examples of copper or brass pipe liners have been reported from: Coleman – van Duesen (Snow 1995a:265), Briggs Run (Snow 1995a:253, 255 figure 6.12), Bauder (Hagerty collection #1730), Rumrill-Naylor (Snow 1995a:318 figure 8.16) and Oak Hill (Hagerty collection #T73; Snow 1995a:346. Conical bowl liners have been recovered from most of these sites as well.

70. Sheet brass effigies have been recovered from the Mohawk Coleman – Van Duesen site, Rumrill 1985:6, and Sand Hill site, Luft collection, Wayne Lenig, personal communication, 1/29/05. In addition to the sheet lead effigies found on Bauder and Rumrill-Naylor sites, Rumrill reports

other examples (geese) from Oak Hill, Rumrill 1988:21. Snow reported a cast lead turtle from Briggs Run in the Jackowski collection but the provenience of this object is unclear, Snow 1995a:252.

CHAPTER 4

1. Trelease 1960:60-84; Rink 1986: 216-21.

2. Floods and poor crops, Van Laer 1908:514. Evacuation of Fort Orange, Huey 1988:37.

3. Van Laer 1908:486.

4. Nucleus for the Colonie's settlement, Van Laer 1908:454-55. A tough company town, Shorto 2004:61, 83-89.

5. Potential for the trade, Van Laer 1927/28:29. For an example of Van Curler's frustration in trying to enforce trade ordinances, see ibid., pp. 24-25.

6. Ibid., pp. 27-28.

7. Venema 2003:46, 50.

8. Van Laer 1927/28:21, 29.

9. Ibid., p. 28.

10. This width dimension referred to the space between the frames. With 10 foot aisles on either side, the actual width of the building was probably closer to 48 feet.

11. Jogues escape, Jameson 1909:244, 246-48. Treaty of friendship and brotherhood, Van Laer 1920 (2):215.

12. Van Laer 1908:690.

13. Schama 1987:19; Van Laer 1922:11.

14. House of commerce closed, Huey 1988:41. Privatizing portions of the fort, ibid., pp. 42, 49.

15. Trelease 1960:82-83. Jesuit accounts in Snow et al. 1996:47-61.

16. Venema 2003:48-52.

17. Working at the Flatts, Van Laer 1922:95. The best farm in the Colonie, Van Laer 1908:743.

18. Renew the former alliance, Van Laer 1922:128-29. Fathered a Mohawk daughter, Wilcoxen 1979.

19. Labatie's brewery, Huey 1988:281, personal communication 1/12/05. Hints of what buildings looked like, Huey 1988:291-93.

20. Ibid., p. 327.

21. Ibid., pp. 328-31.

22. Remained property of the Company, ibid., p. 50. Staats and Van Doesburgh houses, ibid., pp. 53, 335-37; 63, 346-47. Description of cellars, ibid., pp. 339-40, 347-48.

23. Patroon's house and storehouse, Venema 2003:46. Jogues' description, in Snow et al. 1996:32. Court sessions and church, Venema 2003:23, 49.

24. Eight more had been constructed, Van Laer 1920, (1):8. Probably closer to forty, Venema 2003:52.

25. A planned town, ibid., p. 50. The Fuyck, ibid., pp. 13, 52.

26. This was exactly the offense with which Douw was charged in the spring of 1649, Van Laer 1922:70-71. For a profile of Douw, see Venema 2003:249-54.

27. As early as 1647, Huey 1987:19. The best description of this complex site is Peña 1990. A cellar with stone walls, Huey 1987:21.

28. Probably built by Juriaen Theunissen, Venema 2003:305, 462. An illicit trader's house, Moody 2003.

29. Dunn 1994; Huey and Luscier 2005.

30. The farm of Cornelis van Buren, Huey 1984:71; Huey and Luscier 2005. Transferring the farm with "a new house and barns," Dunn 1994:65.

31. *Het Zeepaert,* Huey and Luscier 2005:68. Known for his violent temper, Dunn 2002:35.

32. Brewer 1990:10-11.

33. Livestock, Van Laer 1927/28:21, 27. Box stalls and stabling, ibid., p.21.

34. Huey 1998:28.

35. Van Wijk 1987:165

36. Ibid., pp. 165-69

37. This reconstruction is based on comments from Jan Baart, 10/28/04.

38. Mathook and sith, Cohen 1992:127. Siths, also called "Hainault scythes," were frequently listed in the inventories of tools and materials imported into the Colonie. Van Laer 1908:264, 397. The raw material for these silver/gray schist whetstones comes from Eidsborg near the town of Skien on the southwest coast of Norway. The Benedictine nunnery on the nearby island of Gimsoy received the right to trade these whetstones ca. A.D. 1200 and maintained that monopoly until ca. 1670. Baart 1986; personal communication 10/27/05. Rensselaerswijck inventories also occasionally list "Norse files," possibly a reference to these Norwegian whetstones, Van Laer 1908:192.

39. Greenbush, Dunn 2002. Where the houses of all the mechanics must be built, Van Laer 1908:611.

40. Evidence of an earlier building that had been demolished, Feister 2003. Where Megapolensis lived, Van Laer 1908:828. Carved stones, Feister 2003:5.

41. "They are very friendly," Megapolensis in Snow et al. 1996:43. "We have not… been free from Indians," Shorto 2004:58. Native fields along the Kats-kil, Jameson 1909:206.

42. For land sales, see Dunn 1994:280-81. Van der Donck, in Snow et al. 1996:124.

43. "For a loaf of bread, a knife or even a tobacco pipe," Megapolensis in Snow et al. 1996:39. That the land was still theirs, Dunn 1994:133. The tendency to take anything that was not nailed down, Van Laer 1922:214; Venema 2003:40. A party that could continue for days, Venema 2003:40-41.

44. Sites with components that date to this period include: Winney's Rift, Peebles Island, Lansingburgh, Menands Bridge, Riverside, Little Nutten Hook, Luykas van Alen, Rip Van Winkle and Leeds.

45. Mahicans split into two groups, Dunn 1994:232. Riverside site, Huey et al. 1977. For additional discussion, see Huey 1996:142.

46. "The conquered are obliged," Megapolensis, in Snow et al. 1996:41. Mohawk claim right on conquest, Dunn 1994:112-14.

47. Many deaths, including that of Isaac Jogues, Brandão 1997:147. "To make them both but one people," Jogues, in Snow et al. 1996:21. His Mohawk mother was an adopted Huron, Snow et al. 1996: 69, 73, 81.

48. "Unbearable even to their allies," Thwaites 1896-1901 33:123. Bradley 2005a:182-84.

49. Venema 2003:43. Talk of war "against the Hollanders," Snow et al. 1996:89.

50. Description of Mohawk villages, Megapolensis, in Snow et al. 1996:46. Van der Donck, in ibid. pp. 110-12.

51. The sites dating from 1635 to 1645 include Bauder, Rumrill-Naylor, Van Evera-McKinney, Oak Hill, Duffy Lot and Failing. Sites from the 1645 to 1652 period include Yates II, Mitchell, Janie and Lipe.

52. Populations estimates too high, Snow 1995b:1603. Brandão 1997:158, table C.5.

53. Pig and deer bones at Fort Orange, Huey 1988:362-63. "As fat as any Holland cow," Megapolensis, in Snow et al. 1996:39. Fish, birds and shellfish from Dutch sites, Pipes 2002, 2005; Huey 1988:282-84. Plant remains from Douw's cellar, NYSM collections (A1987.5.403.2).

54. For ceramic frequencies at Fort Orange see Huey 1988:772, table 7. *Hollants Porceleyn,* Baart 2000a; Baart et al. 1990/2.

55. Westerwald stoneware, Gaimster 1997:251-52. Round-bodied wine bottles appear for the first time, Huey 1988:371. For relationship between Portugal and the Republic between 1640 and 1652, see Scammell 1981:296-97.

56. Huey 1988:785.

57. Pipe stem whistles, Huey 1974. For iron mouth harps from Amsterdam, see Baart et al. 1977:476-77; from Fort Orange, see Huey 1988:377; from KeyCorp, see NYSM (A1987.05.406.20). For brass examples marked R from Fort Orange, see Huey 1988:304, 377; from KeyCorp, see NYSM (A1987.05.403.15).

58. Concept of *patria,* Schama 1987:69. Several of these coins and medals have been found on sites within New Netherland and its sphere of influence. A coin struck in 1590 in honor of Prince Maurice was recovered from the Augustine Heerman's ca. 1645 to 1651 warehouse in New York, Cantwell and Wall 2001:154-55, figure 9.20. Two medallions also of Prince Maurice dated 1615 were found at Burr's Hill, a mid 17th-century Wampanoag burial ground in Warren, RI, Gibson 1980:112-14, figure. 104. An undated medal of William, Prince of Orange – probably William II, stadholder from 1647 to 1651 – was found on the Onondaga Indian Castle site during the 19th-century, Beauchamp 1903:69.

59. Brass mirror box covers of Frederick Henry "Prince of Orange, Count of Nassau, 1634" have been found on several Iroquoian sites including Seneca Dann site (RMSC 239/28, Wray 1985:108), the Oneida Thurston site (Pratt 1976:232) and the Susquehannock Byrd Leibhart site (Kent 1984:206-7). An undated mirror box cover of Wilhelm Frederick, Prince of Orange, was recovered from the Seneca Power House site, RMSC 1348/24, Wray 1985:108.

60. Evidence of other 17th-century games from Amsterdam, Baart et al. 1977:455-71. Marbles from Fort Orange, Huey 1988:275, 377. Marbles have also been recovered from the Van Buren and Van Vechten sites.

61. For background on "cabinets of curiosities," see Hamell 1982a.

62. Quartz crystal from Juriaen Theunissen's house site, Moody 2003:36. Effigy pipe from Fort Orange, Huey 1988:303, 696, figure 75. Virtually identical examples have been found on the Thurston site (Oneida), Pratt 1976:225, Plate 34 #6, and Power House site (Seneca), Engelbrecht 2003:58, figure 27. Fragment of a second effigy pipe at Fort Orange, Huey 1988:379.

63. Three silver coins reputedly found at the Oak Hill site are a good example of European objects that may have been a "curiosity" among Native people, Kier 1949. All were apparently two-stuiver coins minted in either Zeeland or Overijssel. As George Hamell has observed, the image of a standing lion clasping a group of arrows in one paw was a piece of iconography that Native people would have noticed, even if they did not understand exactly what it meant.

64. Jogues, in Snow et al. 1996:32.

65. "For the purpose of keeping others out," Van Laer 1908:553.

66. April 1649 court order, Van Laer 1922:70-71. No longer possible to monopolize the trade, Venema 2003:38, 200.

67. "So much merchandise has been sent," Van Laer 1908:486, 561.

68. There are many sources on Edward Bird, among them McCashion 1979:7-9; Bradley and DeAngelo 1981:111-13; De Roever 1987; Huey 1988:299-300, 455-57; den Braven 2003 and Dallel 2004:226-30. Loaned 200 guilders to Brian Newton, De Roever 1987:56; Huey 1988:300. Distributed pipes through Reiner Rycken, Huey 1988:457-58. Hendrick Gerdes, McCashion 1979:8-9; Dallal 2004:227.

69. De Roever 1987; De Haan and Krook 1988.

70. Three examples, one of which was marked EB, were found in pre-1648 contexts at Fort Orange, Huey 1988:299.

71. Hall 1996:119, 127. See Table 5.1 for additional New Netherland examples.

72. The Two Roses was founded in 1622 by Claes Rochusz Jaquet, a glassblower who had trained in the Carel-Soop glasshouse, Michael Hulst, personal communication, 10/24/05. It appears that Jaquet continued to make many of the same styles of beads in his facility after the Carel-Soop glassworks closed in 1624. These included dark blue tubes (IIIa12) from which small circular (IVa12) beads were produced as well as virtually all the monochrome and polychrome varieties that occur on 1630 to 1655 period Mohawk sites. While the site of the Two Roses has not been documented archaeologically, associated waste deposits have suggested a change in color preference, Baart 1988:71-72.

73. "To be bartered to the Indians and other inhabitants," O'Callaghan 1849-1851 (2):340-42.

74. The cheapest, and coarsest, woolens continued to come from Campen. Mid-grade woolens came from Leiden while the most expensive were from Amsterdam. Jan Baart, personal communication, 3/16/01. For examples of cloth seals from these towns, see Wonderly 2001; Baart 2005.

75. Wampum production at Fort Orange, Huey 1988:294-95, 376. An activity for the poor, Peña 2003.

76. Gunstock makers and smiths working together, Venema 2003:280. Evidence for European production includes brazing and other joining or forming techniques not yet practiced by Native craftsmen.

77. First evidence of pewter pipes comes from the Rumrill-Naylor site, Rumrill 1985:13. For pewter pipes from the Mitchell and Janie sites, see ibid. 22-24. Radisson's personal experience with a Mohawk pewter pipe, Snow et al. 1996:78.

78. Although Roger Williams observed that "They have an excellent Art to cast our Pewter and Brass into very neat and artificial Pipes," it is not clear whom he meant by "They," Williams 1973 [1643]:127. At present there is no evidence that the Mohawks were casting objects this sophisticated at that time. For another recent discussion of pewter pipes, see Veit and Bello 2004. The examples illustrated in Figure 4.34 are based on actual specimens. These include: a. a plain, bulbous shaped bowl from the Mohawk Mitchell site (Rumrill collection, NYSM), b. a plain, funnel-shaped bowl from the Mohawk Mitchell site (Rumrill collection, NYSM), c. a funnel-shaped bowl with "panther" effigy from the Mohawk Mitchell and Janie sites (Rumrill collection, NYSM) and the Seneca Dann site (NYSM 20602), d. a funnel-shaped bowl with perching bird from the Mohawk Janie site (Rumrill collection, NYSM) and the Seneca Power House site (RMSC #1345/24, Wray 1964, Plate 9 top), e. a funnel-shaped bowl (?) with monkey smoking a pipe from the Onondaga Lot 18 site (Bradley 2005a:137, figure 14d). George Hamell has suggested that the seated monkey may be a pun on the name of the prominent Mahican sachem, Skiwas, whose Dutch nickname, Aepjen, meant "little monkey." See Dunn 1994:164-67 for more on Aepjen. f. a nesting (or swimming?) bird figure from a ca. 1630-50 period Seneca site (RMSC 501/100, Hamell 1982b, figure 6h).

79. Pewter pipes are essentially unknown in Europe, Wiard Krook, personal communication, 10/25/05. Small-scale casting in Dutch communities, Baart et al. 1977:201, 420-21, and personal communication, 8/10/85. Cornelis Bogardus' pipe mold, Munsell 1865 (3):89.

80. Van Laer 1908:484.

81. Fitzgerald et al. 1995:123.

82. The earliest occurrence of religious rings on Mohawk sites is one L-heart ring at the Van Evera – McKinney site, Wayne Lenig, personal communication, 2/15/05. As many as a dozen rings, primarily IHS-cross and L-heart varieties, have been reported from the later Mitchell and Janie sites, Rumrill 1985:22-23. There has been extensive discussion on the meaning of these devices, see Cleland 1972; Wood 1974. Mandzy provides the most compelling explanation for IHS – that this contraction of IHSOUS is the central motif in the seal of the Society of Jesus, Mandzy 1986:53. There is general consensus that the L-heart motif reflects the sacred heart of Jesus and abbreviation of the Latin word "laudare" or, in English, "to praise." Several other Jesuit-related artifacts have also been reported from the Oak Hill site. See Snow 1995a:335-36.

83. While the Mohawk fired their muskets in salute, Van Laer 1927/28:27-28. Jogues' assessment, in Snow et al. 1996:21.

84. Part of the supplies sent to the Colonie, Van Laer 1908:263-65. Ordinances prohibiting sale, ibid., pp. 426, 565.

85. Winthrop's note on confiscated firearms, Hosmer 1908 (2):161. See Trelease 1960:95-101 for a more detailed review.

86. Vogel 1996.

87. Puype 1985 (1):20-28.

88. This pipe was found by a farmer while plowing and subsequently drawn by Rufus Grider in September 1886, Grider Sketchbook I, p. 47, New York State Library, Manuscripts and Special Collections. Adelbert G. Richmond also drew similar pipes from other Mohawk sites; see Richmond, Book II, p. 217, New York State Library, Manuscripts and Special Collections. Several fragments of similar pipes are known from the Mitchell and Lipe sites. One of the stem fragments from Lipe in the Lenig collection has been incised for a lead or pewter collar.

89. Since these oversized pipes are very unusual, a more detailed description of known examples is provided here. The examples illustrated in Figure 4.39 include an unprovenienced example in the New York State Museum collection (#16849) with a stem bore of 10/64" and a large tulip heel mark (FTO #50). The fragment from the Oak Hill site in the Lenig collection is from a massive pipe, one with a stem bore of 12/64" and a cartouche of four fleur de lis stamped on the heel. This mark was not found at Fort Orange but has been reported from the mid 17th-century Onondaga Indian Castle site, Bradley and DeAngelo 1981:112, figure 2j, 126. The two stem fragments from the Rumrill-Naylor site (Rumrill collection, NYSM) have 10/64" stem bores; one is stamped with the cartouche of four fleur de lis. Several other examples of these very large pipes are known from the Oak Hill site. One in the Hagerty collection is nearly identical to Lenig's, with the same heel mark but a smaller stem bore diameter of +8/64", McCashion 1979:76-77. McCashion also illustrates "the largest Dutch pipe from North America" from the Jackowski collection, ibid., pp. 84-85. This pipe is probably the one found at Oak Hill by Harry Schoff, Snow 1995a:335. Snow also recovered two "large bowl fragments" during his excavations on the site, ibid., p. 356. Though rare, pieces of these very large pipes have also been recovered from Dutch sites in New Netherland. Huey found a bowl and stem fragment (A.FOR.1971.429) with a large tulip heel mark (FTO #50) and a +9/64" stem bore in component 66 at Fort Orange, Huey 1988:785. Brustle also recovered a very large stem fragment with a bore of +9/64" and complex rouletting from cellar #2 at the Flatts. A few of these very large pipes have been reported in Europe. Davey illustrates an example with a large tulip heel mark (FTO #50) identical to three of the pipes described above (NYSM #16849, Fort Orange

and Jackowski's specimen from Oak Hill). Davey identifies these as Gouda pipes dating between 1650 and 1660, Davey 1981:453, #22. Duco lists the tulip as a Gouda mark registered as early as 1643, Duco 2003:128, #61.

90. Received with "great joy," Van Laer 1927/28:27. Kiliaen van Rensselaer used this strategy with other special objects. In 1640, he sent several "very fine blankets" to Van Curler with instructions that they be given to the "most influential" Mohawk and Mahican chiefs "as a sign of peace and friendship," Van Laer 1908:508-9.

91. Old men carving wooden bowls and spoons, Van der Donck, in Snow et al. 1996:120. The antler ladle (RMSC #5000/100) is from the Seneca Steele site, Prisch 1982:23. A similar example from the Oneida Quarry site is illustrated in Bennett 1984: Plate 6, #4.

92. See Sempowski 1989:90-92 and Figure 15 for examples of these forms from contemporary Seneca sites.

93. The burial that contained "a mass of 12,000 wampum beads" was burial #135 at the Power House site. Wray's field notes indicate that it was the grave of a young male and also contained a complete musket with a .62 caliber barrel and a Type II flintlock (see note 96 below) and "a long-stem pewter pipe," Hamilton 1980:24-25. "In general use for buying everything one needs," Van der Donck, in Snow et al. 1996:119. "Girdles of wampum...," ibid., pp. 109-10.

94. Rumrill 1988:20, figure 2.

95. In addition to the examples shown in Figure 4.38 and discussed in Note 88 above, a large, coarsely made stem from Rumrill-Naylor may be the earliest evidence of Native attempts to cast a lead pipe. This piece is illustrated in Figure 5.34b.

96. An example is Burial #135 at the Seneca Power House site. In addition to a complete musket, this burial also contained a cache of six additional locks, a "mass" of gun parts, more than 150 lead balls, a bar of lead

and two antler powder measures, Hamilton 1980:24-25. Based on the recovery of similar Type II locks and brass fittings, this appears to be the same style of musket that Arent van Curler produced at the Flatts.

97. Van der Donck, in Snow et al. 1996:107.

98. The faience pendant from the Lipe site is in the Jan Swart collection, Wayne Lenig, personal communication 2/15/05. Pieces of at least three identical faience wine jugs (*wijnkan*) were recovered from cellar #2 at the Flatts. Three gaming discs from the Seneca Power House site provide another example of how fragments of these white faience jugs were re-used, Wray 1985:109, figure 10d.

CHAPTER 5

1. Ready to seize New Amsterdam, Rink 1986:255-57. Brazil ... one of the Company's few remaining assets, ibid., p. 169.

2. Burghership was the basic organizing principle of Dutch communities, Venema 2003:5-7.

3. Douw... one of the community's wealthiest and most respected members, Venema 2003:250, 254. Philip Schuyler, ibid., pp. 254-55. Wampum's decreasing value, ibid., pp. 158-59.

4. "A jealousy almost verging on fury," Thwaites 1896-1901 (43):129. "I greatly doubt whether Iroquois policy can go so far," ibid., (44):149-51.

5. Trelease 1960:121-22.

6. Venema 2003:203-4, 158-59.

7. "Bung up the casks," Van Laer 1920 (2):212. A new war between the Dutch and Esopus, Fried 1975:22-28; Dunn 1994:144-45.

8. Brothers "only as long as we have beavers," Van Laer 1920 (2):211-12. "To enter into a further alliance," ibid., p. 214. For more details on this embassy, see ibid., pp. 214-19.

9. Diversify into other commodities such as tobacco, lumber and grain, Venema 2003:203-6.

10. "Will never make peace," Lalement, in Snow et al. 1996:137. "No longer in a condition to make war," ibid., p. 140. "If the Mohawk could be defeated militarily," ibid., p. 134.

11. "Great losses on both sides," ibid., p. 140. Also see Van Laer 1932:325-26. For more on the complex and shifting relationships among the Dutch, English, Mohawks, Abenaki and other New England tribes during the 1660s, see Bruchac and Thomas 2006.

12. Rink 1986:262; Shorto 2004:307.

13. Huey 1988:76-78, 108-9, 762.

14. The largest and most complete structure uncovered at Fort Orange, Huey 1987:18. Three very similar windows, probably originally from Beverwijck and decorated by Evert Duyckinck, survive in the collections of the New York Historical Society, Krizner and Sita 2001:18. Another similar enameled window dated 1656 survives from the First Reformed Dutch Church of Albany, AIAH #1984.22. Also see Blackburn and Piwonka 1988:53, figure 12.

15. For background on Van Doesburgh and his wife, see Venema 2003:33, 190. Couple probably moved into town, Huey 1996b, citing Munsell 1870:10-11, 21. House finally collapsed in 1664, Huey 1988:347, and personal communication, 5/12/05.

16. "No business is to be done there...," Van Laer 1932:164.

17. Several efforts were made to repair, Huey 1988:94-95. The landing place for sloop traffic, ibid., pp. 89-90, 92. For information on the courthouses, see Van Laer 1920:10; Huey 1993:27.

18. The source of the refuse, Huey 1988:405. Trash from Adriaen Jansen Appel's tavern, ibid., pp. 467, 473-74.

19. Venema 2003:84.

20. Huey 1993:27-28; Venema 2003: 86-87.

21. Descriptions of the palisade are from Venema 2003:93. No archaeological documentation, Huey 1991:328-29.

22. Venema 2003:94-95.

23. For Juriaen Teunissen's movements, see ibid., p. 291, 303-5, 462. For archaeological evidence of his activities, see Hartgen Archeological Associates, Inc. 2002, Chapter 4, p. 5.

24. Stuyvesant's three boundary markers defining Beverwijck were set 1,200 steps (or 600 paces) from the fort. Venema 2003:51.

25. Wooden houses tended to "wear out in a few years," Van Laer 1908:563. See Venema 2003:64-77 for details and plan views of houses. Preference for stone or brick-lined cellars, Van Laer 1932:176-77; also see Huey 1993:27-29.

26. Venema 2003:74.

27. For background on roads, see ibid., p. 61. For Huey's brief report, see Huey 1984:74.

28. Initial testing and recommendations are summarized in Hartgen Archaeological Associates, Inc. 1986. The subsequent work was done by Collamer and Associates, Inc. 1988a. For a summary on the location of the churchyard, see Venema 2003:86. Church records for November 1670 refer to the "old graveyard" and the "new graveyard," see Munsell 1865 (1):32.

29. Robert Kuhn, personal communication, 8/2/02.

30. While no contemporary view of Beverwijck is known, the Castello plan provides a detailed view of New Amsterdam ca. 1664. See Blackburn and Piwonka 1988:93-95.

31. Hartgen Archaeological Associates 1985. For discovery of deeply buried deposits by amateur excavators, see Times-Union, 3/18/86.

32. Collamer Archaeological Associates, Inc. 1988b.

33. For the initial report and recommendations, see Hartgen Archaeological Associates 1987. Collamer would not discuss what was found during her fieldwork but a representative of the developer stated that "nothing found

on the site appears to be of historic significance"; see Times-Union, 8/25/87. It is not clear whether a report was ever produced. For the report on Hartgen's subsequent work, see Hartgen Archaeological Associates 1997.

34. Initial testing and recommendations are summarized in Hartgen Archaeological Associates 1996a, 1996b. For summaries of the dispute and refusal to permit other archaeologists to view the excavation or examine the artifacts recovered, see Hartgen 1997, 2003. Current status of the collection and lack of a report is based on discussions with Tammis Groft, curator, AIHA, most recently June 2006.

35. For a review of the archaeology, see Moody 2005. For information on changing ownership and occupancy, also see Venema 2003:90; Bradley 2005b:9.

36. For other discussions of the Bronck house, see Reynolds 1929:66-67; Blackburn and Piwonka 1988:138. For more on Pieter Bronck, see Venema 2003:294-96.

37. More than 30 tin-glazed tiles were recovered from cellar #2. The majority (20) have the vase of flowers (bloemvaas) motif with ox head corners, Korf 1979:118, Figure 363. Another dozen depict small animals on a white background. These also have ox head corners, Korf 1979:148, Figure 504, 507. Two tiles have Wan Li corners, Korf 1979:142, Figure 484/273. A small number of tiles with the same motifs were recovered from cellar #1.

38. This style of hearth continued to be used in Dutch houses well into the 18th-century. See Blackburn and Piwonka 1988:146 and 150 for discussion.

39. For a summary on Douw and his land dealings, see Huey and Luscier 2004:66; Dunn 1994:65-66. Papscanee as Douw's primary residence, Peter Christoph to Paul Huey, personal communication, 3/24/86.

40. In addition to glass beads, EB pipes and evidence of firearms, Van Buren is the only other Rensselaerswijck farm site that has produced stone pipes, worked marine shell, brass projectile points and other similar trade-related objects. The gray-green soapstone pipe bowl (#A.PX.1992.59) from Van Buren illustrated in Figure 5.19a is virtually identical to an example illustrated by Richmond and mentioned in note 88, Chapter 4 above. The unfinished pipe from the Flatts is made of a hard gray limestone and was found by Paul Huey on the surface near cellar #1.

41. First settlement in June 1653, Fried 1975:24. "Not to sell any more brandy," Van Laer 1920 (1):88.

42. Vos was an old Rensselaerswijck hand who arrived in the Colonie in August 1642. An excellent shot, he was hired to serve as the Rensselaerswijck "court messenger," or the man who enforced the court's orders, Van Laer 1908:829. In this capacity Vos served as a bounty hunter, bringing the wayward Van den Bogart back from Oneida country in 1647, Gehring and Starna 1988:xxi. Many complaints were lodged against Vos for selling liquor during 1657 and 1658. In response, he threatened to "tie a rope around the neck" of anyone who denounced him and "throw them into the kill," Van Laer 1920 (2):26. Although Vos' primary residence was at Katskil, he maintained a house in Fort Orange during this period. Huey may have found a portion of that house during his excavations, Huey 1988:341-42.

43. Decision to relocate into a centralized community, Fried 1975:29-30. For information on the 1658 palisade, see Bridges 1974 and Feister and Sopko 2003. For a summary on the First Esopus War, see Fried 1975:33-42.

44. Diamond 2004 (1):73.

45. O'Callaghan and Fernow, 1853-87 (13):195-99.

46. Establishment of New Dorp, Fried 1975:52-53. Among the backers were several prominent Beverwijck merchants, among them Volckert Jansz

Douw and Philip Schuyler, Diamond 2004 (1):11. "We are in great danger of drawing upon us a new war," O'Callaghan and Fernow, 1853-87 (13):228-29. Fried 1975:55-62.

47. Evidence for the burning of the town was found in Strata Group 11, Diamond 2004 (1):76. Evidence of Van Imbroach's construction was in Strata Group 16, ibid., p. 79.

48. For more on Van Curler and the founding of Schenectady, including specific citations for quotes, see Bradley 2005b:12-13.

49. See Dunn 1994:279-86 for details of these sales.

50. A distinction between the Mahican and the Katskil, Van Laer 1920 (2):222. For Aepjin's efforts to mediate, see Dunn 1995:185-212. "Katskil remain in our league as brothers," Van Laer 1932:327.

51. For Lalement's comments on the Loups, see Snow et al. 1996:140, 143. For sale of Mahican lands by the Mohawks, see Dunn 1994:116-17.

52. Lalement, in Snow et al. 1996:140.

53. The Greene County sites include Four Mile Point, the Bronck House Rockshelter, Rip Van Winkle and Leeds. The sole Columbia County site known at present is Little Nutten Hook. It is likely that additional sites exist along lower Kinderhook and Stockport Creeks.

54. Poncet, in Snow et al. 1996:102.

55. Lalement, in Snow et al. 1996:133.

56. "One would never believe how few they are," ibid., pp. 132, 137. Brandão estimates the Mohawk population in 1659-60 at 4,500, dropping to 2,700 by 1665, Brandão 1997:165, table C.5. Snow's population estimates for the period, once again, seem out of line, Snow 1995b:1603. "No longer in a condition to make war" and "within two finger-breadths of total destruction," Lalement, in Snow et al. 1996:140, 142.

57. "Help them repair their stockades," Van Laer 1920 (2):45. Repair request, ibid., pp. 212-13. Their villages "have no palisades," Snow et al. 1996:137.

58. Kuhn and Snow 1986. Also see Snow 1995a:403-10. Thanks to Wayne Lenig for sharing the information from his father's excavations.

59. The sites dating between 1652 and 1658 include Printup, Yates III, Philip Failing, Fisk and Prospect Hill. Those from the 1658 to 1666 period include Freeman, Cromwell II, Allen, Brown, Shineman, Fort Plain Cemetery and Jackson-Everson. As with the Mohawk sites discussed in previous chapters, much of the information on these sites and their chronological placement has come through the generosity of Wayne Lenig and the cumulative wisdom of the Van Epps – Hartley Chapter , NYSAA.

60. See Snow 1995a:371-75. These excavations were conducted during the mid-1960s by Dr. Kingston Larner and other members of the Van Epps – Hartley Chapter of the New York State Archaeological Association.

61. "Dogs and rascals" and to "live with them as brothers," Van Laer 1920 (2):222.

62. See Venema 2003:258-62 for more discussion of wealth.

63. Analysis of faunal remains has been done by Marie-Lorraine Pipes. In addition to the brick maker's house, Quackenbush Square (Pipes 2004) and the Flatts (Pipes 2005), she has also analyzed faunal assemblages from the DEC and DASNY sites.

64. Examples of both 8 1/4" and 9" wide delftware plates with broad undecorated rims were recovered from the Van Doesburgh house, Huey 1988:412-13, personal communication, 8/1/05. These plates were made primarily in the city of Delft and became popular during the 1650s, Jan Baart, personal communication, 10/6/04.

65. Fragments of at least three faience wine jugs (*wijnkan*) and a porringer were recovered from cellar #2 at the Flatts. One wine jug was found in the Van Doesburgh cellar, Huey 1988: 414-15. For the lobed dish at Fort Orange, see ibid., p. 369.

66. Porcelain from cellar #1 at the Flatts, Paul Huey, personal communication, 8/1/05. The two plate fragments illustrated in Figure 5.27 are #A.S.F. 1972.1362 and 1582. Porcelain from the Van Doesburgh cellar, Huey 1988:411-12.

67. Van Laer 1974 (2):121-25.

68. The majolica was probably made by the elder Verstraeten while his son Gerrit, who died in 1657, made the faience, Jan Baart, personal communication, 10/6/04. Also see Baart 2000a and Van Dam 1982:89-90. For examples from the Monte Cristi wreck, see Wilcoxen 2000:61 and figure 8. For more on the Monte Cristi wreck, see Hall 1996.

69. For more on Japanese porcelain, see Vialle 2000 and Baart 2000b. For Dutch motifs on K'ang Hsi porcelain, see Wilcoxen 1992.

70. This piece was recovered from the Staats-Van Twiller house area early in the excavation, Paul Huey, personal communication, 9/21/05.

71. For Dutch domestic sites where only bulbous bowl pipes (and no EB marked examples) were recovered, see the Appel's tavern refuse, component 77, and the Staats-Van Twiller house, component 86, at Fort Orange, Huey 1988:473-74, 479, 493-95.

72. A bodkin was recovered from the Persen house, Kingston, Diamond 2004:106. Brass spectacle frames, tortoise shell comb and bodkin were recovered from the Van Doesburgh house, Huey 1988:445-46; personal communication, 9/21/05.

73. Identification of the Flatts comb as elephant ivory was made by Joseph McEvoy. For the tortoise shell comb from the Van Doesburgh house, see Huey 1988:445.

74. Moody 2005:127-28.

75. For Van Curler's travels, see O'Callaghan and Fernow 1853-87 (1):386, 503. The shells are a small Music Volute (*Voluta musica*) and a Fighting Stromb (*Strombus pugilis*), both of which have a natural range extending from the West Indies south to Brazil, Morris 1975: 228, 169.

76. The case in which they were shipped was marked JVR, Van Laer 1932:45-46. Note that the letters JVR are reversed, a common die-cutter's error. For seals from the Staats-Van Twiller house, see Huey 1988:490-92.

77. For background on the discovery of this bodkin, see Bennett 1984:14-15. For more information on Sara Roelofs, see Venema 2003:166-67.

78. Rink 1986:199.

79. "For merchandise received to my satisfaction," Van Laer 1932:10. For other examples, see Venema 2003:264-67.

80. Rink 1986:200; Venema 2003:191-99.

81. In addition to the Flatts and Van Buren, Dutch sites of this period include the Van Doesburgh house (component 96) at Fort Orange and the brick maker's house, Moody 2005. In all these locations, trading appears to have been a significant part of the household's business.

82. Baart 1988:71-72.

83. In addition to consumer demand, a change in production might be part of the reason for this shift to beads with finished ends. In 1657, Claes Claesz Jaquet abandoned the old Two Roses glasshouse on the Keizergracht and built a new one on the Rozengracht., ibid., p. 72.

84. The illustrations in Figure 5.33, as in Figure 4.35, are based in large part on drawings made by Gene MacKay for Hamell 1982b. The examples illustrated in Figure 5.33 are based on the following: I. a flanged bulbous bowl with a distinct heel, from Seneca Dann site (NYSM #21136), Ia. a flanged bulbous bowl with a distinct heel and "person with blanket roll-style" figure, from the Onondaga Indian Castle or Indian Hill site (NYSM #15199), the Seneca Dann site (RMSC AR37831) and the Cayuga Ganz site (private collection), II. a plain, funnel-shaped bowl, IIa. a funnel-shaped bowl with "bird-man-style" figure, from Seneca Dann site (RFC/RMSC -/28). IIb. a funnel-shaped bowl with "sitting dog-style" figure, from the Seneca Marsh site (RFC/RMSC 1345/24), IIc. a "man-bird-style" figure, from the Allen site (Rumrill collection, NYSM), IId. a modified funnel-shaped bowl with an "erect bird-style" figure, from Seneca Dann site (RFC/RMSC 5000/28). Examples not illustrated include a "heron-style" figure from the Printup site (Rumrill collection, NYSM) and a different style of monkey playing or smoking a pipe from the Seneca Dann site (NYSM #35550).

85. Two objects labeled "lead tubes" in the Rumrill collection (Fda18-41) appear to be collars for wooden or stone pipes. An example from the Jackson-Everson site, Rumrill collection (NYSM A2005.13AX.99.5), is mentioned in Figure 5.22b. Another finely made example (possibly part of a gift?) was recovered from cellar of the Van Doesburgh house at Fort Orange, Huey 1988:351 and p. 705, figure 83b.

86. George Hamell has observed that the bear/man figure illustrated in Figure 5.36b might also be described as a "piasa" or chimeric figure with a human face, antlers, an eagle's claws and wings, a body covered with scales and a serpent's tail. In 1673, Father Jacques Marquette recorded that a pictograph of such a manitou was painted high on the bluff above the Mississippi where the city of Alton, Illinois, now stands.

EPOLOGUE

1. Lalement, in Snow et al. 1996: 131-32. As a Frenchman and a Jesuit, Lalement had a very different view of Fortuna than his Dutch contemporaries, one more rooted in a medieval rather than neoclassical tradition. For more on Fortuna and her wheel, see Patch 1927:145-80; Pickering 1970:168-69.

2. O'Callaghan and Fernow 1853-87 (3):143. Richard was Jeremias' brother, Kiliaen's youngest son. For more on "Surrendering the Land," see Merwick 1990:134-87.

3. Quartering of soldiers, Huey 1988:107. O'Callaghan and Fernow 1853-87 (3):67-68. "The Mahican were not mentioned," Trelease 1960:228.

4. Van Laer 1932:386-87. For the loss of Douw's farm, see Ferris 1973:7. For rebuilding, see Huey 1993:28-32. For Van Curler's death, see Bradley 2005b.

5. O'Callaghan and Fernow 1853-87 (3):163-64. Note the misprint in the O'Callaghan – Camper instead of Campen. Exception was revoked, Trelease 1960:215-16.

6. Dutch patterns of trade were so radically altered that Dutch commercial activities in North America were "destroyed," Merwick 1990:168. The ethnic Dutch merchant establishment was supplanted and anglicized at a surprisingly rapid pace, Rink 1986:266. For a contrary view, see Israel 1990:292-99.

7. The farmhouse at the Flatts had collapsed and had to be completely repaired, Van Laer 1932:407. The farm was sold to Philip Schuyler, Van Laer 1932:444, 450n.

8. More Mohawk warriors near Montreal, Thwaites 1896-1901 (63):179.

9. The Dutch Reformed Church continued to be governed under the Classis of Amsterdam, Huey 2005a:11. For Dutch architecture, see Huey 1993:28-32. Many residents continued to describe themselves as living in

Beverwijck or even the Fuyck, Merwick 1990:173.

10. To make Albany into "an English place," ibid., p. 202. The garrison for an occupying force as much as to protect the local population from outside invasion, Merwick 1981. Also see Huey 1988:114-15.

11. To impress them with his potential as a friend and protector, Trelease 1960:249.

12. Richter 1992:140-41; Trelease 1960:249.

13. "As servants and souldjers" of the English, ibid., p. 238. Settle at Schaghticoke, ibid., p. 235. Within ten years, the governor would begin to refer to the Five Nations as his subordinate "Children" instead of his equal "Brethren" and command rather than suggest how they should act, Richter 1992:155.

14. Proximity to "the king's highways" determined where one lived, Merwick 1990:202. Records would be kept in English, ibid., p. 197. Shift to property tax, ibid., pp. 200-201.

15. Robert Livingston as court secretary, ibid., p. 253; Leder 1956:6. Shift in court proceedings away from Dutch precedents toward those of the English, ibid., pp. 206-8. Lutheran church, Fisher 2004:7-9.

16. Trade as "a Prerogative Royall," Merwick 1990:210. Rights to trade in Albany denied, ibid., p. 211. Merchants could either trade for furs or trade overseas, but not both, ibid., pp. 212-13.

17. Ibid., 209.

18. Creation of counties, Munsell 1853 (2):39. Establishment of wards, Merwick 1990:203-4.

19. See Leder 1956:97-98 for the "humble petition" sent to Dongan on behalf of "the Inhabitants of His Magestys Burgh of Albany." To participate in the trade, one had to be a "freeman" and "actual Inhabitant," Weise 1884:202. The mayor and sheriff would remain appointed, ibid., p. 200.

20. "With all the joy and acclamations imaginable," ibid., p. 203. Not clear that everyone was so enthused, Merwick 1990:205.

21. Haley 1988:132-42.

22. For summary on Mohawk sites of this period, see Snow 1995a. Here again, important additional information comes from the Swart and Rumrill collections, NYSM and through the generosity of Wayne Lenig.

23. Baart 1988:69; Karklins 1974:66; Hudig 1923:77-79. For more on beads from Mohawk sites, see Rumrill 1991.

24. Amsterdam glasshouses after 1697, Baart 1988:69, 72-73. By early decades of the 18th-century, several new beads styles occur on Native sites. These include large oval monochrome varieties, especially clear (IIa10), white (IIa15) and dark blue (IIa57,) as well as a revival of polychrome styles (IIb32&34, IIbb13, IIb'2&3, IIb'7 and "Roman" beads IIj1&2). While no archaeological evidence for production of these beads has been reported, Van der Sleen found many examples of them, as well as later wire-wound varieties, in and around Amsterdam, 1963a, 1963b.

25. At least one CAMPEN cloth seal has been recovered from White Orchard, see Cnj 3-27, Rumrill collection, NYSM. Also see examples from Oneida Sullivan and Onondaga Indian Hill sites, Bennett 1973, figure 13R; Bradley 1980. For more on stroud cloth, the textiles made in and around Bristol for export to America and other colonies, see Jennings 1975:99.

26. The best sources on Bird, his followers and imitators are De Roever 1987 and Den Braven 2003. For Adrian van der Cruis and his use of other makers, see Duco 2003 #418; Den Braven 2003:15-17. For Jacobus de Vriend, see Duco 2003 #297.

27. Examples include Willem Claesz Boot (1676), whose mark was the goblet or roemer (ibid., #243); Pieter Soutman (1675), who used a PS monogram

(ibid., #598 and 599); and Jan Kunst (1689), whose mark was two figures or prince and princess (ibid., #178). Examples of these pipes have been recovered from eastern Iroquois sites dating from the last quarter of the 17th-century, Bradley and DeAngelo 1981.

28. Evert Bird moved to Gouda in 1684 and worked as a tavern keeper until he died in 1692, De Haan and Krook 1988:17; Den Braven 2003:14.

29. The orb was registered to Dieter Jansz Gleijne in 1674 (Duco 2003 #29). The first detailed discussion of the HG and crowned HG marks is McCashion 1975. The crowned HG was registered to Hendrick Gloudijse Marte in 1694 (ibid., #474). It is possible Hendrick Gloudijse Marte made pipes stamped with a plain HG prior to that date, but no such mark is listed in the Gouda records. Examples of these pipes have been recovered from eastern Iroquois sites dating from the last quarter of the 17th-century, McCashion 1975; Bradley and DeAngelo 1981.

30. For a summary on Bristol pipe makers, see Walker 1971.

31. The exception might be McCashion's "London pipes" (1994:31) but, since these pipes are unmarked, they could just as easily be from Gouda or another town in the Republic.

32. For component 66 at Fort Orange, see Huey 1988:760. My thanks to Paul Huey and Joe McEvoy for their thoughts on this feature and its pipes. For additional discussion, see Huey 2006.

33. See Alexander 1979 for a discussion of Evans pipes and their distribution. See Huey 2006:11-12 for a more detailed discussion on the occurrence of Evans and Tippett pipes in New York. The one example of an Evans pipe from an upstate site is a bowl fragment from the Mohawk White Orchard site, Jan Swart collection (2.33.34 NYSM).

34. The available information comes from the KeyCorp and Lutheran Church Lot sites in Albany, the Schuyler Flatts and Van Buren farm sites, and Mortar Hill, a small site on the north side of the Mohawk River in Scotia. This site, documented by Gary Bernhardt, may have been the farm of Johannes and Stephanus Groesbeck or the tavern of Jacques Cornelissen van Slyck, Huey 2005b.

35. Huey recovered a pipe stem whistle made from an HG-marked funnel bowl pipe during testing beneath Broadway, Huey 1974:109. Other examples have been found at KeyCorp and Lutheran Church Lot, Chuck Fisher, personal communication, 9/2/05.

36. The orb, HG and crowned HG marks are discussed in note 29 above. McCashion identified the CDP mark as that of Cornelis Dircxz Peck, who may have started in Amsterdam but is listed as a Gouda pipe maker between 1667 and 1679, McCashion 1994:36-37. Duco also identifies this as the mark of Cornelis Dircksz Peck, a Gouda pipe maker between 1654/59 and 1690, Duco 2003 #799.

37. There was another reason Dutch material continued to dominate the trade during the last quarter of the 17th-century. The Industrial Revolution came to the Republic first, especially in terms of textiles, ceramics and munitions. England would not catch and surpass the Dutch in terms of production until the 18th-century. The Indian trade was another example of "England's apprenticeship" to the Dutch in economic matters, Wilson 1966; Haley 1988. The formula developed by Van Rensselaer and Van Curler was so successful that, like Edward Bird's pipes, it was quickly copied. When the Hudson's Bay Company was organized in 1670, its inventory of goods – smoking pipes, blankets and good quality flintlocks in addition to the usual kettles, knives, axes, awls and glass beads – was taken

directly from the Dutch. This decision was based on the recommendations of their special consultant, Pierre Radisson, the same man who, as an adopted Mohawk in the early 1650s, had learned firsthand what Native people wanted, Rich, ed. 1942:xv, 243-49. For a list of the trade goods Radisson recommended, see ibid., p. 108.

38. Blackburn and Piwonka 1988:79. There is not a good biography of Schuyler at present. This sketch is drawn from Blackburn and Piwonka 1988:79-89; Trelease 1960:209-10; the *Dictionary of American Biography,* Johnson, ed. 1928 (16):476-77; and the *American National Biography,* Garraty and Carnes, eds. 1999 (19):460-61.

39. Since Iroquoian languages have no labial sounds (that is *b, p* or *m*), this was how the Mohawks pronounced Schuyler's first name. Quote from Bond 1952, in Blackburn and Piwonka 1988:79.

40. Koot 2005.

41. For the tea table and chairs, see Blackburn and Piwonka 1988: 86-88, #45 and #46. The fireback was donated to the Albany Institute in 1910 by Mrs. Richard P. Schuyler. A note that accompanied the donation indicates that this fireback was "from the Schuyler family home at the Flatts."

REFERENCES

Alexander, L. T. 1979. Clay Pipes from the Buck Site in Maryland. In *The Archaeology of the Clay Tobacco Pipe. II. The United States of America,* edited by P. Davey, pp. 37-62. International Series 60. British Archaeological Reports, Oxford, England.

Anselmi, L. M. 2004. *New Materials, Old Ideas: Native Use of European Introduced Metals in the Northeast.* Ph.D. dissertation, University of Toronto.

Baart, J. 1986. Tools, Implements and Specialized Organization in Towns ca. 1200 A.D. In *ZAM Zeitschrift fur Archaologie des Mittelalters,* 4:379-389. Rheinland-Verlay Gmbtt, Koln.

—. 1988. Glass Bead Sites in Amsterdam. *Historical Archeology* 22(1):67-75.

—. 1994. Dutch Redwares. *Medieval Ceramics* 18:19-27.

—. 1995. Combs. *In One Man's Trash is Another Man's Treasure,* edited by A. van Dongen, pp. 174-187. Museum Boymans-van Beuningen, Rotterdam, the Netherlands.

—. 2000a. Het ontstaan van het 'Hollants porceleyn'. In *Lost and Found. Essays on medieval archaeology for H. J. E. van Beuningen.,* edited by D. Kicken, A. M. Koldeweij and J. R. ter Moten, pp. 51-62. Rotterdam Papers 11. Museum Boymans-van Beuningen, Rotterdam.

—. 2000b. Japanese Porcelain Finds in Amsterdam. In *The Voyage of Old Imari Porcelain,* edited by A. Hiwatashi, pp. 216-220. Kyushu Ceramic Museum, Nagasaki.

—. 2005. Cloth Seals on Iroquois Sites. *Northeast Historical Archaeology* 34:77-88.

Baart, J., W. Krook and A. Lagerweij. 1977. *Opgravingen in Amsterdam.* Fibula-van Dishoeck, Haarlem.

—. 1986a. Herstellung und gebrauch von Trinkglas in Amsterdam (1580-1640). In *Spechterglaser.* Glasmuseum Wertheim, Wertheim.

—. 1986b. Opgravingen aan de Oostenburgermiddenstraat. In *Van VOC tot Werkspoor,* pp. 83-151. Matrijs, Utrecht.

—. 1990/2. Italiaanse en Nederlandse witte faience (1600-1700). *Mededelingenblad Nederlands Vereniging van Vrienden van de Ceramiek* 138:4-48.

Barnes, D. R. and P. G. Rose. 2002. Matters of Taste. *Food and Drink in Seventeenth-Century Dutch Art and Life.* Albany Institute of History and Art. Syracuse University Press.

Beauchamp, W. M. 1902. *Metallic Implements of the New York Indians.* New York State Museum Bulletin 55. University of the State of New York, Albany, NY.

—. 1903. *Metallic Ornaments of the New York Indians.* New York State Museum Bulletin 73. New York State Education Department, Albany, NY.

—. 1905. *A History of the New York Iroquois.* New York State Museum Bulletin 78, Archaeology 9. New York State Education Department, Albany, NY.

Bennett, M. 1979. The Blowers Site, OND 1-4. An Early Historic Oneida Settlement. *Chenango Chapter, NYSAA, Bulletin* 18(2):1-25.

—. 1984. Recent Findings in Oneida Indian Country. *Chenango Chapter, NYSAA, Bulletin* 21(1).

—. 1991. The Thurston Site, MSV 1-2. *Chenango Chapter, NYSAA, Bulletin* 24(3):1-19.

Bennett, M. and D. Clark. 1978. Recent Excavations on the Cameron Site (OND-8). *Chenango Chapter, NYSAA, Bulletin* 17(4).

Blackburn, R. H. and R. Piwonka. 1988. *Remembrance of Patria. Dutch Arts and Culture in Colonial America 1609-1776.* Albany Institute of History and Art, Albany, NY.

Braat, J. *et al.* 1998. *Behouden uit het Beouden Huys. Catalogus van de voorwerpen van de Barentsexpeditie (1596) gevonde op Nova Zembla.* Rijksmuseum, Amsterdam.

Bradford, W. 1952. *Of Plymouth Plantation, 1620-1647.* Alfred A. Knopf, New York, NY.

Bradley, J. W. 1980. Dutch Bale Seals from 17th-century Onondaga Iroquois Sites in New York State. *Post-Medieval Archaeology* 14:197-200.

—. 1996. Maps and Dreams: Native Americans and European Discovery. In *One Man's Trash is Another Man's Treasure,* edited by A. van Dongen, pp. 27-39. Museum Boymans-van Beuningen, Rotterdam.

—. 2001. Change and Survival among the Onondaga Iroquois since 1500. In *Societies in Eclipse,* edited by D. S. Brose, C. W. Cowan and R. C. J. Mainfort, pp. 27-36. Smithsonian Institution Press, Washington, DC.

—. 2005a. *Evolution of the Onondaga Iroquois: Accommodating Change, 1500-1655.* Nebraska University Press, Lincoln, Nebraska.

—. 2005b. Visualizing Arent van Curler: A Biographical and Archaeological View. *de Halve Maen* 78(1):3-14.

Bradley, J. W. and M. Bennett. 1984. Two Occurrences of Weser Slipware from Early 17th-century Iroquois Sites in New York State. *Post-Medieval Archaeology* 18:301-305.

Bradley, J. W. and S. T. Childs. 1991. Basque Earrings and Panther's Tails: The Form of Cross-Cultural Contact in Sixteenth-Century Iroquoia. *MASCA Research Papers in Science and Archaeology* (Metals in Society: Theory Beyond Analysis) 8:7-18.

Bradley, J. W. and G. DeAngelo. 1981. European Clay Pipe Marks from 17th-Century Onondaga Iroquois Sites. *Archaeology of Eastern North America* 9:109-133.

Brandão, J. A. 1997. *Your Fire Shall Burn No More: Iroquois Policy Towards New France and Its Native Allies to 1701.* University of Nebraska Press, Lincoln, NE.

Brasser, T. J. 1978. Mahican. In *Northeast,* edited by B. G. Trigger, pp. 198-212. Handbook of North American Indians. vol. 15, W. C. Sturtevant, general editor. Smithsonian Institution, Washington, D.C.

Brewer, F. I. 1990. Ceramics from the Nicoll-Sill House. *The Bulletin: Journal of the New York State Archaeological Association* 101:10-22.

Bridges, S. T. 1974. *The Clinton Avenue Site, Kingston, New York.* Masters thesis, New York University.

Bruchac, M. and P. Thomas. 2006. Locating "Wissatinnewag:" John Pynchon's Influence on Pocumtuck Diplomacy. *Historical Journal of Massachusetts* 34(1):56-82.

Brumbach, H. J. 1975. "Iroquoian" Ceramics in "Algonkian" Territory. *Man in the Northeast* 10:17-28.

—. 1995. Algonquian and Iroquoian Ceramics in the Upper Hudson River Drainage. *Northeast Anthropology* 49:55-66.

Brumbach, H. J. and S. Bender. 2002. Woodland Period Settlement and Subsistence Change in the Upper Hudson Valley. In *Northeast Subsistence-Settlement Change A.D. 700-1300,* edited by J. P. Hart and C. B. Rieth, pp. 227-240. New York

State Museum Bulletin 496. New York State Education Department, Albany, New York.

Burke, T. E. J. 1991. *Mohawk Frontier: The Dutch Community of Schenectady, New York, 1661-1710.* Cornell University Press, Ithaca, NY.

Cantwell, Anne-Marie and Diana diZerega Wall. 2001. *Unearthing Gotham. The Archaeology of New York City.* Yale University Press, New Haven, CT.

Cassedy, D. F., P. A. Webb and J. W. Bradley. 1996. The Vanderwerken Site: A Protohistoric Iroquois Occupation on Schoharie Creek. *The Bulletin: Journal of the New York State Archaeological Association* 111/112:21-34.

Ceci, L. 1989. Tracing Wampum's Origins: Shell Bead Evidence from Archaeological sites in western and coastal New York. In *Proceedings of the 1986 Shell Bead Conference,* edited by C. F. Hayes, pp. 63-80. Research Record No. 20. Rochester Museum and Science Center, Rochester, NY.

Cleland, C. E. 1972. From the Sacred to Profane: Style Drift in the Decoration of Jesuit Finger Rings. *American Antiquity* 37(2).

Cohen, D. S. 1992. *The Dutch-American Farm.* The American Social Experience Series. New York University Press, New York, NY.

Colden, C. 1727 and 1747. *The History of the Five Indian Nations.* 1973 ed. Cornell University Press Ltd., London UK and Ithaca, NY.

Collamer and Associates, I. 1988a. *Dutch Reformed Church Burial Ground, c.1676-1881. Key Corp Parking Garage, Albany, New York.*

—. 1988b. *Stage 1A &1B Cultural Resource Investigation [for] 532-554 Broadway, Albany, New York.*

Craddock, P. T. 1995. *Early Metal Mining and Production.* Smithsonian Institution Press, Washington, D.C.

Curtin, E. V. 2004. The Ancient Mohicans in Time, Space and Prehistory. In *The Continuance – An Algonquian Peoples Seminar.* Selected Research Papers – 2000, edited by S. W. Dunn, pp. 5-18. New York State Museum Bulletin 501. Albany, New York.

Dallal, D. 2004. The Tudor Rose and the Fleurs-de-lis: Women and Iconography in 17th-century Dutch Clay Pipes found in New York. In *Smoking and Culture. The Archaeology of Tobacco Pipes in Eastern North America,* edited by S. M. Rafferty and R. Mann, pp. 207-240. The University of Tennessee Press, Knoxville, TN.

Davey, P. 1981. *The Archaeology of the Clay Tobacco Pipe,* V. British Archaeological Reports, Oxford, England.

De Haan, R. and W. Krook. 1988. Amsterdam. In *De Kleipijp als Bodemvondst,* edited by F. Tymstra and J. van der Meulen, pp. 16-38. Translated by W. Krook. Pijpelogische Kring Nederland, Leiden.

De Roever, M. 1987. The Fort Orange "EB" Pipe Bowls: An Investigation of the Origin of American Objects in Dutch Seventeenth-Century Documents. In *New World Dutch Studies: Dutch Arts and Culture in Colonial America 1609-1776,* edited by R. H. Blackburn and N. A. Kelley, pp. 51-62. Albany Institute of History and Art, Albany, NY.

—. 1995. Merchandises for New Netherland. In *One Man's Trash is Another Man's Treasure,* edited by A. van Dongen, pp. 71-93. Museum Boymans-van Beuningen, Rotterdam, the Netherlands.

Den Braven, A. 2003. *EB Pijpen, Inzicht in Het Pijpmakersbedrijf Bird (1630-1683).* Bachelor thesis, University of Amsterdam.

Diamond, J. E. 1999. *The Terminal Late Woodland/Contact Period in the Mid-Hudson Valley.* Ph.D. dissertation, State University of New York, Albany.

—. 2004. *Archaeological Excavations at the Matthewis Persen House, Kingston, NY.* Prepared for the County of Ulster Department of Buildings and Grounds.

Duco, D. H. 1975. Pijp en tabak in Amsterdam. *Nieuwsbulletin Pijpenkamer Icon* 1(2).

—. 2003. *Merken en merkenrecht van de pijpenmakers in Gouda.* Pijpenkabinet, Amsterdam.

Dunn, S. W. 1994a. *The Mohicans and Their Land, 1609-1730.* Purple Mountain Press, Fleischmanns, New York.

—. 1994b. Settlement Patterns in Rensselaerswijck: Locating Seventeenth Century Farms on the East Side of the Hudson. *de Halve Maen* 67(3):62-74.

—. 1997. Settlement Patterns in Rensselaerswijck: Farms and Farmers on Castle Island. *de Halve Maen* 70(1):7-18.

—. 2000. *The Mohican World 1680-1750.* Purple Mountain Press, Fleischmanns, NY.

—. 2002a. Settlement Patterns in Rensselaerswijck: Crailo at Greenbush. *de Halve Maen* 75(3):49-56.

—. 2002b. Settlement Patterns in Rensselaerswijck: The Farm at Greenbush. *de Halve Maen* 75(2):23-36.

—. 2003. Influences on New York's Early Dutch Architecture. *Dutch Barn Preservation Society Newsletter* 16(2):1-6.

— (editor) 2004. *Mohican Seminar 1. The Continuance – An Algonquian Peoples Seminar.* New York State Museum Bulletin 501. New York State Education Department, Albany, NY.

— (editor) 2005. *Mohican Seminar 2. The Challenge – An Algonquian Peoples Seminar.* New York State Museum Bulletin 506. New York State Education Department, Albany, NY.

Engelbrecht, W. 2003. *Iroquoia: The Development of a Native World.* Syracuse University Press, Syracuse, New York.

Fagan, B. 2000. *The Little Ice Age: How Climate Made History 1300-1850.* Basic Books, New York.

Feister, L. M. 2003. Archaeology at Crailo State Historic Site: Excavations to 1994. Manuscript, New York State Office of Parks, Recreation and Historic Preservation, pp. 1-46, Peebles Island, Waterford, NY.

Feister, L. M. and J. S. Sopko. 2003. *Archaeology at the Senate House State Historic Site, Kingston, Ulster County, New York, 1970-1997.* New York State Office of Parks, Recreation and Historic Preservation. Bureau of Historic Sites.

Fenton, W. N. and E. Tooker. 1978. Mohawk. In *Northeast,* edited by B. G. Trigger, pp. 466-480. Handbook of NorthAmerican Indians. vol. 15, W. C. Sturtevant, general editor. Smithsonian Institution, Washington, D.C.

Fernow, B. 1897. *The Records of New Amsterdam from 1653 to 1674 Anno Domini.* Knickerbocker Press, New York, NY.

Fisher, C. L. 2004. *Cultural Resources Survey Report for PIN 1754.38.321. Pearl Street Reconstruction Part I: Archaeological Mitigation Report.* New York State Museum, Division of Research and Collections.

Fitzgerald, W. R. 1990. *Chronology to Culture Process: Lower Great Lakes Archaeology, 1500-1650 AD.* Ph.D. dissertation, McGill University.

Fitzgerald, W. R., D. H. Knight and A. Bain. 1995. Untanglers of Matters Temporal and Cultural: Glass Beads and the Early Contact Period Huron Ball Site. *Canadian Journal of Archaeology* 19:117-138.

Fitzgerald, W. R., L. Turgeon, R. H. Whitehead and J. W. Bradley. 1993. Late Sixteenth-Century Basque Banded Kettles. *Historical Archeology* 27(1):44-57.

Fried, M. B. 1975. *The Early History of Kingston and Ulster County, N.Y.* Ulster County Historical Society, Marbletown, Kingston, NY.

Funk, R. E. 1976. *Recent Contributions to Hudson Valley Prehistory.* Memoir 22. New York State Museum, Albany, NY.

Funk, R. E. and R. D. Kuhn. 2003. *Three Sixteenth-Century Mohawk Iroquois Village Sites.* New York State Museum Bulletin 503. New York State Education Department, Albany, New York.

Gaimster, D. 1997. *German Stoneware 1200-1900. Archaeology and Cultural History.* British Museum Press, London.

Garraty, John A. and Mark C. Carnes, eds. 1999. *American National Biography.* 24 vols. Oxford University Press, Oxford.

Gehring, C. T. 1978. *A guide to Dutch Manuscripts Relating to New Netherland in United States Repositories.* University of the State of New York, Albany, NY.

Gehring, C. T. and W. A. Starna. 1988. *A Journey into Mohawk and Oneida Country, 1634-1635.* Syracuse University Press, Syracuse, NY.

Gibson, S. G. 1980. *Burr's Hill: A 17th-Century Wampanoag Burial Ground in Warren, RI.* Haffeneffer Museum of Anthropology, Brown University, Providence, RI.

Goodby, R. G. 2002. Reconsidering the Shantock Tradition. In *A Lasting Impression. Coastal, Lithic and Ceramic Research in New England Archaeology,* edited by J. E. Kerber, pp. 141-54. Praeger, Westport, CT.

Green, J. N. 1977. *The Loss of the VOC Jacht VERGULDE DRAECK, Western Australia 1656.* BAR Supplementary Series 36 (i), Oxford, England.

Hagerty, G. W. 1963. The Iron Trade Knife in Oneida Territory. *Pennsylvania Archaeologist* 33(1):93-114.

—. 1985. *Wampum, War and Trade Goods West of the Hudson.* Heart of the Lakes Publishing, Interlaken, NY.

Haley, K. H. D. 1988. *The British and the Dutch: Political and Cultural Relations through the Ages.* George Philip, London.

Hall, J. L. 1996. *A Seventeenth-Century Northern European Merchant Shipwreck in Monte Christi Bay, Dominican Republic.* PhD dissertation, Texas A&M University.

Hamell, G. R. 1978. Wooden Smoking Pipes of the Seneca Iroquois of Western New York State: Sixteenth and Seventeenth Centuries. Manuscript in the author's possession.

—. 1982a. One Culture's "Truck" is Another Culture's Treasure: Cabinets of Curiosities and Northeastern Native American Ethnological Specimens of the 16th through 18th Centuries. Manuscript in the author's possession.

—. 1982b. Smoking Pipes and related artifact morphology. Manuscript in the author's possession.

—. 1983. Trading in Metaphors: The Magic of Beads. In *Proceedings of the 1982 Glass Trade Bead Conference*, edited by C. F. Hayes, pp. 5-28. Research Record No. 16. Rochester Museum and Science Center, Rochester, NY.

—. 1987. Mythical Realities and European Contact in the Northeast during the Sixteenth and Seventeenth Centuries. *Man in the Northeast* 33:63-87.

—. 1988. Arent van Curler and the Underwater Grandfather. Manuscript in the author's possession.

—. 1992. The Iroquois and the World's Rim: speculations on color, culture and contact. *American Indian Quarterly* 16(4):451-69.

—. 1996. Wampum. *In Encyclopedia of North American Indians,* edited by F. E. Hoxie, pp. 662-64. Houghton Mifflin Company, Boston, MA.

Hamilton, T. M. 1980. *Colonial Frontier Guns.* The Fur Press, Chadron, NE.

Hart, J. P. and H. J. Brumbach. 2003. The Death of Owasco. *American Antiquity* 68(4):737-52.

—. 2005. Cooking Residues, AMS Dates, and the Middle-To-Late Woodland Transition in Central New York. *Northeast Anthropology* 69:1-33.

Hart, S. 1959. *The Prehistory of the New Netherland Company.* City of Amsterdam Press, Amsterdam.

Hartgen Archaeological Associates, I. 1985. *Archeological Investigations at KeyCorp Plaza, South Pearl at Norton and Beaver Streets, Albany, New York.*

—. 1986. *Dutch Reformed Church Burial Ground, c. 1656-1882. Key Corp Parking Garage, Beaver St. & Hudson Ave. Albany, New York.*

—. 1987. *Phase IB End-of-Field-Work letter, 102 State Street site.*

—. 1996a. *End of Field Work Letter, Phase I Archeological Investigations, Dormitory Authority of the State of New York Office Building.*

—. 1996b. *Phase IA Literature Review and Phase IB Archeological Investigations, Dormitory Authority of the State of New York Office Building.*

—. 1997. *Phase IA Archeological Resources Assessment for the 110 State Street Building Project (102-110 State Street), Albany, NY.*

—. 2002. *On the Outside Looking In: Four Centuries of Change at 625 Broadway. Archeology at the DEC Headquarters.* Hartgen Archeological Associates, Inc., Rensselaer, NY.

—. 2005. *Beyond the North Gate: Archeology on the Outskirts of Colonial Albany.* Hartgen Archeological Associates, Inc., Rensselaer, NY.

Hartgen, K. 1997. Preserving Albany's Past: The Battle over the Broadway-Maiden Lane Archeological Site. *de Halve Maen* 70(1):1-6.

—.2003. Archaeology, Historic Preservation, and Albany's Past: The Battle over the DASNY Building Project. In *People, Places, and Material Things: Historical Archaeology in Albany, New York,* edited by C. L. Fisher, pp. 153-66. New York State Museum Bulletin 499. New York State Education Department, Albany, NY.

Heckewelder, J. 1971 [1876]. *History, Manners, and Customs of the Indian Nations Who Once Inhabited Pennsylvania and the Neighboring States.* Arno Press/New York Times, New York, NY.

Hosbach, R. E. and S. Gibson. 1980. The Wilson Site (OND 9), A Protohistoric Oneida Village. *Chenango Chaper, NYSAA, Bulletin* 18(4A):1-167.

Hosmer, J. K. 1908. *Winthrop's Journal.* 2 vols. Charles Scribner's Sons, New York, NY.

Huey, P. R. 1974. Reworked Pipe Stems: A 17th-Century Phenomenon from the Site of Fort Orange, Albany, New York. *Historical Archaeology* 8:105-111.

—. 1984. Dutch Sites of the 17th-Century in Rensselaerswyck. In *The Scope of Historical Archaeology. Essays in Honor of John L. Cotter,* edited by D. G. Orr and D. G. Crozier, pp. 63-85. Laboratory of Anthropology, Temple University, Philadelphia, PA.

—. 1985. An Historic Event at the Schuyler Flatts in 1643. Manuscript, New York State Office of Parks, Recreation and Historic Preservation, Archaeology Division, Peebles Island, Waterford, NY.

—. 1987. Archaeological Evidence of Dutch Wooden Cellars and Perishable Wooden Structures at Seventeenth and Eighteenth Century Sites in the Upper Hudson Valley. In *New World Dutch Studies: Dutch Arts and Culture in Colonial America 1609-1776,* edited by R. H. Blackburn and N. A. Kelley, pp. 13-35. Albany Institute of History and Art, Albany, NY.

—. 1988. *Aspects of Continuity and Change in Colonial Dutch Material Culture at Fort Orange, 1624-1664.* Ph.D. dissertation, University of Pennsylvania.

—. 1991. The Archeology of Fort Orange and Beverwijck. In *A Beautiful and Fruitful Place: Selected Rensselaerswijck Seminar Papers,* edited by N. A. M. Zeller, pp. 327-39. New Netherland Publishing, Albany, NY.

—. 1993. Early Albany: Buildings brfore 1790. In *Albany Architecture,* edited by D. S. Waite, pp. 21-58. Mount Ida Press, Albany, NY.

—. 1996a. A Short History of Cuyper Island, Towns of East Greenbush and Schodack, New York, and its Relation to Dutch and Mahican Culture Contact. *Journal of Middle Atlantic Archaeology* 12:131-47.

—. 1996b. The East Side of Broadway from Maiden Lane to Steuben Street, Albany. In *End of Field Work Letter Phase I Archeological Investigations, Dormitory Authority of the State of New York,* edited by I. Hartgen Archeological Associates, pp. 1-11. Hartgen Archeological Associates, Inc., Troy, NY.

—. 1998. Schuyler Flatts Archaeological District National Historic Landmark. *The Bulletin: Journal of the New York State Archaeological Association* 114:24-31.

—. 2000. *A Preliminary Survey of Potential Archaeological Sites Within the Area of Beverwyck and Colonial Albany.* Manuscript, New York State Office of Parks, Recreation and Historic Preservation, Peebles Island, Waterford, NY.

—. 2003. A Chronology of Events in the History of the Schuyler Flatts through 1672. Manuscript, New York State Office of Parks, Recreation and Historic Preservation, Archaeology Division, Peebles Island, Waterford, NY.

—. 2005a. Introduction. *Northeast Historical Archaeology* 34(1-14).

—. 2005b. Research on the "Mortar Hill" Site in the Town of Glenville, Schenectady County, New York. Manuscript in possession of the author.

—. 2006. From Bird to Tippet: The Archeology of Continuity and Change in Colonial Dutch Material Culture after 1664. Paper presented at the conference *From De Halve Maen to KLM: 400 Years of Dutch-American Exchange,* Albany, NY.

Huey, P. R., L. M. Feister and J. E. McEvoy. 1977. Archeological Investigations in the Vicinity of "Fort Crailo" during Sewer Line Construction under Riverside Avenue in Rensselaer, NY. *The New York State Archeological Society Bulletin* (69):19-42.

Huey, P. R. and A. Luscier. 2004. Some Early Rensselaerswyck Farms: A Documentary and Archaeological Review. *De Halve Maen* 77(4)63-74.

Hurst, J. G. e. a. 1986. *Pottery Produced and Traded in North-West Europe 1350-1650.* Rotterdam Papers VI. Museum Boymans-van Beuningen, Rotterdam, the Netherlands.

Israel, J. I. 1990. *Dutch Primacy in World Trade, 1585-1740.* Clarendon Press, Oxford.

Jameson, J. F. (editor) 1909. *Narratives of New Netherland, 1609-1664.* Charles Scribner's Sons, New York.

Jennings, F. 1975. *The Invasion of America. Indians, Colonialism, and the Cant of Conquest.* W. W. Norton and Company, Inc., New York, NY.

Johnson, Allen, ed. 1928. *Dictionary of American Biography.* 20 volumes. Charles Scribner's Sons, New York.

Karklins, K. 1974. Seventeenth Century Dutch Beads. *Historical Archeology* 8:64-82.

—. 1985a. Early Amsterdam Trade Beads. *Ornament* 9(2):36-41.

—. 1985b. *Glass Beads. The 19th-Century Levin Catalogue and Venetian Bead Book and Guide to Description of Glass Beads.* Studies in Archaeology, Architecture and History. Parks Canada, Ottawa, Canada.

Kent, B. C. 1984. *Susquehanna's Indians.* Anthropological Series, No. 6. The Pennsylvania Historical and Museum Commission, Harrisburg, PA.

Kenyon, I. T. and W. R. Fitzgerald. 1986. Dutch Glass Beads in the Northeast: An Ontario Perspective. *Man in the Northeast* 32:1-34.

Kenyon, I. T. and T. Kenyon. 1983. Comments on 17th-Century Glass Trade Beads from Ontario. In *Proceedings of the 1982 Glass Trade Bead Conference,* edited by C. F. Hayes, pp. 59-74. Rochester Museum of Science Center, Rochester, NY.

Kidd, K. E. and M. A. Kidd. 1970. A Classification System for Glass Beads for the Use of Field Archaeologists. *Occasional Papers in Archaeology and History* 1:46-89.

Kier, C. F. J. 1949. Pieces of Silver. *Pennsylvania Archaeologist* 19(1-2).

Koot, C. 2005. An Adaptive Presence: the Dutch Role in the English Caribbean after the "Fall" of New Holland. Paper presented at the 28th Rensselaerswijck Seminar, Albany, NY.

Korf, D. 1979. *Tegels.* De Haan, Haarlem, the Netherlands.

Krizner, L. J. and L. Sita. 2001. *Peter Stuyvesant: New Amsterdam and the Origins of New York.* The Library of American Lives and Times. The Rosen Publishing Group's PowerPlus Books, New York, NY.

Kuhn, R. D. 1994. The Cromwell Site. *The Bulletin: Journal of the New York State Archaeological Association* 108:29-38.

—. 2004. Reconstructing Patterns of Interaction and Warfare between the Mohawk and Northern Iroquoians during the A.D. 1400-1700 Period. In *A Passion for the Past: Papers in Honour of James F. Pendergast,* edited by J. V. Wright and J. L. Pilon, pp. 145-166. Archaeology Paper 164. Canadian Museum of Civilization, Gatineau, Quebec.

Kuhn, R. D. and R. E. Funk. 2000. Boning Up on the Mohawk: An Overview of Mohawk Faunal Assemblages and Subsistence Patterns. *Archaeology of Eastern North America* 28:29-60.

Kuhn, R. D. and D. R. Snow (editors). 1986. *The Mohawk Valley Project: 1983 Jackson-Everson Excavations.* The Institute for Northeast Anthropology, SUNY. Albany, NY.

Largy, T. B., L. Lavin, M. E. Mozzi and K. Furgerson. 1999. Corncobs and Buttercups: Plant Remains from the Goldkrest Site. In *Current Northeast Paleoethnobotany,* edited by J. P. Hart, pp. 69-84. New York State Museum Bulletin 494, New York State Education Department, Albany, NY.

Lavin, L. 2002. Those Puzzling Late Woodland Collared Pottery Styles: An Hypothesis. In *A Lasting Impression: Coastal, Lithic, and Ceramic Research in New England Archaeology,* edited by J. E. Kerber, pp. 155-178. Praeger, Westport, Connecticut.

—. 2004. Mohican/Algonquian Settlement Patterns. In *The Continuance – An Algonquian Peoples Seminar. Mohican Seminar 1,* edited by S. W. Dunn, pp. 19-28. New York State Museum Bulletin 501. New York State Education Department, Albany, NY.

Lavin, L., M. E. Mozzi, W. J. Bouchard and K. Hartgen. 1996. The Goldkrest Site: An Undisturbed, Multi-Component Woodland Site in the Heart of Mahican Territory. *Journal of Middle Atlantic Archaeology* 12:113-129.

Leder, L. H. (editor) 1956. *Livingston Indian Records,* 1666-1723. Pennsylvania Historical Association, Gettysburg, PA.

Lenig, W. 1998. Prehistoric Mohawk Studies: The Mohawk Valley Project and Beyond. Fort Johnson, New York. Manuscript in the author's possession.

—. 1999. Patterns of Material Culture During the Early Years of the New Netherland Trade. *Northeast Anthropology* 58:47-74.

—. 2000. In Situ Thought in Eastern Iroquois Development: A History. *The Bulletin: Journal of the New York State Archaeological Association* No. 116:58-70.

—. 2003. The Swart Collections and Mohawk Archaeology. Paper presented at the Iroquois Conference, Rensselaersville, NY.

—. 2005. Fort Plain, Fort Plank, Fort Rensselaer and Canajoharie. Manuscript in the author's possession.

Mak, G. 2000. *Amsterdam.* Translated by P. Blom. Harvard University Press, Cambridge, MA.

Mandzy, A. 1986. Symbols, Saints and Scenes: Jesuit Christianization Rings from Seneca Sites. The *Iroquoian* 12:49-63.

Martin, S. R. 1999. *Wonderful Power: The Story of Ancient Copper Working in the Lake Superior Basin.* Wayne State University Press, Detroit, MI.

McCashion, J. H. 1975. The Clay Pipes of New York State. Part One: Caughnawaga 1667-1693. *The Bulletin: Journal of the New York State Archaeological Association* 65:1-18.

—. 1979a. A Preliminary Chronology and Discussion of Seventeenth and Early Eighteenth Century Clay Tobacco Pipes from New York State. In *The Archaeology of the Clay Tobacco Pipe II. The United States of America,* edited by P. Davey, pp. 63-149. BAR International Series. International Series 60. British Archaeological Reports, Oxford, England.

—. 1979b. An Unique Dutch Clay Tobacco Pipe from the Blowers Oneida Site. *Chenango Chaper, NYSAA, Bulletin* 18(1):1-25.

—. 1992. The Clay Tobacco Pipes of New York (Part IV). *The Bulletin: Journal of the New York State Archaeological Association* 103:1-9.

—. 1994. The Clay Pipes of New York State. Part V: The White Orchard site. *William Beauchamp Chapter, NYSAA, Bulletin* 6:1-39.

McCashion, J. H. and T. Robinson. 1977. The Clay Tobacco Pipes of New York: Under the Sidewalks of New York. *The Bulletin: Journal of the New York State Archaeological Association* 71:1-18.

Melius, W. B. and F. Burnap. 1902-1907. *Index of the Public Records of the Counties of Albany, State of New York 1630-1894. Grantors.* 14 volumes. Argus Company, Albany, NY.

—. 1908-1911. *Index of the Public Records of the Counties of Albany, State of New York 1630-1894. Grantees.* 12 volumes. Argus Company, Albany, NY.

Merwick, D. 1981. Becoming English: Anglo-Dutch Conflict in the 1670s in Albany, New York. *New York History* 62(4):389-414.

—. 1990. *Possessing Albany, 1630-1710. The Dutch and English Experiences.* Cambridge University Press, New York, NY.

Milton, G. 1999. *Nathaniel's Nutmeg or, The True and Incredible Adventures of the Spice Trader Who Changed the Course of History.* Penguin Books, New York, NY.

Moody, K. 2003. Traders or Traitors: Illicit Trade at Fort Orange in the Seventeenth Century. In *People, Places, and Material Things: Historical Archaeology of Albany, New York,* edited by C. L. Fisher, pp. 25-38. New York State Museum Bulletin 499, New York State Education Department. Albany, NY.

—. 2005. Quackenbush Square House. In *Beyond the North Gate: Archaeology on the Outskirts of Colonial Albany,* edited by K. Hartgen, pp. 89-160. Hartgen Archeological Associates, Inc., Rensselaer, NY.

Morison, S. E. 1971. *The European Discovery of America. The Northern Voyages, A.D. 500-1600.* Oxford University Press, New York, NY.

Morris, P. A. 1975. *A Field Guide to Shells of the Atlantic.* The Peterson Field Guide Series. Houghton Mifflin Company, Boston, MA.

Munsell, J. 1853-1859. *The Annals of Albany* 10 volumes. Joel Munsell, Albany, NY.

—. 1865. *Collections on the History of Albany from its Discovery to the Present Times* 4 volumes. Joel Munsell, Albany, NY.

Neill, A. B. 1991. Recrudescence at the Thurston site MSV-1. *Chenango Chaper, NYSAA, Bulletin* 24(2):1-22.

Neurdenburg, E. 1948. *De Zeventiende Eeuwsche Beeldhouwkunst in De Noordelijke Nederlanden.* J. M. Meulenhoff, Amsterdam.

O'Callaghan, E. B. 1849-1851. *Documentary History of the State of New York* 4 volumes. Weed, Parsons, Albany, NY.

O'Callaghan, E. B. and B. Fernow. 1853-1887. *Documents Related to the Colonial History of the State of New York.* 15 volumes. Weed, Parsons, Albany, NY.

Patch, H. R. 1927. *The Goddess Fortuna in Mediaeval Literature.* Harvard University Press, Cambridge, MA.

Pearson, J. 1883. *A History of the Schenectady Patent.* Joel Munsell's Sons, Albany, NY.

Peña, E. S. 1990. *Wampum Production in New Netherland and Colonial New York: The Historical and Archeological Context.* Ph.D. dissertation, Boston University.

—. 2003. Making "Money" the Old-Fashioned Way: Eighteenth-Century Wampum Production in Albany. In *People, Places, and Material Things: Historical Archaeology of Albany, New York,* edited by C. L. Fisher, pp. 121-27. New York State Museum Bulletin 499. New York State Education Department. Albany, NY.

Pipes, M. L. 2002. Dormitory Authority of the State of New York, Faunal Analysis and Interpretation. Manuscript report.

—. 2004. *The Quackenbush Square Parking Garage Site, Faunal Analysis and Interpretation.* Manuscript report.

—. 2005. Schuyler Flatts: Analysis and Interpretation of a Mid-Seventeenth Century Colonial Dutch Faunal Assemblage from Upstate New York. Paper presented at the conference *From De Halve Maen to KLM: 400 Years of Dutch-American Exchange,* Albany, NY.

Pratt, P. P. 1976. *Archaeology of the Oneida Iroquois, Volume 1.* Occasional Publications in Northeastern Anthropology. Man in the Northeast, Inc., George's Mills, NH.

Prisch, B. C. 1982. *Aspects of Change in Seneca Iroquois Ladles A.D. 1600-1900.* Research Records 15. Rochester Museum and Science Center, Rochester, NY.

Purchas, S. 1906. *Hakluytus postumus, or Purchas His Pilgrimes.* 20 volumes. James MacLehose and Sons, Glasgow, UK.

Puype, J. P. 1985. *Dutch and other Flintlocks from Seventeenth Century Iroquois Sites.* Proceedings of the 1984 Trade Gun Conference, Part 1. Research Record No. 18. Rochester Museum and Science Center, Rochester, NY.

—. 1996. Dutch firearms from the 17th-century. In *The Arsenal of the World. The Dutch Arms Trade in the Seventeenth Century,* edited by J. P. Puype and M. van der Hoeven. Batavian Lion International, Amsterdam.

Reynolds, H. W. 1929. *Dutch Houses in the Hudson Valley Before 1776.* Payson and Clarke, for the Holland Society of New York, New York, NY.

Rich, E. E., ed. 1942. *Minutes of the Hudson's Bay Company, 1671-1674.* The Champlain Society, Toronto.

Richter, D. K. 1992. *The Ordeal of the Longhouse: The Peoples of the Iroquois League in the Era of European Colonization.* University of North Carolina Press, Chapel Hill, NC.

Rietbergen, P. J. 2004. *A Short History of the Netherlands.* sixth ed. Bekking Publishers, Amersfoort.

Rink, O. A. 1986. *Holland on the Hudson: An Economic and Social History of Dutch New York.* Cornell University Press, Ithaca, NY.

Ritchie, W. A. 1961. *A Typology and Nomemclature for New York Projectile Points.* New York State Museum and Science Service Bulletin 384. New York State Education Department, Albany, NY.

—. 1965. *The Archaeology of New York State.* Natural History Press, Garden City, NY.

Ritchie, W. A. and R. E. Funk. 1973. *Aboriginal Settlement Patterns in the Northeast.* Memoir 20. New York State Museum, Albany, NY.

Rumrill, D. A. 1985. An Interpretation and Analysis of the Seventeenth Century Mohawk Nation: Its Chronology and Movements. *The Bulletin: Journal of the New York State Archaeological Association* 90:1-39.

—. 1988. Art Form or Artifact Type? *The Bulletin: Journal of the New York State Archaeological Association* 96:19-25.

—. 1991. The Mohawk Glass Trade Bead Chronology, ca.1560-1785. *Beads, Journal of the Society of Bead Researchers* 3:5-45.

Salisbury, N. 1982. *Manitou and Providence. Indians, Europeans, and the Making of New England, 1500-1643.* Oxford University Press, New York, NY.

Scammell, G. V. 1981. *The World Encompassed: The first European maritime empires c. 800 to 1650.* University of California Press, Berkeley and Los Angeles, CA.

Schama, S. 1987. *The Embarrassment of Riches: An Interpretation of Dutch Culture in the Golden Age.* Vintage Books, New York, NY.

Sempowski, M. L. 1989. Fluctuations Through Time in the Use of Marine Shell at Seneca Iroquois Sites. In *Proceedings of the 1986 Shell Bead Conference,* edited by C. F. Hayes, pp. 81-96. Research Record No. 20. Rochester Museum and Science Center, Rochester, NY.

Sempowski, M. L. and L. P. Saunders. 2001. *Dutch Hollow and Factory Hollow. The Advent of Dutch Trade Among the Seneca.* Research Records No. 24. 3 volumes. Rochester Museum and Science Center, Rochester, NY.

Sheaf, C. and R. Kilburn. 1988. *The Hatcher Porcelain Cargoes.* Phaidon – Christie's Limited, Oxford, UK.

Shorto, R. 2004. *The Island at the Center of the World.* Doubleday, New York, NY.

Simmons, W. S. 1970. *Cautantowit's House: An Indian Burial Ground on the Island of Conanicut in Narragensett Bay.* Brown University Press, Providence, RI.

Smith, M. T. and M. E. Good. 1982. *Early Sixteenth Century Glass Beads in the Spanish Colonial Trade.* Cottonlandia Museum Publications, Greenwood, Mississippi.

Snow, D. R. 1995a. *Mohawk Valley Archaeology: The Sites.* The Institute for Archaeological Studies, University at Albany, SUNY.

—. 1995b. Micronchronology and Demographic Evidence Relating to the Size of Pre-Columbian North American Indian Populations. *Science* 268:1601-04.

—. 1995c. Migration in Prehistory: The Northern Iroquoian Case. *American Antiquity* 60(1):59-79.

Snow, D. R., C. T. Gehring and W. A. Starna. 1996. *In Mohawk Country. Early Narratives about a Native People.* Syracuse University Press, Syracuse, NY.

Starna, W. A. and J. A. Brandão. 2004. From the Mohawk - Mahican War to the Beaver Wars: Questioning the Pattern. *Ethnohistory* 51(4):725-750.

Stokes, I. N. P. 1915-1928. *The Iconography of Manhattan Island, 1498-1909.* R.H. Dodd, New York, NY.

Thwaites, R. G. 1896-1901. *The Jesuit Relations and Allied Documents.* 73 volumes. The Burrows Brothers, Cleveland, OH.

Trelease, A. W. 1960. *Indian Affairs in Colonial New York: The Seventeenth Century.* Cornell University Press, Ithaca, NY.

Trudel, M. 1973. *The Beginnings of New France, 1524-1663.* McClelland and Stewart, Ltd., Toronto.

Tuck, J. A. and R. Grenier. 1981. A 16th-Century Basque Whaling Station in Labrador. *Scientific American.* pp. 80-190.

—. 1989. *Red Bay, Labrador. World Whaling Capital A.D. 1550-1600.* Atlantic Archaeology Ltd., St. John's, Newfoundland, Canada.

Turgeon, L. 1997. The Tale of the Kettle: Odyssey of an Intercultural Object. *Ethnohistory* 44(1):1-29.

—. 1998. French Fishers, Fur Traders, and Amerindians during the Sixteenth Century: History and Archaeology. *William and Mary Quarterly* 3d series, 55:585-610.

—. 2001. French Beads in France and Northeastern North America during the Sixteenth Century. *Historical Archeology* 35(4):58-82.

Turnbaugh, W. A. 1976. The Survival of a Native Craft in Colonial Rhode Island. *Man in the Northeast* 11:74-79.

—. 1984. *The Material Culture of RI-1000, A Mid 17th-Century Narragansett Indian Burial Site in North Kingston, Rhode Island.* Department of Sociology and Anthropology, University of Rhode Island.

Van Dam, J. D. 1982/4. Geleyersgoet en Hollants Porceleyn. Ontwikkelingen in de Nederlandse aardewerk-industrie 1560-1660. *Mededelingenblad Nederlands Vereniging van Vrienden van de Ceramiek* 108.

Van der Sleen, W. G. N. 1963a. A Bead Factory in Amsterdam in the Seventeenth Century. *Man* (article 219):172-74.

—. 1963b. Bead-Making in Seventeenth-Century Amsterdam. *Archaeology* 16(4):260-63.

Van Dongen, A., ed. 1995a. *One Man's Trash is Another Man's Treasure.* Museum Boymans-van Beuningen, Rotterdam.

—. 1995b. "The Inexhaustible Kettle." In *One Man's Trash is Another Man's Tresure,* edited by A. van Dongen, pp. 115-171. Museum Boymans-van Beuningen, Rotterdam, the Netherlands.

Van Gelder, H. E. 1965. *De Nederlandse munten.* Uitgeverij Het Spectrum, Utrecht/Antwerpen.

Van Laer, A. J. F., ed. 1908. *Van Rensselaer Bowier Manuscripts.* University of the State of New York, Albany, NY.

—. 1916-1919. *Early Records of the City and County of Albany, and the Colony of Rensselaerswijck (1656-1657).* Revised version of Jonathan Pearson 1869 ed. 4 volumes. State University of New York, Albany, NY.

—. 1920. *Minutes of the Court of Fort Orange and Beverwyck 1652-1656.* 2 volumes. University of the State of New York, Albany, NY.

—. 1922. *Minutes of the Court of Rensselaerswyck 1648-1652.* University of the State of New York, Albany, NY.

—. 1924. *Documents Relating to New Netherland, 1624-1626, in the Henry E. Huntington Library.* Henry E. Huntington Library and Art Gallery Press, San Marino, CA.

—. 1926-1932. *Minutes of the Court of Albany, Rensselaerswijck and Schenectady 1685-1686.* 3 volumes. State University of New York, Albany, NY.

—. 1927-28. Arent van Curler and his Historic Letter to the Patroon. *The Dutch Settlers Society of Albany Yearbook* 3:18-29.

—. 1932. *The Correspondence of Jeremias van Rensselaer.* University of the State of New York Press, Albany, NY.

—. 1935. *Correspondence of Maria van Rensselaer 1669-1689.* University of the State of New York, Albany, NY.

—. 1974. *New York Historical Manuscripts: Dutch.* 4 volumes. Geneological Publishing Company, Baltimore, MD.

Van Wijk, P. 1987. Form and Function in the Netherlands' Dutch Agricultural Architecture. In *New World Dutch Studies: Dutch Arts and Culture in Colonial America 1609-1776,* edited by R. H. Blackburn and N. A. Kelley, pp. 161-170. Albany Institute of History and Art, Albany, NY.

Veit, R. and C. A. Bello. 2004. "Neat and Artificial Pipes:" Base Metal Trade Pipes of the Northeastern Indians. In *Smoking and Culture. The Archaeology of Tobacco Pipes in Eastern North America,* edited by S. M. Rafferty and R. Mann, pp. 185-206. The University of Tennessee Press, Knoxville.

Venema, J. 1998. *Deacons' Accounts 1652-1674, First Dutch Reformed Church of Beverwyck/Albany, New York.* Pictou Press; Wm. Eerdman's, Maine; Michigan.

—. 2003. *Beverwyck: A Dutch Village on the American Frontier, 1652-1664.* Verloren/Hilversum–State University of New York Press, Hilversum, The Netherlands - Albany, NY.

Vialle, C. 2000. Japanese Porcelain For the Netherlands: The Records of the Dutch East India Company. In *The Voyage of Old Imari Porcelain,* edited by A. Hiwatashi, pp. 176-183. Kyushu Ceramic Museum, Nagasaki.

Vogel, H. P. 1996. The Republic as arms exporter 1600-1650. In *The Arsenal of the World. The Dutch Arms Trade in the Seventeenth Century,* edited by J. P. Puype and M. van der Hoeven. Batavian Lion International, Amsterdam.

Walker, I. C. 1971. *The Bristol Clay Tobacco-Pipe Industry.* City Museum, Bristol, Bristol.

Weise, A. J. 1884. *The History of the City of Albany.* E. H. Bender, Albany, NY.

Wilcoxen, C. 1979. Arent van Curler's Children. *The New York Genealogical and Biographical Record* 110(2):82-84.

—. 1982. New Data on Schuyler Flatts Found in the Account Book of Jeremias van Rensselaer. Manuscript, Office of Parks, Recreation and Historic Preservation, Archaeology Division, Peebles Island, Waterford, NY.

—. 1987. *Dutch Trade and Ceramics in America in the Seventeenth Century.* Albany Institute of History and Art, Albany, NY.

—. 1992. The Dutch "Tulip Plate" and Its Chinese Prototype. *American Ceramic Circle Journal* 8:7-24.

—. 2000. Dutch Fayence from a Seventeenth-Century Shipwreck. *American Ceramic Circle Journal* 11:52-67.

Williams, R. 1973 [1643]. *A Key into the Language of America.* Wayne State University Press, Detroit, MI.

Willoughby, C. C. 1935. *Antiquities of the New England Indians.* The Peabody Museum of American Archaeology and Ethnology, Harvard University, Cambridge, MA.

Wilson, C. 1966. *England's Apprenticeship: 1603-1763.* St. Martin's Press, New York.

Wonderley, A. E. 2005. Effigy Pipes, Diplomacy, and Myth: Interactions between St. Lawrence Iroquoians and Eastern Iroquois in New York State. *American Antiquity* 70(2):211-240.

Wonderly, D. E. 2001. The Importance of Cloth Seals found on Two 17th-century Oneida Occupations (MSV 4 and MSV 6). *Chenango Chapter, NYSAA, Bulletin* 28(1):15-27.

Wood, A. S. 1974. A Catalog of Jesuit and Ornamental Rings from Western New York State. *Historical Archeology* 8:83-104.

Wray, C. F. 1964. The Bird in Seneca Archeology. *Proceedings of the Rochester Academy of Sciences* 11(1):2-28.

—. 1985. The Volume of Dutch Trade Goods Received by the Seneca Iroquois, 1600-1687 A.D. *Bulletin KNOB* 84(2/3):100-112.

Wray, C. F. *et al.* 1991. *Tram and Cameron. Two Early Contact Era Seneca Sites.* Research Record No. 21. Rochester Museum and Science Center, Rochester, NY.

Zandvliet, K. 2002. *Mapping for Money: Maps, plans and topographic paintings and their role in Dutch overseas expansion during the 16th and 17th centuries.* Batavian Lion International, Amsterdam.

INDEX

flat-handled 23, flensing 23, iron 50, ovate 14; mat hook 104; pitchfork 104; projectile points 51, 80; replacement process of discussed 81; scissors 50; scrappers 51, 80; splitting wedges 104; stone 11, 14, 80; use of lead in 83; used in metal working 24, 51; whetstone 104; woodworking 121; and *passim*

trade assemblages of 1652-1664, *see also* Independent Traders, Private Traders, West India Company; contents discussed 169-71

trade goods, 44; changes in 116-17; English 122; French 122; increased demand for types of 115; items used by Independent Traders 45-46, Private traders 117, 120-21, WIC traders 71-75; lack of on native sites 74-75; objects for 44, 50-51, 71-75, 79; on Mohawk sites 45; private traders assemblages recycled by natives 50-51; used in land payments 80; and *passim*

trash pits, Fort Orange contents of 63; mentioned 3

traders, *see also* Independent Traders, Dutch influence of 79; Private Traders, West India Company; private assemblage of discussed 120-23; rise of 115-16; and *passim*

Tribes Hill Creek, 13

Trico, Caterina, 62

Troy, 9, 58

U

Unuwat's Castle, probable location of 65

utensils, for cooking, drinking and eating described 109-10, 121

V

Van Buren, Cornelis, and wife drown in flood of 1648, 98; artifacts from 98; farm site of 98

Van Buren site, 151

Van Curler, Arent, appointed magistrate of Albany 176; attitude toward natives 87; built patroon's house 89, construction of 90; buys land from Mahicans 100; drowns in Lake Champlain 177; fathers a Mohawk daughter 93; helps Isaac Jogues escape 90; Killian van Rensselaer's grandnephew 5; land purchases of 92, 100; leaves for the Republic 90, 116, returns 91; letter to Van Rensselaer 89; marriage to

Anthonia Slachboom 90; meets with Mohawks and Katskill Indians 156; on embassy to Mohawks 136; primary responsibilities 86; purchases houses in Beverwijck 151; raises horses 92, 100; receives lease of the Flatts 90; relationship with Mohawks and Mahicans 86, 87, 89; revived fur trade 86-87; secretary, bookkeeper, business agent and *commis* of Rensselaerswijck 62, 116; starts Schenectady (Great Flats) settlement 136, 154-55; travels of 165; mentioned 2, 134-35; and *passim*

Van den Bogart, journal of visit to Mohawk and Oneidas 60, 66, 74; mentioned 89

Van der Cruis, Amsterdam merchant 185

Van der Donck, Adriaen, Dutch view of Indians in *Description of New Netherland* 107

Van Doesburgh, Hendrick Andriessen, gunstock maker, glass windows in house of 142; house, contained garbage 143, site profile of 140-42; house of 94, 97, 139, 140-42; wife of Marietje Damen 139

Van Imbroch, Gysbert, surgeon, house of 154

Van Nes, Cornelis, possible house of 100

Van Krieckenbeeck, Daniel, Fort Orange commander, killed in attack on Mohawks 58

Van Rensseaer, Jan Baptist, made director of Rensselaerswijck 134; returns to Amsterdam 168; directs family fortune 168

Van Rensselaer, Jeremias, given Staats-Van Twiller house 139; Greenbush house of 105; farm destroyed by flood 177; Johannes van Twiller cousin of 139; meets with Mohawk and Katskill Indians 156; on embassy to Mohawks 136; Rensselaerswijck director 168; and *passim*

Van Rensselaer, Johannes, patroonship goes to at Killian's death 168

Van Rensselaer, Killian, a director of West India Company 56-57; death of 90, 105, 169; fur trade interest of 75, 79; house location 95; patroonship of 2, 5, 59; plan of 59, 115-16; requests of 87; storehouse location 95, 116; mentioned 5, 66; and *passim*

Van Rensseaaler, Richard, appointed magistrate of Albany 176; returns to the Republic 177; sells house to Pieter Schuyler 177